What Others Are Saying about This Book . . .

Martenson's irresistible wit is not to be missed.

—Kyra Davis, *Lust, Loathing, and a Little Lip Gloss*

A fun, wry, and truly eye-opening
look into real-life world of matchmaking.

—Joanne Rendell, *The Professors' Wives' Club*

Marla's quick wit will have you rolling on the floor.

—Megan Castran, International "You Tube Queen"

Imagine this: a professional matchmaker giving us a witty,
often hilarious, insight into the fascinating underbellies
of dating and making it in Beverly Hills. Priceless.

—F. G. Gerson, *21 Steps to Happiness*

Sharper than a Louboutin stiletto,
Martenson's book delivers an insider's look at the
image-obsessed world of Los Angeles dating.

—Nadine Haobsh, *Beauty Confidential*
and *Confessions of a Beauty Addict*

I absolutely love this book! A witty, smart read for anyone
who's ever wondered what the other half is really thinking.

—Lisa Daily, DAYTIME TV dating coach
and author of *Stop Getting Dumped*

Also by Marla Martenson

Excuse Me, Your Soul Mate Is Waiting

Good Date, Bad Date

Diary of a Beverly Hills Matchmaker

Marla Martenson

To Kelly,
Great to meet you.
love, Marla Martenson

BETTIE YOUNGS BOOKS

Cover design by Mark Clements and Jane Hagaman

BETTIE YOUNGS BOOKS PUBLISHING COMPANY
Del Mar, CA
www.BettieYoungsBooks.com

If you are unable to order this book from your local
bookseller, you may order directly from the publisher.

Library of Congress Control Number: 2010900644

ISBN 978-0-9843081-0-1
10 9 8 7 6 5 4 3 2 1
Printed on acid-free paper

Contents

Acknowledgments...vii

Chapter 1. Matchmaker, Matchmaker! Make Me a Match 1

Chapter 2. Magnets 11

Chapter 3. How Dreams Change..21

Chapter 4. Scrambled Eggs...31

Chapter 5. Lucy and Ricky..41

Chapter 6. The Pig Party...47

Chapter 7. But I Look So Young for My Age 55

Chapter 8. You're Smooth, but Not That Smooth......................................65

Chapter 9. Cupid, Angels, and the Day from Hell 73

Chapter 10. "A Toast to Your Success . . ."..83

Chapter 11. "If Ya Think I'm Sexy . . ." 93

Chapter 12. Kiss My Botox 103

Chapter 13. Goddess Plan...111

Chapter 14. Darling, José Eber You're Not...121

Chapter 15. One Percent of the Population 129

Chapter 16. Two Life Lines..137

Chapter 17. Back at the Double D Ranch 147

Chapter 18. Women of Leisure...155

Chapter 19. Butterflies...165

Chapter 20. Baggage..175

Chapter 21. I Am Not Obsessed!...181

Chapter 22. The "H" Word 189

Chapter 23. The Glam Fix 195

Chapter 24. Law of Attraction 203

Chapter 25. Adolfo's Christmas Present 209

Chapter 26. Imagine My Surprise 215

Chapter 27. Shift Happens..225

Chapter 28. Volumptuous...233

Chapter 29. Slings and Arrows 237

Chapter 30. Rollercoaster Boogie...243

Chapter 31. Showtime..249

Chapter 32. "How It Ends and How It All Begins . . ."..............................257

Acknowledgments

First, all my love and thanks to mi amor, Adolfo. You fill my life with love and make life an adventure and always exciting—as well as giving me plenty of material for my books!

To my wonderful mother, the one and only Donna Reed, "park angel" who looks out for everyone in the hood. Thanks for supporting me in all of my dreams to be a writer and for saving me from those times when I wanted to become anything from the fastest tap dancer in the world to a ventriloquist.

A million thanks aren't enough to my friend and mentor—among other things—Bettie Youngs. You have changed my life in so many ways. I know that the fun is just beginning. Special thanks to wonder woman Peggy Lang, my fabulous editor. Thanks to Clayton Stroope of Thriving Ivory for letting me use the lyrics from *Flowers for a Ghost,* and for your amazing voice coming out of my iPod, uplifting me on my morning hikes in my attempt to whittle myself back down to a size two.

And thanks to all of my friends, family, and readers for your love and support.

one

Matchmaker, Matchmaker!
Make Me a Match

A chichi decorator came up with the color of one of the walls in my Beverly Hills office by matching paint swatches to the silky dark chocolate Godiva heart-shaped ganaches that sit in a crystal dish alongside Teuscher Irish Cream truffles, and chocolate cordials of cherries soaked in black port and wrapped in gold foil. We do pamper our clients. I mention this so you'll know that there are many aspects of my job that I absolutely adore. Such niceties distract me from fantasies of . . . dismemberment.

> Hi Marla, Scott, here. I'm so glad I joined your dating agency; I can see this is going to be verrrrry interesting. . . . Hey, the gal you lined me up with last evening was gorgeous, but I would really like my matches to be a 10 or, ideally, a 10+. And the gal needs to back up her beauty with an income of her own and her own living quarters. No roommate situations. I don't waste my time with someone who doesn't live up to my expectations—you know, long legs, firm small butt, double-D's, thin arms, blonde hair.
> SCL

Ahem.

Dear Scott,

> To paraphrase the deathless sentiments of Roseanne Barr, I'll get my wand. Oh, wait, it's in the repair shop, utterly depleted. I'm having to make do with our back-up magic lamp, but the genie keeps

laughing and muttering about peace in the Middle East being an easier request as he disappears in a puff of smoke. He's such a joker. But since you have so much to offer, it shouldn't be too difficult to find the woman of your fantasies since all the 10+s in our database say that a man willing to plough up his bald scalp with those cute little tufts of implanted hair is a real turn-on. And most "gals" don't mind giving up their stilettos to avoid towering over a man of your stature.

Of course, I don't write this. This is my first email of the day at Double D Dating Service here in Beverly Hills where I'm the head matchmaker. Double D is not the company's real name, as you may have guessed, just my own special pet name for it. I dash off a breezy professional response to Scott as if diplomacy were my mother tongue.

Dear Scott,
   I'm so glad you enjoyed your evening with a gorgeous woman. A new and interesting experience, huh? Well, we do have an ever-growing list of many stunning women, eager to meet you. I'll get back to you later in the day with another name.
Marla

Something is nagging at me. Oh, my conscience. It's not bothering me at all about the direct lie: *eager to meet you.* I've left in a little dig. I change that one snarky line about dating gorgeous women being a new experience to simply "An interesting experience indeed," and hit send. Next email.

Dear Marla,
   I really found Sandy to be attractive, fun, intelligent, and cultured. We had a great time. The only thing is, I am wondering if she has a big butt. She was wearing one of those puffy dresses. She says that she does all kinds of activities like dance classes, working out at the gym, and hiking, but I just can't be sure how big her butt is. Is there any way you can let me know if it's big or if the dress she was wearing just gave that illusion?
Joseph

Joe, don't you know that when we bring a woman into our service, it means that we have carefully inspected her butt from every angle and therefore certify it is also a 10 along with the rest of her? I'm so glad you asked though, because you must never ever consider dating a woman with flesh on her butt. Oversized curves belong above the waist only. Makes perfect sense. How could nature have created such a serious design flaw?

Sigh. I find it so comforting to type out what I truly want to say to some of these clods before writing the response I must write. God forbid Gary should ever see this stuff. I am, after all, good at what I do. Pictures of my successes hang on the chocolate-colored wall above fresh pale pink hydrangeas: two of happy couples at their respective posh wedding receptions and several more couples on honeymoons at places like Bellagio on Lake Como in Italy, or snorkeling with humpback whales off Vava'u, Tonga, in the South Pacific, or skiing in Aspen. I do still believe in love—the soul-mate kind of love. I think deep down, the Scotts and Josephs do too. They just rarely know it.

Dear Joseph,
    Sandy's dress probably created the wrong illusion. Call her for another date; I think you will be pleased to find that in addition to being beautiful, intelligent, and a most remarkable woman, she's also fit and trim.
Marla

I polish off my vanilla soy latte, ready for the next email, when I hear Gary, my boss, barking at Charlotte, the other matchmaker in the office. She hangs her head as she follows him into his office. He doesn't usually come in on Thursdays, so this isn't looking good for Charlotte.

I step outside the artistically etched glass double doors of my office to check with Alana at the front desk. "What's going on?" I ask in a stage whisper.

Alana, a petite blonde in her twenties with big brown eyes and a gorgeous smile, is just about to say something when Gary strides over. "Back to work!" he tells me. Then to Alana he says,

"Find the Harrison file. . . . And never wear those shoes here again. If you want to look like Peter Pan, work somewhere else."

I can't help but turn to check out Alana's shoes. Ohh, they're darling: green flats with little cut-outs of stars.

"Marla, I hope you have some makeup in your bag," Gary says. "You're looking washed out again. Do you go to the gym before work or something? Don't you two get it that we're all about glamour and sex appeal here? Our clients don't want Peter Pan and Miss Grundy lining up their matches."

"Right," I say, feeling my face redden to the roots of my already red hair. "I'll touch up." Gary can be a nice guy, but he does go on rampages.

Back in my office, I pile all my black matchmaking catalogues on my desk to hide from Gary's view. I eat a chocolate. Then another. One more. Call it an early lunch. Mmmmm. Better. Deep breaths, a few affirmations. *I am young and hot-looking. I am a terrific matchmaker. I am lucky to have this job.*

Back to work. Next email.

Dear Marla,

Denise looks like she's pushing forty. Not to say there's anything wrong with that. I live in Newport, so I can't help but date forty-year-olds occasionally, but when it comes to being set up with someone through an exclusive agency such as yours, I don't want to waste "matches." And we need to talk about Natasha, the last gal you lined me up with—a bit low-brow, don't you think? I will send you a few photos of females that I find attractive so hopefully that will help you see the caliber of beauty I'm seeking. I want to date ONLY beautiful women, and I just won't settle for anything less.

Let me know if anyone in your stable meets my criteria.

Thanks, Dave.

I had matched him with Natasha because of the astonishing bounty of her bosom. But as to Denise—she's nowhere near the accursed four-oh. But if she were, how could any man in his fifties possibly be expected to tolerate a crone of such advanced years?

His comment reminds me that I haven't "touched up" yet. I pull out my compact and scrutinize time's deepening etch in the tiny lines around my eyes. I pat them over with mineral powder, add a dusting of blush to my cheeks, a brighter lipstick, and heavy gloss.

I sit back and ponder the photo of Denise, a gorgeous twenty-eight-year-old woman, and all I can do is shake my head. This beautiful young woman is Dave's fourth reject. Before I worked in the matchmaking field, I honestly had no idea how shallow, picky, selfish, and entitled some clients could be. After six years of feedback, demands, and expectations, I'm still thrown for a loop now and then. I don't want to pass judgment on people; I want to keep an open heart, but geez.

It's times like this when I need an anchor, a sane voice, someone who lives far away from the zany nuttiness of Beverly Hills. I call my friend Shelly in Federal Way, Washington, where we both grew up—it's a little suburb of Seattle, a land far away from this town's obsession with age, looks, and perfection.

"Listen to this," I tell her and then read her Dave's email—anonymously, of course.

I hear a gasp on the other end of the line.

"My reaction exactly," I tell her.

"What is he? Some rich stud?"

"Well, rich anyway. I'm supposed to find matches for these guys. They all want perfect 10s—even if they're dweebs who'd be lucky to rate a 5!"

"What about the women?"

"Yeah, some days the gold-diggers and airheads get to me too."

"Guess I don't have to envy you anymore, thinking that you have the perfect life in Los Angeles," Shelly teases. "At least you're not still a waitress in Chicago."

Shelly is referring to my life seven years ago. Memories of my fourteen years spent waiting on tables jolt my sense of perspective, spurring me to work ever harder and continue with the exasperating emails,.

I see Charlotte walk past my door, head held high, but I can tell she's gotten the ax. She starts cleaning out her office. We weren't close, so I won't be going over and chatting. I'll get the scoop later from Alana. After Charlotte leaves, Gary sticks his nose in my door.

"You look better," he says. "You'll have to meet Charlotte's noon appointment. I'm not replacing her, so you'll be taking her people." He closes the door and leaves before I can say anything.

In other words, double the work, same pay. Oh boy!

Dutifully, I meet Andy and take him into the "selling office" with its stunning wall fountain sheeting water over pink-veined slabs of granite and pooling in a pink copper basin beneath two spotlights angled to form a soft heart-shape. The arty painting on the opposite wall captures dancers, hungry with passion, a slash of pink light falling on the woman's tan face and cleavage. Its subtle eroticism is designed to inspire rich guys to pay top dollar for what they imagine will be the world's classiest women. I offer the new client something to drink, and we settle in to chat about what he is looking for in a lady and what his lifestyle is like.

Andy has just flown in for the day to buy a sex life, I mean meet someone, and then he'll jet back to Dallas. He has the most charming Southern accent.

He's forty-six years old with three kids: aged eight, ten, and twelve. He explains that he would like to meet women under thirty because he'd like the option of having another child.

Uh-huh. Right. He's eager to go through diapers and babysitters and soccer games for the fourth time. I've found that men usually claim to want one more kid as an excuse to date younger women.

I learn that Andy likes riding horses, racing cars, playing golf, working out at the gym, and traveling. He says that although he isn't a redneck, he's a redneck at heart—whatever that means. "Do you prefer a fresh-faced girl-next-door look, or more of a Pamela Anderson type of look?" I ask him.

He mentions blonde hair and nice legs, then pulls on his goatee and says, "Well, now I'll tell you, my ex-wife wears a C-cup, but she has nice nipples."

I stop taking notes. *And so . . . ?*

Then I get it. This guy expects me to know what a woman's nipples are like! I focus on my clipboard and remind myself that he will be paying $40,000 to find the right woman. Maybe more. I manage not to hiss at him.

After the meeting, I walk Andy down to the taxi stand. He turns to me and says, "I want you to be honest. Do you think that I have a chance to meet the right girl? Am I going to be too difficult to match up?"

"Not at all, Andy! You're a great catch with a wonderful lifestyle." Lots of gorgeous L.A. women are closet rednecks. "I'll start looking for matches for you this week. Have a safe trip." I want to add: and I'll be investigating nipple potential for you, sir!

I'm also remembering a recent client who broke up with a thirty-two-year-old woman he really liked because he said that she had big areolas. Yes, big areolas! She was perfect in every way: sweet, charming, financially secure, intelligent, cute as a posy with a rockin' body, but he said that he dreaded when she took off her blouse. After dating him, she felt so insecure that she called a plastic surgeon to see if he'd take a look at her areolas. Yikes!

I guess I should change our questionnaire to include nipple preferences. I could put in something subtle like, "How do you feel about headlights on a Duesenberg?" I've seen older guys fall over themselves laughing at this line. I had to look it up. Fabulously snazzy old car with, you know, big headlights, wink, wink.

Something has gone too far though.

+¦+

I don't mind telling you that when I first took this job, I considered myself young and hot-looking, but after working with some of these guys and hearing their smug criticism over every aspect of a woman's body, I'm a bit crestfallen. Getting bombarded with male mating preferences is very disconcerting. Now that I'm fortyish, I look in the mirror, and I see someone who looks pretty darn good looking back at me. So why are so many men obsessing over the extra ounce of flesh, the telltale frown line, and nipple perfection? Gimme a flippin' break!

I push past the clueless effrontery of these men every day, but once in a while, I catch myself judging my most intimate anatomy by their standards. I get so many of these emails every week, they slither around in my head nagging at me about how I'm officially "undesirable"—according to what most of my male clients think they want and *must* have. How could these idiots close themselves off to the wonders of love for something so damn insignificant?

I take a deep breath or two. I'm already a little wired with caffeine, but I *cannot* get through the rest of this day without another soy latte. 'Bucks is just down the street, and I still have a few minutes left of my lunch break.

I need this job, I remind myself while in line for my midday fix. And, I mean, who doesn't want an ideal mate? A dream lover is the stuff of fantasies. Yet, who among us is ideal? The pain of being dumped or disappointed is what keeps people going to shrinks, buying self-help books, bravely enduring elective surgery—and hiring us.

Bolstered by another caffeine infusion, I slog through the rest of the day, interviewing men who are willing to spend up to $100,000 to get the woman of their fantasies. (The women do not pay. This figures: If you're a gorgeous woman, it is unlikely you are going to need to pay anyone to find you a date.) I keep current on the feedback. Both the man and woman are to report on how they found their date: strong mate potential? Problems? Did everyone "behave" themselves? I think you know what I mean.

Gary has left for the day, and Alana comes into my office with the scoop. "Charlotte was fired because two clients complained she didn't pay attention to what they were looking for. You know what *that* means!"

"Yeah. They'll now be my problem," I say.

At six o'clock, I still have an hour to go before quitting time. I grab my cell phone and call my friend Bobbie in Del Mar. I'm not going to whine, I just want to hear her upbeat stuff. Her life is exciting. She usually picks up on the first call. I love that. Hate phone tag.

"Hi, it's Marla."

We chat a bit and Bobbie invites me to an upcoming social event—something to do with farm animals?

I'm so tired, I just say, "Sounds wonderful."

"Are you at home yet?" she asks.

"No. Everyone else in our building gets off at five, but I still have another hour of work."

"You work till seven? Marla, honestly, you deserve combat pay! Especially with the bizarro demands from some of your clients! Do something fun tonight!"

"I should finish chapter 4 of my new book, but I just don't have the juice. Maybe I'll do some window-shopping down on Rodeo. That's always good for a lift."

"Is Adolfo working?"

"Of course. My nights are pathetic, I know."

"Marla, you should just open your own matchmaking service. You'd be fabulous and then you could make your own hours!"

"Thanks. People have suggested I do that, but honestly, I like being able to hand over the big problems to Gary."

There is a pause. "Sweetie, something's wrong. I can tell. I'm a little worried about you," Bobbie says. "I mean, excuse me, your soul is limping."

I chuckle. She's doing a little riff off the title of my first book, *Excuse Me, Your Soul Mate Is Waiting.*

The office line is ringing, and Alana is long gone.

"I gotta go," I say. "I love you. Talk to you soon."

I pick up the office phone, schedule an appointment, and get back to the emails, back to the guys who are looking for gorgeous, starving waifs with double D cups—"tits on a stick," as Bobbie calls them.

Affirmations

I am a terrific Beverly Hills matchmaker happily playing Cupid all day long.

I have many wonderful friends like Shelly and Bobbie whose friendship keeps me from screaming at highly inappropriate times.

Heaven has blessed me with perfectly lovely areolas, thank you very much!

two

Magnets

'**ve** taken off my Jimmy Choo eight-strap platform pumps that originally cost seven hundred dollars—and that I bought online for only a hundred fifteen bucks after I got my signing advance on my first book—and put on my walking shoes from Target. I'm just about to shut the computer off when my email chime sounds. Why do I even bother looking in my inbox at this hour?

Hi Marla, Scott here.
  I'm still waiting for the 10+ lovelies you promised.
SCL

Oops.

Dear Scott,
  Our 10+ young women are very popular and booked well in advance, or they often date one client steadily—which is what we want for you too, right? I'm sure I can have a name for you by tomorrow though.
Marla

There's a second email. It's cc'd to me, but primarily addressed to Gary.

Gary and Marla,

None of the twenty-three women I've dated through your service are up to my standards. I demand that you cancel my contract and give me my money back immediately or I'll see you in court.
Nathan

OgodOgodOgodOgod. I blow my breath out about a dozen times. I know Gary will handle this if it gets really ugly, but I'll have to try to talk the guy out of it first. *Shit!*

Dear Nathan,

Picture if you will the jurors listening to you plead your case: six horny guys slobbering over the gorgeous women you turned down, and six women who must be restrained from forming a lynching party. See what I'm saying, Nathan?

I start to write a foray into an amicable resolution, but you know what? I can't deal with this tonight. Nathan will just have to wait. I shut down the computer, turn off the lights, and lock up.

+‡+

Do I really need this job? I ask myself as I head up Rodeo Drive toward Wilshire. Enough to put up with all the crap?

I hated being a waitress. I made a solemn vow to myself that I would *not* still be waitressing at forty. My thirty-five-year-old self would think I was so dang successful now, I should stand up and cheer. I make good money and have sold two books. The first one is just about to be released, so it hasn't earned enough yet to allow me to focus on writing full time.

Is Bobbie right? Is my soul limping? Right now, I'm fondly remembering my waitressing days in Chicago, where I had more time for creative pursuits before and after work. Or are my Oakleys too rose-tinted as I glance into the past?

Wow! Isn't that Reese Witherspoon in that Rolls driving by? I walk a little faster and almost catch up at the light at Wilshire. The Rolls turns and I follow. I can see it turn again onto North Canon. I bet she's going to Spago. I walk a little faster and am half a block away when I see a swarm of photogs, their cameras flashing like firecrackers. I can see a blonde making it inside the restaurant before being totally mauled.

I have to smile as I head back to Rodeo. She's living the life I was pursuing. At the age of twenty, I left Washington and moved to Los Angeles to pursue my dreams of an acting career—along with thousands of Kelly McGillis wannabes and Don Johnson posers. People used to mistake me for Molly Ringwald and even ask me for my autograph. I would walk down the street and hear, "Hey, Molly!" I'd wave and blow kisses. When I was waiting tables, a few customers thought I was Molly. I went along with it at first and signed their napkins. Finally, I asked the obvious. "Why in the heck would Molly Ringwald be waiting tables in West Hollywood?"

I have pictures of me playing up the Molly look, but I also loved Madonna. The photos of me dressed in her "like a virgin" days: hilarious! None of this got me anywhere in show biz, however. So to pay the bills, I moved on to waitressing along with the rest of the dreamers—just until I landed a part in some big movie that would make me famous. And rich. And allow me to live in Beverly Hills.

Not that doing anything in Beverly Hills isn't a trip, if you know what I mean. In one of the first of my many stellar jobs, which was just across the street from where I'm right now, fogging up a window—sighing over a red Louis Vuitton handbag that I've already priced at $1,110—I often worked the busy Saturday lunch shift where I lost some of my naiveté very quickly. Ron, the manager-host, told us to seat the "beautiful people" outside on the patio so that passers-by could see them frequenting his dining establishment. The "less attractive" tourists were seated inside upfront, and the uglier ones, as he called them, were "positioned in the back." I felt sorry for those poor schmucks— because they also got the slowest service. And the smaller portions. Sometimes they even got the least appealing or slowest selling food items. "What do you recommend on the menu?" the ugly folks would ask in good faith. "Oh, the dirt sandwich with onions and sauerkraut is my favorite. You'll enjoy it."

I begged to wait on the outdoor diners—celebrities, the rich and famous, the spoiled patrons juggling Chanel, Gucci, and Armani shopping bags. I was a bit jealous, of course, of all these privileged people, shopping and dining in Beverly Hills while I worked my ass down to a size zero at two restaurant jobs just to get by. I was waiting on Joan Collins, who came to the restaurant with a party of six. *Dynasty* was a top-rated TV show, and I did my best to please its star villainess, pouring more of *this*, fetching another *that*. And then disaster struck. She called me over to her table. Her fork was missing. "This is an outrage!" she barked.

For all my work, she left me a $2 tip on a $120 tab. The woman was clearly typecast as Alexis, right?

+¦

My dream of getting work as an actress got squeezed into the crannies as the years flew by, and I accepted—but never liked—the restaurant work. I mean *I* should be the one wearing fabulous designer suits at power lunches and dripping with bling at dinner—not serving these hoity-toities. I mostly just got lonelier and felt worse about myself. By age twenty-seven, I was still living alone, away from my family, and struggling financially.

But I was about to ride off into the smoggy sunset with Mr. Fabulous who would, I hoped, save me from the drudgery of two jobs so I could return to acting. I was working in a French restaurant in West Hollywood. Neither Tom Cruise nor Rob Lowe had taken notice of the adorable cashier at Le Bistro Brasserie, so I flirted with Bruno, the cute French sous chef who didn't speak much English. I spoke French, so he chatted me up *tout suite*. I let him talk me into letting him crash at my place a few times— he lived forty-five minutes away and knew I walked to work from my little apartment. Success story that he was, he had no car and spent a fortune on taxi fares at night after work.

I must confess that I suffer from RAA syndrome, Rescues Abandoned Animals, and so I helped the guy out. Like, four times a week. He camped on my sofa. You can see where this is going. I mean a bed is so much more comfy than a lumpy couch.

Bruno soon had an epiphany: Marriage would save us money. Somehow, it sounded sexy in French. Deep down I knew that he was using me, but I was so lonely. I said, *oui.*

What *was* I thinking?

A few years later, Bruno had a chance to work with two brothers who were opening a restaurant in Chicago. He asked me if I wanted to move so far away from sunny California. The only thing I knew about Chicago was that Oprah and Phil Donahue were there, and as one of my guy waiter friends who had visited many times told me, "It's colder than a witch's tit." I had also heard that there was acting work available. I was sick of L.A. and said *oui* once more.

I loved the Windy City and made some good friends, but the restaurant partners turned out to be very bad people, so, after a year and a half, we broke off our association with them. Bruno decided to take a job in Beverly Hills and move back to L.A. We didn't have enough money to pay a moving company, so he went ahead of me; I stayed the summer, working two jobs waitressing in order to save enough for the move. I was so exhausted from waiting on tables day and night that when I came home, I often collapsed on the floor in tears, my three-and-a-half-pound Yorkshire terrier, Daphne, my only comfort. But at least I looked good. According to my friends, the fifteen pounds I dropped gave me a "gaunt catwalk allure."

I finally made it back out to L.A. to be with Bruno, who had by then found his true passion in life: playing poker with the guys. I hardly ever saw him. I should have thought, *Yay!* I was so depressed, though, I thought I might have a nervous breakdown. I told Bruno that it looked like our marriage was falling apart and that maybe we should just end it. He said that would be just fine with him, since he wasn't all that attracted to me in the first place. *Aaaarrrrgggghhhh!* I hated L.A., I couldn't find a job, and I missed Chicago and my friends. I spent a lot of time crying my eyes out. On top of that, I just never got picked out of the studio cattle calls. I felt like I was nothing. After ten months back in the City of Angels—from hell—I decided to go back to Chicago and start a fresh life. This should have been a "woo-hoo moment," but I was still a mess. Scars? It's a wonder my heart still worked. I still have nightmares about those times.

After seven years of marriage, I filed for divorce, packed two suitcases, and put Daphne in my roomy Gucci knock-off handbag. My dad was living nearby in Anaheim with his second wife—my parents having divorced when I was about twenty-seven. He drove me to the airport. Waterworks gushing, I nodded as my dad kept pointing out that this was the best thing I could have done for myself. He was right. My outlook and therefore my luck was about to change.

Oh. My. God. I smell Italian food, and it draws me right out of my memory of those moronic times with Bruno. I've wandered along, enjoying the profusion of flowers blossoming along the center divide of Rodeo Drive. The pleasant summer evening is still light at almost eight. Most of the shops have closed, so I have the place virtually to myself. The flowers perfume the streets, but my nose also detects . . . money. No kidding. The air smells like new cars and aroma therapies and salons and perfume and leather goods. *Eau de Moolah*—that's the scent along this street. I've reached the Rodeo Collection, small, yet the most expensive shopping turf on the planet. You can't really tell from the outside though. Part of it is sunken with all this ivy cascading over the brick walls and marble columns. There's an open courtyard three levels down with trees and a small waterfall. The pizza smell that is making my stomach growl is wafting up from a new upscale restaurant.

I love Italian food, but somehow I managed not to bulk up on it back in Chicago, where I worked in an Italian restaurant for the steady income. It was the first time I actually took charge of my life, and I began making a good deal of money doing TV commercials and getting small parts in films and print modeling work. I even had a couple of lines in the Mel Gibson film, *What Women Want*. Mel was very nice. I got to stand just a few feet from where he was doing his scene. I was so surprised to see what a heavy smoker he was. He would stand in front of the camera, puffing on a cigarette, and then when it was time to do his scene, he threw the lit cigarette on the floor in front of him. After his scene, he would pick it back up and start smoking again. Cig addictions—don't even get me started.

I was happy there for five years. Chicago holds a special place in my heart—but life was about to call me back to California. I was home for Christmas at my mom's house in Federal Way when the call came that my father was in the hospital with cancer. I called the airlines, got a ticket, and jumped on the next plane to Los Angeles, crying the whole way down and as I walked into the hospital. I looked at him lying in his bed, knowing that the time had come for us to pay the ultimate price for those damn cigarettes. The hold that cigarettes get on people is like a vise around the throat. Okay, I didn't mean to go there, but knowing that he was going to suffer just about killed me.

The doctor came into the room and coldly announced that the diagnosis was terminal and that Dad had six months to live, at the most. Then he just turned around and walked out the door.

Neither of us could look at each other.

Then Dad said, "You think it's too late for me to start eating that tofu and carrot juice you're always trying to foist off on me?" We laughed and I hugged him.

Back in Chicago, it took me only five days to pack everything, close bank accounts, tell my boss I was leaving, say good-bye to dear friends like Rita—who would take care of Daphne for me—and hire a moving company. When I got back to California, Dad was no longer in the hospital. He had deteriorated so much that he was put into a nursing home. I spent days and nights at his side, crying and praying for help getting through this.

Mercifully he died a few days later. I was living at my aunt's house, waiting for my things to cross the country from Chicago on a moving truck. The second hardest thing that I've ever had to do in my life was to drive over to the cremation place and pick up my dad's ashes. I paid the four hundred dollars and was handed a cardboard box that weighed about ten pounds. I hid it in the back of the closet of the guest room that I was staying in.

That night, lying on the inflated mattress that was my bed for the next two months, I felt and heard a buzzing sound in my left ear. Then I heard the words in my dad's voice, "We did okay, didn't we? I love you."

"I love you too," I said.

I always feel Dad at my side in stressful times. Like right now.

I think he's telling me to do what makes me happy. I feel in my heart that he helped me right after I moved back to L.A., back to Hollywood.

I planned on getting an agent and a job—in any line of work except waitressing—and start auditioning again. I finally found a cute little studio apartment in Hollywood that accepted dogs, a small miracle, and Daphne and I moved in. Decorating the place helped me cope with the loss of my dad, but I still felt very lost and lonely.

I did some French translation work and was also cast in bit parts as an actress. I began doing "audience work." Yep, they actually pay people to sit in the audience at tapings of game shows and late-night talk shows. I had no idea "audience work" existed as a profession until my girlfriend, Anouchka, introduced me to it. It paid a pittance—six dollars per hour cash, sometimes more—but it was interesting. Getting on the *Judge Judy* show, for instance, paid a whole $40 for just sitting on your butt, staying awake, and looking interested while people bickered, ranted, and endured magisterial sarcasm.

One evening, I walked to a pharmacy up on Sunset Boulevard to get some vitamins. There I met an adorable little Polish woman from New York who also lived in the neighborhood. Sabrina and I became solid friends. We went to plays and comedy clubs together—it was a lot of fun. She introduced me to one of her girlfriends who was an agent. She signed me right away. In the meantime, Sabrina was always talking about a guy who lived in her building. She told me he was dating a gal, but it wasn't serious.

I didn't really care to hear about a guy who was "in a relationship," but every time I saw Sabrina, she kept talking about this guy. She told me that he played piano at a place in Playa Del Rey.

I can't explain this, but I felt like my dad was nudging me. I was just kind of glowing with expectation the night I decided to go to the piano bar with Sabrina to secretly check him out.

Adolfo.

I liked his music, the way he played the piano, and just . . . the way he looked: Latin, handsome, with a warm smile. He came over and sat with us during his break. When he was done for the evening, we all went over to Sabrina's apartment and had a drink. We sat next to each other on her couch, and our lips, I don't know . . . they just . . . somehow . . . locked like magnets.

Affirmations

I will receive a belated tip from an old actress for $62.37 (adjusting for inflation and interest accrual).

My happy clients shower me with appreciation.

My Dad watches over me.

three

How Dreams Change

'm back home after my walk on Rodeo, finishing off some pasta and a green salad, catching a little CNN. Afterward, I take my laptop to my sofa, my treasured forest-green velvet loveseat, and check my Double D Dating Service email.

Hi, Marla,

This Scott sounds like yet another short, fat, bald guy. So, no way, José. Barry does look interesting, but he's just too old. And if Andy already has three kids, why does he want another one? I'm sorry but none of these men is even close. Keep trying.

Best,

Cheryl

She's holding out for George Clooney. Yeah. Right. I keep Cheryl in a different file—one I seldom use. She and a few others are sort of my secret weapons. She's a femme fatale.

Hello there, Marla,

I am liking to meet Scott who has those dimples. Also Barry looks so nice. He sure has those nice pecs for a gentleman of his so many years. I think I do not want to meet the man with already three kids. Andy. Him no. I got a new black dress to wear. You know I so much want to go on nice dates to nice places. Tell to them that please?

Sonia

Yes. I will tell to them that. I want to keep Sonia happy. I'm having a lot of luck with my Russian girls. Sonia is a stunner and is well educated, but her accent makes men think she's less intelligent. I feel better knowing I have at least one name to give out tomorrow, and I know there will be more, of course. Nothing from Gary about Nathan's demand for his money back. This issue makes my dinner churn.

I check my personal inbox and see that my publisher is asking for chapter 4 by the end of the week. I must get up and write, but . . . the loveseat is so comfy. I'll just wait for Larry King and watch a few minutes of his show first. Oh, I love this sweet little sofa. It's a remnant of my single days in Chicago and has seen more action than the Shady Lady Ranch in Nevada. Well, that's a slight exaggeration, but it always reminds me of that night Adolfo and I first kissed on Sabrina's sofa.

He likes to say that I kissed him, but, honestly, we kissed each other.

I didn't check the size of his pecs or ask if he could take me out on expensive dates or try to discover if he fit my list of what I want in a mate. I never felt that he was appraising my cup size— I'd lost so much weight at the time from all the chaos and emotional upheaval with my dad's death and moving that I had to take a deep breath to fill an A cup. Yet, the magic happened.

When we'd left Sabrina's, he'd walked me to my car. We exchanged phone numbers. He called me every day after that, and he took me out every night he was off. He broke things off with the girl he was casually dating, telling her he could no longer see her because he had met someone special. It wasn't too long after that this "loveseat" earned its name.

For the five years after my divorce from Bruno, I'd had no luck in the dating arena. I got my heart dragged around in the dirt a couple more times. I dated a lot. I really wanted to be in a wonderful relationship. However, for some reason, I just couldn't find or attract an available man. They never wanted to get serious or even admit that I was their "girlfriend." I thought I just really loooooved one guy, but when the time seemed right, he didn't propose. We broke up and three months later, he was engaged to somebody else. Strangely, it didn't occur to me that the guys I dated were schmucks or that we were simply not right for each other. I confess that I sorta needed watching over at the time. And wowser, does Adolfo ever love to watch over!

Anyway, the week after meeting Adolfo, my career picked up. I was booked to work for a whole week as an extra on the Jim Carrey film, *The Majestic*. I was in the courtroom scene, which was filmed in a beautiful old hotel in downtown Los Angeles. The story takes place in the fifties, so they dressed us all in fabulous clothes from that era. It was fascinating watching Jim do his scene over and over and over again until he was completely satisfied. He's so intense and definitely a perfectionist. I can see why he is a superstar.

I started collecting Daphne at my apartment and then excitedly rushing over to Adolfo's after work. I was guarding my heart, though. In Chicago, I'd made the mistake on many an occasion of being the first to bring up the subject of "Where is this going?" or "Are we exclusive?" It only backfired on me each and every time.

So, with Adolfo, I vowed to never utter a word about where the relationship was going. To my astonishment, Adolfo started to introduce me to his friends as his girlfriend after only two weeks. Was he for real? Had I slipped into a parallel universe where handsome men could experience a sense of commitment and not fear sudden loss of manhood? I was in complete shock.

One afternoon, I was in the between-jobs limbo and spending the day at his place. Adolfo decided to take me to Malibu for lunch. We were driving along Sunset Boulevard, and he looked over at me and said, "I asked God to send me someone special. He did. You are the love of my life. My heart and soul."

Naturally, I melted inside. But even if I felt the same way, my love wounds hadn't healed, and I didn't respond fully. *You know these passionate Latin lovers,* I cautioned myself. *He thinks he's in love, but next month, he'll use this line on someone else. Why else is he still single?*

Later, back at his apartment, he announced to me that he had written me a song. "It's called 'Tu Eres Mi Estrella,'" he said.

I also speak Spanish, so I knew instantly he was telling me, "You are my star."

He took out his guitar, started strumming, and then sang to me in Spanish. In English, some of his lines translate as:

I want to tell you now, that I feel your spirit
When I look deep in your eyes.
I want to tell you again,
Even though I'm so far, you still live inside of me

I'm not giving you up, I won't, and I won't give you up
Because you are my star
And I carry you inside
And you are like an earthquake
That trembles my life, my heart
You're like the silver moon that shines and shows me the
*　　way all night*

This was by far the most romantic thing that any man had ever done for me. Any doubts I had tucked away in my damaged little heart vanished, ghostly wisps, fading with the sunlight. There we were, two blissful, joyful, love-silly souls, needing little else but the moon and the stars. He would go on to record the song, which would be played on the TV shows *One Life to Live* and *Prison Break*. He made a lot of money on it.

So my love life was going well, and my career was going well, too. I auditioned for the lead in an episode of *Unsolved Mysteries*. I was reading for the part of a woman whose husband had been murdered with an ax. The ironic thing was that when I was up in Seattle staying with my mom for a couple of weeks after my dad died, I saw a story on the news about a realtor who was showing a house and was murdered with an ax. It was the same story. They hadn't solved the case and were now doing a segment on it. In my audition, I had to pretend that I just got the news over the phone that my husband was dead and react to it. I was shaking and trying to cry and everything. I did my best, but when I walked out of the room I thought, *there is no way I am getting that part. I was so bad.* But surprisingly, my agent called me the next day with the news. I'd gotten the job. Now, I'm the type of person who gets excited when the potted rose on my balcony gets a new bud. This was *huge* for me. My acting career was finally going somewhere.

I was also booked to do a scene with Andy Dick on his show. He is so funny and super nice. I had a blast, but the acting work proved sporadic, and my savings dwindled. I needed to get a steady job. Every day I would go sit on my front steps in the sun and try to talk myself into applying for work at some restaurants, but I just couldn't bring myself to do it. I'd made myself a vow.

Six months after we met, Adolfo invited me to his hometown, Mexico City, for New Year's to meet his family. One night, his parents, brothers, and sister were sitting in the living room chatting, and Adolfo stood up and pulled his wallet out of his back pocket. He extracted one of those little laminated calendars and said, "We need to pick a date for the wedding." I choked as if I'd just swallowed a whole jalapeño chili pepper, swigged my tequila, and looked at his parents. They seemed thrilled, so I jumped up and threw my arms around him.

"Honey," he said, "my family loves you as much as I do, and we want you to be part of us."

The heavens opened and showered us with golden confetti. I saw it for sure. I, Marla Renee Martenson, was engaged to my soul mate and man of my dreams. Adolfo took me to a little jewelry store next to his parents' home.

"We have to have something to show everyone that we are really engaged," he said. "Pick something out."

"But there isn't much here," I told him.

"It's okay, we just need something."

So I selected a simple silver ring with a small cubic zirconia. We walked over to the church, and I showed his parents. They kissed me and congratulated us. I could have been wearing a ring out of a crackerjack box for all I cared. I was now a part of this wonderful family. The wedding would be in ten months, right there in Mexico City.

✝

Just before we got married, Adolfo asked me to move in with him, telling me there was no need to worry about paying rent, so I didn't need to earn much money.

Really? Honestly? Okay, then. No hay problema. I got to do what I wanted when I wanted. What an amazing concept.

Leisurely days turned into exciting nights. I got dressed up to go to fashionable piano bars around the beautiful, wonderful City of Angels—whole choirs of angels, cherubim and seraphim belting out the *Hallelujah Chorus*. I'd go alone or bring friends to hear the love of my life play his music at clubs. Suddenly, there were weekends in wine country, nights off that allowed movies and theatre instead of working late. It was glorious!

Eventually, though, as happy as I was wifeing it full time, I got tired of not having my own money, and when I found myself in credit card debt for a total of ten grand, I had a little talk with myself that went something like this: "Marla, time to get your ass in gear and make some dinero!"

So, back to job hunting. After weeks of calling, trekking around, doing interviews, schlepping résumés, and filling out reams of applications, I was getting discouraged; then Adolfo's friend took over the management of a video dating service and needed part-time help at the front desk. She told him that if I wanted the job, it was mine. I accepted and found that I thoroughly enjoyed videotaping new clients and interviewing them to learn all about what they were looking for in a partner.

What I discovered was that regardless of what men and women say they want and need from a partner it all boils down to this: a man wants someone who is beautiful, slim, and sexy; a woman wants a "good-guy" who is successful and has a sense of humor. There you have the secret of the ages as to finding successful matches, reduced to a bouillon cube that is the basis of many a stew.

I enjoyed doing the interviews for a year and a half, but when the owner sold the business, I was once again out of a job. I checked out the "Help Wanted" section in *Backstage West,* a newspaper for actors. There was an ad that stated simply, "Talent scout, fun job, Beverly Hills," and the phone number. I told my friend Francine, about it.

"It's a scam! Don't apply!" she warned.

"How bad can it be?" I said. "I'm savvy. The interview is only four miles from my apartment. What do I have to lose? I'm going to check it out!"

"You'll be sorry," she said, "when you're in Bangladesh, taking orders from some fat old geezer whose real intention is to put the make on you in some sleazy backstreet hotel!"

The next day, I showed up for an interview. I loved the look of the art deco ten-story building on Roxbury. I could definitely picture myself working in this neighborhood. The place turned out to be an upscale matchmaking service that catered to wealthy men seeking goddesses, models, and ex-prom queens: none other than the Double D—which was looking for a recruiter, a hired representative to go out and scout for "talent," meaning a fresh supply of goddesses. Given my experience in the dating industry, I was hired on the spot.

Afterward, I called Francine and gloated. "I'll be sitting in a plush office in the center of Beverly Hills, looking out into the hustle and bustle of power brokers making mega-deals. I'll lunch with clients who flash their little plastic cards representing unlimited credit lines in five-star restaurants. . . ." Wicked, I know. Sometimes my inner devil just kicks down the doors.

So I'd found true love with my husband and held a dream job. How could I ever find anything to whine about again?

Well, there was that little matter of my dream of acting. I had little time to audition. Was I going to have to let that dream die? Dead dreams are not the stuff of happiness. I didn't notice so much at first because after about two months of successful recruiting, I was offered a full-time job in the office as a matchmaker, and then as head matchmaker.

I still went on weekend auditions, but they rarely led to anything. I swear I wasn't weird about the waning possibility of an acting career. I didn't make bitter offhand remarks or drink too much wine to drown any sorrows over my wasted talent. Somehow, though, Adolfo sensed something. One day three years ago, I was in the living room, and Adolfo came out of the music studio in the second bedroom of the apartment.

He came up to me and said, "I have something to tell you."

"What is it, mi amor?"

"God told me to tell you to write. You need to be a writer."

I was completely shocked. Even though I'd always wanted to be a writer from a young age, I had never pursued it or even shared that dream with Adolfo. He only knew about my interest in acting.

In grade school, I used to write letters to my favorite authors, telling them how I wanted to be just like them. I sent fan letters and felt so disappointed if I didn't get a reply. I vowed to always answer my fan mail when *I* became a famous writer. *When*, not *if.*

In junior high, I was writing poetry and short stories nonstop. I got sidetracked, though, after seeing Ann Miller in a movie, and my focus shifted to tap dancing, then to acting. Yes, it was final. I would be a movie star. Yet, through all my many directions and experiments, I journaled and never lost the dream of being a writer. I just never told anyone.

"I can't believe you are saying this," I told Adolfo. "How did you know?"

"I have this vision of you being a successful writer." His face held the intent glow of sincerity. "Forget about the acting, Marlita. You need to write."

"But I still love acting. I don't want to forget about it."

"I'm telling you Marla, I got the message, and you'd better follow up on it." His voice was gentle. "I'm very perceptive. Don't waste your time and gasoline going on all these auditions that never pan out. Focus on writing. I see you as a bestseller."

Again, I marveled at his words. This wasn't just something to keep my mind off the virtual impossibility of an acting career. He truly believed in me.

I remember one day while driving to an audition, hearing Salma Hayek on a radio interview. She said, "As women, we need to make our own projects. We can't just sit around waiting for someone to give us a job." Hearing her say that with such confidence and knowing what she had accomplished in her life had already planted a seed in my head. So, Adolfo's intuition or revelation was perfectly timed.

"Well . . . I have been keeping a lot of notes since I started in the matchmaking industry. I have an idea for a dating book."

His smile always won me over. "Excellent, put it together. I am so proud of you Marlita."

From that day on, he has always guided me and kept me on track, not only with my writing, but with getting out of debt, saving for retirement, prioritizing my goals, and being more creative. He likes to tease me by saying, "Don't forget, I am responsible for you being a writer."

✚

I see I've missed Larry King. I force myself to open my book file on my laptop and work on my *book,* but first I want to jot down a few things in my journal:

Having a writing career is like working two jobs again, matchmaking by day, hitting the computer keyboard at night, early mornings, and on weekends. The matchmaking job starts to feel draining and frustrating when it sucks the energy away that I covet for my writing time. If I feel tired and frustrated from writing, though, I don't seem to mind as much because it feels like this is who I truly am. I am a writer. How could I have ever forgotten to nurture this side of myself?

Now perhaps a line for a book:

Attention! Attention! Profound truth coming at you: love really does lift us up where we belong. When you're with the right person, you can talk honestly about the future, and they won't go away. Not only that, your lover sees who you really are and encourages that true self, just as you encourage it in your loved one.

Attention all you clueless dickheads! You know who you are. You do things like rejecting twenty-three gorgeous women because their areolas aren't perfect. You are going to attract women who insist that your bank accounts are perfect, and you will never figure out how to love each other for your true selves.

Huh? Is it appropriate to say *clueless dickhead* in the book? I guess the threat of litigation has made me cranky. What about *myopic dweebs?* No? Priority-challenged simpletons? Okay, I'll work on it.

Affirmations

I keep my inner devil in her corner around irritating clients.

I am a *New York Times* bestselling author.

I am madly in love with the love of my life.

four

Scrambled Eggs

I slept on it, and I tried. Really. I'm sorry, but if a guy tells a fabulous woman *adios* because of totally superficial issues— as is the case with Nathan-who-wants-his-money-back and Areola Man—there is no more accurate terminology than *clueless dickhead.* However, I'm willing to compromise and settle for code: If you see *C.D.* anywhere in my story, you'll know I don't mean compact disc.

I figured this out driving to work this morning as I dreaded having to deal with Nathan's threat. I didn't sleep well last night, and I just don't have any energy, which, in turn, forced me to splurge on a *venti*-size vanilla soy latte. At work, I boot up, slurp my coffee, refill the water in the wall fountain in my office— which is much smaller than the big one in the sales office—scroll past the spam, and click on my inbox icon. I see my boss's name, and my heart does a whammo ka-thump. Holding my breath, I click to open the file.

> Marla: I'll handle Nathan. —G

Oh, thank God! Deep breaths. Ah, the lovely feeling of oxygenated blood returning to white knuckles and cold feet, the gut kinks relaxing. It helps. Next email.

> Dear Marla,
> This last girl you set me up with led me off on another wild

goose chase. Turns out she's about to go into foreclosure and needs
20K to pay debts, including money for lawyers. She hinted that I
should pay for a nanny, personal trainer, and assistant for her so
that she could "devote more time to me."

You have to admire the audacity, right? I mean I'd only known
her two weeks. In essence, the only thing she has is her looks. She's
a 10, no doubt about that, but I got the feeling she's used to working that to get what she wants. And actually? Dumb as cheese. She
couldn't follow any real conversation.

I told her it was too early in our relationship to lend her
money or subsidize her lifestyle. Within hours I was dumped.
Ted

Dear Ted,
I'm on a mission to find you a smart, down-to-earth, lovely
woman.
Marla

Ted is a *mensch* and deserves just what I said I'd find. Miss
Chaching, on the other hand, will not be seeing any of my nicer
guys anymore. However, my down-to-earth lovely woman files are
running low. Note to Luisa, a recruiter: find some really *nice* gals.

As I plow through the morning, I realize I'm starting to feel
not just tired but drained and achy. A follow-up email from Gary
comes in around ten thirty.

Marla: I've spent the morning talking to Nathan. He's out of
our hair, but I don't want any more of this. We need new talent.
Our numbers are getting low. I'm telling our recruiters to step it
up. It's been a long time since you've brought anyone in. Get with
it. Don't make any assumptions. Approach *every* beautiful woman
you see and give her your card.
—G

I'm getting a headache.
I hate recruiting with a passion, but our numbers are way
down. I'm going to have to cruise for women. Yep, that's what I
said.

Just before noon, I get an email from a client, Serena Smythe. It's horrendous but juicy. I must share it with Alana. I hit print and rush out to the lobby.

"Listen to this. I cannot believe this feedback." I perch on the arm of the mocha-colored leather sofa across from Alana's desk and start to read.

Dear Marla,

I actually have decided not to continue dating through your service. I'm sure that you must have some nice guys over there, but honestly? After tonight, I am taking a loooong break from the dating scene. I met Stuart at the wonderful Italian restaurant on Third Street called Matteo. It is actually my favorite restaurant in Los Angeles. Or was. I found him to be a very brilliant and interesting man and enjoyed his stories of his travels around the world. And I was also impressed that he is an orthopedic surgeon. I did find it odd, however, that he mentioned several times that he liked my shoes and especially my choice of color for the polish on my toes. I'd never had a date comment on something like that. Well, after the main course and while we were waiting for dessert, Stuart started sort of squirming. He suddenly disappeared under the table and started caressing my ankles. I sat there in total shock expecting him to pop back up with some kind of explanation, but when I felt his tongue slide from my toes to my ankle and then work it's slimy way up my leg, my reflexes took over, and I gave him a swift kick. With a God-awful moan, Mr. Foot Fetish slowly crawled out from under the table, and then collapsed in a bloody heap beside my chair. *Everyone* in the restaurant put down their forks and glasses and stared. His nose was hemorrhaging and his pants were unzipped. He swore at me profusely, called for an ambulance, and then yelled, "Find your own way home, bitch!" Good thing that Cedars Sinai is located practically across the street. This thing gave me the creeps, big time. So, thanks, but no thanks to any more dates.

Sincerely,

Serena

"Oh. My. God." Alana says. "I'm kinda freaked out here! Remember when he came in for his first meeting with Gary? I was wearing my four-inch, open-toed candy-apple-red Jimmy

Choo's that I bought on eBay? Well he commented on my pedicure. Twice!"

"I wondered why none of his last five dates wanted a second date with such a nice looking, charming, rich guy," I said. "I'm going to have to discuss this with Gary."

I also have to contact his previous referrals and ask them for a little more detail on their dates with him. Gary will then tell the guy that any further reports such as Serena's will constitute a nonrefundable breach of contract. If he has the nerve to ask for another referral, I'll give him one of my girls who has seen everything—like Jolene, a southern girl who once showed me a small handgun, a Taurus CIA—Carry It Anywhere.

Now with Serena dropping out, I have one less nice woman to match up. She'd have been a great one to introduce to Ted.

By one o'clock, all I can think about is spending my lunch break lying down on the little foldaway cot in the office kitchen/lounge. The thought of food turns my stomach. I haven't felt this bad since I discovered I was pregnant.

This thought makes me sit straight up in my chair.

I'm feeling more achy flulike than the general cruddiness I felt back then, aren't I? I just need more rest, right? I drag a pink and copper pillow off the front sofa, haul myself into the small back room, unfold the cot, and lie down.

Adolfo would be thrilled if I *am* pregnant, but the situation is impossible.

✝

When Adolfo and I met, I was well into my thirties, and, of course, had never had kids. He was forty-one, had never married or fathered a child. I never actually wanted kids. It never even crossed my mind. I don't seem to get all goo-goo eyed like some of my friends who, upon seeing a baby in a stroller, run over with arms flailing as they coo and make ridiculous faces and strange noises until the mother wheels the poor kid away. Now, should a puppy or a kitten cross my path, well, I'm as delighted as a kid playing in a mud puddle.

When Adolfo and I got married, he did mention that he

would like to have one child. I still wasn't keen on it, especially since we lived in an apartment, and I had to work full time. And honestly, giving birth was always on my list of scary, painful, and extremely undesirable things to do, right up there with bungee jumping and stretching an earlobe piercing to accommodate Ubangi bones.

"How could I possibly handle having a baby?" I asked.

"Honey, don't even worry about it. I will bring a nanny from Mexico."

"Oh really? And she will live here with us in our little apartment? And I suppose at least half of my salary would go to paying her."

"We'll buy a house."

"But we can't afford to buy a house now, so how would we do that?"

"Don't worry, honey. I will handle everything."

Well, I was very nervous about it, so I waited until I was almost forty before I agreed to stop taking my birth control pills. (I figured that was about as far as I could push it.) I had been taking them for most of my adult life. No accidents for me.

One night in bed I told Adolfo, "Look, just forget about this baby thing. It's not going to happen. My eggs are too old—scrambled, actually."

"No, I am not giving up. I am sure that we still have a chance. You would make such an amazing mother."

"But you don't even trust me to take the camera outside of the house because you're afraid that I'll lose it, yet you would trust me with your child?"

He just rolled his eyes.

Then one day at work I realized that my breasts had been hurting for over a week, which had never happened before. I told the other matchmaker at the time, Leslie, "I feel a bit nauseous."

"Maybe you're pregnant," she said.

"Wow, maybe. Nah, I doubt it."

"Go to Rite Aid and get a test."

I walked over to Rite Aid, bought the kit, and went into the bathroom down the hall from my office. I peed on the stick and waited a couple of minutes for the results. What the @#$#@&!!#^!! The word in the window spelled *PREGNANT.* I started to shake and then sob. I went out into the hallway and dialed Adolfo's cell phone.

"Hi, honey." I tried to keep my voice even. "What are you doing?"

"Oh, I am out in front of Mastro's. I had to meet the piano tuner."

"Oh, you're in Beverly Hills. Well, wait there. I need to see you about something."

"No, honey, I have to go. I'll see you later."

"I need to see you now!"

I ran over to Canon Drive as fast as my four-inch high-heel-clad feet would carry me. When I saw him, I was still crying.

"Marlita, what's wrong? What happened?"

I grabbed the pregnancy test from my purse and started flailing it around, hyperventilating, tears streaming down my face.

"Are you pregnant? Are you pregnant?" he yelled.

A guy in a business suit walked by, obviously wondering what the commotion was. I dashed into a doorway to hide. I handed Adolfo the results. Romantic approach, huh?

Yet Adolfo held both of my hands and kissed my forehead, my cheeks, my nose, looked deeply into my eyes and kissed me tenderly on the lips. For him, I would try to be happy.

I was nauseous twenty-four/seven, dragging myself from bed to work and work to bed. At the same time, I was writing my first book, *Excuse Me, Your Soul Mate Is Waiting.* I'd sold it partially written along with a proposal, and the publisher needed me to meet incremental deadlines. At about seven weeks along, I miscarried.

I had thought I'd feel only relief, but I felt an acute sense of the loss of something precious. I grieved, but I knew it was probably just not meant to be. I had to work all that day, and all I wanted to do was go to bed. Adolfo couldn't understand. He blamed my vegan diet. That had to be it. It couldn't be the fact that because of my age, I was a high risk for miscarriage. I ate very healthily and was under a doctor's care, but most women's eggs are not viable after forty.

"I am sick of this tofu bullshit. You need to eat real food."

"Well, tofu is real food to me, so I am not going to change my diet."

He was so disappointed, I was truly sad for him, and I continued to feel as if I'd lost a small part of myself, that part of me that could have loved a child. My life was so full, however, with work, writing, friends, household obligations, errands, taking care of Daphne—now an elderly dog, working out, and grocery shopping. I was completely overwhelmed trying to figure out how I was supposed to fit in taking care of a baby as well, and doing it throughout my forties. I imagined men coming in the middle of the night with a straight jacket to haul me away after I'd accidentally placed the baby in the refrigerator instead of the formula.

People still tell me, "Oh, you have plenty of time to have kids."

And I say, "Oh yeah? Well I just had a hot flash!"

Three weeks after my miscarriage, I'd gotten a little strength back and went to the nail salon for a manicure. My phone rang. I answered it with my free hand.

"Honey, I've been trying to call you like six times." Adolfo's voice carried urgency.

"Why? What's going on?"

"Something bad happened," he said.

I immediately braced myself.

"Your brother died."

My brother? My brother! *My brother.* The words hit me like I was on a collision course with a comet. I slumped into the chair sobbing, the whole salon looking over at me, wondering what was going on.

"My brother died," I choked out between sobs. One of the manicurists ran over to hug me. I threw some money on the table and drove home, where I tossed a few winter clothes into a suitcase. I called Gary on his cell phone and told him what had happened and that I wouldn't be in to work. I took Daphne for a walk and then headed to the airport.

My uncle picked me up in Seattle. My brother, Brett, had been living in Utah, although we hadn't known where for the past five years. Because of an alcohol addiction, he'd been estranged from us. I had been thinking of him so much the last few months and was planning to hire a detective to find him after I paid off my credit card debt. I felt so guilty and ashamed that I didn't just do it anyway. We learned that he had been living with his girlfriend, an apparent drug user whose children had been taken away from her. When he died, she looked through his address book and found the number of one of his friends in Seattle. She contacted him, and it was he who showed up on my mother's doorstep.

I had hoped that Adolfo would one day get to meet my brother. They would have hit it off immediately. Brett was crazy about music; it was his life. Actually the beginning of his downfall was when he became obsessed with heavy metal music as a late teen. The people he gravitated to and their lifestyle offered the dangerous path he chose.

My uncle helped us a lot, including tracking down where my brother's body was being held, and he arranged for the cremation and for the ashes to be sent to us. It was a terribly sad thing, and both mom and I came down with some kind of horrible flu that left me sick for a whole week.

I'll never forget when the doorbell rang, and I opened the door to find a smiling UPS man.

"Good afternoon. I have a package for you. It's very heavy. It must be bars of gold," he said with a grin.

"It's my brother's ashes," I said, fresh tears brimming.

"Oh . . . I'm sorry." His expression changed instantly, registering dismay.

Another box of ashes, another broken heart.

My dear friend from grade school, Kevin, led the memorial by the ocean. Many of Brett's old friends came and said some kind, loving, and funny things. Barely choking back tears, I couldn't say a word. After the service, we went to the edge of the water and spread his ashes in the same place where we had said good-bye to my grandparents.

I was back on the job a week later. The shallow demands of my clients seemed laughable: A woman concerned that a guy was living in a condo and not a house and drove a Toyota instead of a Porsche; a man refusing to call a lady because her eyes were the wrong color. "I want to meet a woman with blue eyes because I can see her soul." To even imagine that we are only as good as the car we drive, our eye color, or cup size is really just plain sad. It was after Brett's death that I started bringing candles to the office.

I have no trouble remembering the prayers I said then. "Thank you God for my wonderful Adolfo, my soul mate with brown eyes, my rock. Thank you for sending me what seems to be one of the few men in Los Angeles who sees the whole picture and cherishes being with his best friend through all the weird things life can throw at you. Thank you. Thank you. Thank you."

I still say that prayer.

†‡

Actually, my boobs don't hurt. I don't think I'm pregnant. I'm just sick. Half-hour break over all too soon, I haul myself off the cot, fold it up, and roll it back between the fridge and the wall.

Back in my office, I look at my day-planner to see what I can reschedule over the weekend. Oh, no! I've got tomorrow afternoon and evening devoted to Bobbie and some kind of party for . . . ? I penciled in farm animals? I have no memory of what this is about. Why did I say I'd go?

I start to call her and plead a case of the plague when I realize that the parties Bobbie takes me to are often attended by celebs, so there might be some single women at this event who qualify as 9s or 10s, and who, for some reason, are having trouble getting dates and would agree to go out with well-heeled older men who rate as 5s. That shouldn't be too hard to find. With Gary on his rampage, I don't dare let this party opportunity pass.

And what am I thinking? I don't have time to be sick. I've got to finish chapter 4. To get through the afternoon, I load up on Alka Seltzer nondrowsy daytime cold medicine.

Affirmations

I am kidless and that's okay.

I am as healthy as a fitness coach.

I am a prodigious writer.

Gorgeous, skinny, young nubile women who want to date 5s will flock to me.

five

Lucy and Ricky

'm home and feeling really crappy. I guess it's a mélange of cold and flu. I am hopped up on mega doses of cold meds, trying to get some writing done. Adolfo, who works at home in his recording studio during the day, is freaking out over a parade of ants in the bathroom. He's been rather edgy since I told him that Gary fired Charlotte. He asked me a hundred questions. What did she do? Do you ever do what she did? How does he talk to you? What does he want you to do now?

"Should I go get the white klieg lights to shine in my eyes while you ask the questions, inspector?" I asked a bit crossly.

He backs off. "Sorry, honey. It's just that this would be a terrible time for you to lose this job."

So now he's at war with the ants. Los Angeles in the summertime *is* one massive colony. Daily armies of them march through the kitchen, bathroom, and occasionally even have the nerve to traverse my computer screen while I'm writing. I long for a room of my own like Adolfo's, where I could write in peace while he natters and frets over ants to his heart's content without bothering my concentration.

As I'm working on a troublesome section of chapter 4, he is scurrying around cleaning them up, blaming me for the invasion—everything negative is my fault—and complaining that I spend too much time at the computer. I should be doing housework since we have an overnight guest coming, Bobbie. I'm picking her up from Union Station at 2:40. She's coming up on the train to Los Angeles from Del Mar. I checked out the e-vite. We are going to a fundraiser for factory-farmed animals that Jane Velez-Mitchell is cosponsoring to support Proposition 2, which requires that calves raised for veal, egg-laying hens, and sows be confined in ways that are humane—namely, that the animals be able to lie down, stand up, fully extend their limbs, and turn around freely for the majority of the day, as opposed to the tiny crates that they are confined to now. The cruelty to animals is really disgusting. For a pig party, it should be a big deal. I was thrilled over the invitation once I realized Jane was behind it. I'm a huge fan of hers. Bobbie, also an author, and I met Jane at Book Expo of America. We were invited to Jane's booth at the Expo, where the three of us became friends.

I confess I'm looking forward today to gawking at those in the movie industry. Stargazing is the number two sport in Hollywood and Beverly Hills. Shopping is number one, of course, and name-dropping is number three. Watching bizarro people while sipping a latte is number four. From the rich and famous to the actual stars to the wannabe's and weirdoes, it's all about theatrics in Los Angeles. I want to rack up a big score, so I can one-up people in Monday morning conversations about the weekend. Just kidding. Sort of.

+̣+

"I found what caused the ant invasion," Adolfo yells, rushing through the living room holding a half-eaten cough drop. "You left this candy in the trash!"

"No, I didn't." I'm trying to write, but I must defend myself. "That's a cough drop. I don't eat cough drops. I *hate* cough drops."

He opens a kitchen drawer, "Look, half of my cough drops are gone. I know you've been eating them." He is relentless in his crusade to lay blame for the ants and now also for the cough drops he doesn't remember using. I'm not unhappy about getting out of the house today.

Bobbie says that the moment God created man, He took one look at the poor fellow and all his limitations and said, "Oh, surely I can do better than this!" And hence, He created woman.

In that spirit, I take a look at my big strong man standing there with a teeny piece of cough drop in his hand, looking like Javert accusing Jean Valjean and I laugh. He is not amused.

"Are you going to pick up all the bags you left in the living room?" nags Adolfo.

"Yes, yes," I say. "Just give me fifteen minutes to finish this paragraph I'm working on. I *have* a deadline."

"Can't they cut you some slack? You only just finished your first one."

"Right, but they're already getting advance orders, so they asked me to speed up the second one."

"You shouldn't be writing so much. You're sick!" he says.

"I know I'm sick, but I have to get this done."

"You push yourself too much. I told you that you would get sick." Adolfo hands me a Hall's cough drop. "No excuses. Here, suck on this cough drop."

"I hate cough drops! I don't want it."

"Just eat it. Your throat is scratchy, right?"

"Just a little scratchy; it's my lungs that feel funny, more than my throat."

"Your lungs?" He rolls his eyes. "Oh, my God. Eat the cough drop!"

"Okay!" I unwrap the cough drop and put it in my mouth. As soon as he leaves the room, I spit it out.

Bobbie says we're a real-life Ricky and Lucy. She affectionately calls him Ricardo, as do many of our friends. Like Ricky, Adolfo is a Latin musician, performing in night clubs, married to a red-head, only I'm nothing as ditzy as Lucy.

I check the time and gasp. It's 1:35. I have to leave in about twenty minutes. I drop more fizzing cold tablets into a glass and sip as I work on my hair and make-up. Standing in front of my closet, I tap my foot along to "Sweet Caroline" now playing in Adolfo's recording studio—our second bedroom.

What exactly does one wear to a Beverly Hills pig party? I try on a white Nicole Miller puffy sort of dress with lace, a gift, which looks great on the hanger, but once on my body, makes me look like a giant marshmallow even with the gold belt that came with it.

"What's *that?*" Adolfo asks standing in the bedroom doorway.

"How long have you been standing there peeking?" I ask.

He is grinning.

"This is an expensive designer dress that I got as a gift. But it doesn't do anything for me," I moan.

He nods solemnly. "Give it away."

I change in my closet, donning a black slip.

"Wow, that looks nice," says Adolfo, eyeing me up and down. "But you can't wear it outside. It's too sexy."

"This isn't the dress, silly, it's the slip."

"Okay, well, I'm not against you wearing it while you dust. You do know how to dust, right honey?"

"Enough already," I say, putting on a blue wrap-around dress, a DKNY bought on sale—two years ago.

"Honey, you look beautiful in anything and everything— which is why I do the dusting myself. And the vacuuming. And the grocery shopping. And the cooking. Oh, and by the way, I am taking the job of doing the laundry away from you."

"What? That is my job! You have no idea how to do the laundry. You cram so many clothes in the washer that there's no way they can get clean."

He's laughing. "Marlita, you are the one who has no idea how to do the laundry. I grew up with maids. I saw how they did the laundry. You have to pack it all in."

"Watch me pack this in," I say, adjusting the dress and heisting my no longer A-cup boobs to a prominent position so that the dress reveals maximum cleavage. He is observing me closely, so I pull my shoulders back and thrust my chest out for added emphasis.

Ricky smiles sheepishly. "Lucy, honey, do we have time for a quickie before you have to pick up Bobbie?"

I glance at the time. 2:02. "Oh, no!" I've allowed our banter to distract me. "Sorry, honey. Gotta go!" I give him a quick kiss and fly out the door.

Affirmations

I keep my dreams alive.

Like ants parading across my computer, my work station is alive and teeming with ideas.

I'm a champion at Beverly Hills sports.

I have friends in high places whose names I can drop all over the place.

six

The Pig Party

I am a vegetarian and *love* animals, especially pigs. One of my dreams is to have one as a pet some day. In my opinion, pigs are friends, not food. Bobbie on the other hand grew up on a farm and has another view of farm animals.

"Nothing like a thick pink cut of prime rib," she says, smiling.

I take comfort that she is so opposed to the maltreatment of animals.

We're both excited about the party, which is taking place in the garden of a Beverly Hills mansion. I'm hoping for a stroll through the stunning backyard of some wildly rich and famous person. We have to park what feels like miles away, and as we approach the party, a bevy of skinny models prances around in skimpy animal print costumes that display their beautifully tanned bodies. They greet us and plead for donations, "which can easily be put on your credit card, say for a small deduction of only $75 *per month.*" I offer them my dating service cards instead.

"These girls need a pork-chop," Bobbie says, not caring if any of them hear the remark.

As we pick up our name tags, I watch to see what the costumed women do with my card. One, wearing a red cockscomb hat and a white Playboy-Bunny-style suit literally covered with white feathers, is looking it over carefully. So is a black sheep in a wooly bikini. Another, in faux cowhide, tucks it into her scanty halter top. A gal in pig ears and a little pink satin outfit with a curly tail at the butt tosses it in the trash.

We make our way toward the red carpet entrance. Photogs snap pictures in hopes of selling them to the tabloids. I'm dying to be photographed, but no one seems interested in us.

"It's my hair," I tell Bobbie. "If my hair looked better, I think I'd be asked to pose."

"I'm going to get really serious about taking off those five pounds," Bobbie says.

"I should have worn a lower cut dress." *I should be younger and more glamorous.*

Oh, no! I stand still on the lawn. How did that thought sneak into my brain? More affirmations for me tonight.

Bobbie has walked ahead. She turns to look at me. "What's wrong?"

I catch up with her. "Nothing. I'm good. We're great-looking, right?"

"We're totally hot!"

A good number of guests have arrived, all heading to the wine-bars, all straining to see who is attending. I recognize a couple of my female clients—both carrying drinks and wearing low-cut designer dresses that showcase enormously enhanced cleavages.

Two buffet lines are loaded with what a hostess proudly calls vegan delicacies.

"Isn't vegan delicacy an oxymoron?" Bobbie asks. She's eyeing the separate dessert tables—which none of the female 9s and 10s will go near. Three different bars offer wine, vodka martinis, or beer. I pick up an already poured Merlot, hoping it will kill off whatever bugs I'm fighting, though it hasn't harmed the gnat that's swimming in it.

"There's Jane!" I say, but such a crowd has gathered around her that I can't get close.

She waves at us, and we wave back. At that, a young woman on the outer fringe of the crowd around Jane turns to me.

She has the kind of long blonde hair the movie guys love to film in slow motion while she's swishing it from side to side. Slow motion hair. I hate this bitch.

Oh, no! I'm letting stuff chink my rainbow. This isn't me. More affirmations needed.

Bobbie elbows me. "She's not wearing any rings on her left hand. You're trolling, aren't you? Go for it."

I approach the young woman and chat about our mutual connection to Jane. Her name is Heather. I notice her handbag is a Louis Vuitton knockoff. Aha! She'd love to have the real thing. I give her my card, just as a handsome man brings her a martini. Dang, I was getting my hopes up. As I leave them, a photographer snaps the happy couple's picture.

"I don't expect to hear from Heather," I say to Bobbie. "Her boyfriend's really great-looking."

"In this town, great-looking guys often like to pick out decorator pillows," Bobbie says. "I bet you'll hear from Miss Heather."

The babes in animal outfits are mingling with the crowd. I hand out a few more cards before Bobbie and I plant ourselves at the tall bar tables next to the swimming pool, which is filthy, its water the color of avocados.

"I understand the enthusiasm for going green," I say, "but this is ridiculous."

"If I were having an event at *my* mansion, I'd have asked Jeeves to see about possibly removing all the nasty dead tree branches," remarks Bobbie.

This strikes us both as hilarious and our giggles start up just as a gorgeous, well-dressed man approaches, wearing ultra-cool sunglasses against the glare of the setting sun. D&G, I think. He must be six foot five.

Bobbie recognizes him right off. "That's Matt Grant, the bachelor from *The Bachelor* TV show!" she gushes. "Is this guy an adorable hunk, or what? C'mon, let's go talk to him!"

"I love his English accent. He's a 10 for sure," I tell Bobbie as we walk past a rose cemetery—a former rose bed where dry thorny things now stand. "Boy, would I love to have him as a client to match up! I can just imagine saying, 'Hi, Amy, I have a guy for you! Twenty-seven, from London, gorgeous, went to Cambridge, financier and business development manager. Never married, no kids, down-to-earth, charming, stylish, well traveled, polite, and sexy as hell.'"

Bobbie says, "She'd clear her calendar at the speed of light."

We catch up with him, and Bobbie says, "Excuse me, Matt," as she sidles up alongside him. "Are you and that little blonde—Monkey—still together as the tabloids are reporting?"

Laughing amiably, the well-dressed hunk says, "No, we're not. That didn't last too long, did it?"

"Because I was surprised you stayed on the show. I mean if I looked around and saw that I wasn't going to get interested in any of the matches, I'd split," Bobbie informs him, adding, "and certainly none of the girls were in your league."

Matt laughs and says, "Well, then I wouldn't have the chance at some of the amazing opportunities I have now—like meeting the both of you, now would I?" Always gallant, this guy.

The pig girl walks over, her pink stilettos clacking along the slate pathway. She's the one who threw my card away. She's wearing her long blonde hair in pigtails, of course, the ends brushing her cupcakes, all nice and plump with saline. The cute pink ears on her pink headband bob as she looks at my nametag.

"Marla, I so enjoyed our chat earlier. I see you're friends with . . ." she turns to Matt, ". . . someone special." She stretches her pink glossy lips into what seems like genuine radiance. "I'm Fawn. It's so fabulous to meet you, Matt." She manages to angle herself so that she cuts me off from Matt's line of sight.

"A pleasure," he says dryly.

"Hi, Fawn," Bobbie says, stepping forward and slightly in front of Matt. "I'm Bobbie."

"Hi." She merely glances at Bobbie.

A woman, probably in her sixties, very chic, appears at Matt's side.

"Hannah!" he says. "How great to see you!" He turns toward Bobbie and me. "Great chatting with you. Excuse me."

They link arms and stroll off, but another cluster forms around him. Poor guy. He probably can't get out of here fast enough.

I turn to Fawn. "So, you might be interested in meeting an attractive man of means through our dating service?"

"What makes you think *I* need help getting a date?" She gives me a once-over. "Nice dress. Didn't I see it in an ad for a Kmart sale? Few years back?" She turns abruptly and walks off, swaying so that the little curly tail on her butt glides right and left.

"Oink!" Bobbie says. "What a skank!"

I'm stunned and check my hemline for any hanging threads that might suggest shabbiness.

"There's nothing wrong with your dress," Bobbie says.

"Every now and then women get offended at being approached," I say without enthusiasm.

"This went way beyond that. We need another drink."

I manage to hand out a few more cards to pretty women. Bobbie nudges me. She points out Heather's boyfriend chatting up another great-looking guy. Heather is looking off in another direction.

"I bet you'll hear from her," Bobbie says.

The sky is almost dark, and the film showing animal cruelty is about to start, to be followed by an award ceremony. The cow girl, the chick, the black sheep, and Fawn the pig are prancing around on the stage, assisting.

"I've had about enough of this," I say to Bobbie, "Want to head over to Mastro's in Beverly Hills to hear Adolfo play for a bit?"

"Absolutely! We're out of here."

⁺⁺

Mastro's Steakhouse is one of the most happening places in town. It's just up the street from Spago, and the place is busy seven nights a week. Their steaks are world famous, the seafood delectable, and people love the giant-sized martinis smoking with dry ice. The biggest draw is the celebrity-watching. And it has a world-class piano bar—home to simply the best entertainer in all of Los Angeles, my hubby, Adolfo!

We find a place to park on a side street about three blocks away so that we don't have to pay for parking. As we walk around the corner, I see Mikey, the homeless guy who has been living on the same street and in the same location for the past six months.

"See that guy?" I say to Bobbie. "Some people call him Grate Man because he lives in front of that grate that shoots out hot air. Adolfo gives him at least a five after work, twenty if the tips have been big."

Bobbie says, "I'd hate to be homeless. At least this guy lives in a perfect climate and gets to see the celebs at Mastro's. He's not too pitiful-looking. What's his problem?"

"Evening," I say to him as we pass. I whisper to Bobbie, "He kinda looks like an actor I used to see at the casting calls. This town is hard on people's dreams." I point at the building just ahead with the red carpet on the sidewalk. "There's Mastro's."

"Are there any places in Beverly Hills that don't have a red carpet?"

"I know, it's ridiculous. Everyone wants to feel like a celebrity. Including me." I strike a pose between the gold ropes.

We make our way up the winding staircase and pass what appears to be an eighty-year-old man, arm-in-arm with a twenty-something bleached blonde, revealing maximum DD cleavage. Let's just call her "Dee Dee."

Bobbie says, "Marla, look out so you don't get crushed. Double-wide load coming through."

We move to the side so the odd couple can pass, but Dee Dee trails behind the geezer. I slip her my card with a wink as we make our way to the landing at the top of the stairs.

"Wow," Bobbie says, as we enter the dimly lit and packed restaurant, "great piano."

Upstairs, the piano is the first thing you see as you enter—that and a gorgeous bar. Stacked stone walls, leather upholstery, rustic yet contemporary. Terraces outside.

"Is this place cool, or what?"

"I told you!" I say. "Hey, don't stare, but at the last table against the wall in the back is David Beckham. He comes here a lot. Adolfo says he's a super nice guy." I rack up more stargazer points.

Bobbie cranes to see, as we take a seat at the piano, and wave to Adolfo who winks at us as he sings. "Hi, beautiful ladies," he says between the lyrics.

The place is busy as usual, and Adolfo's tip jar is filling up.

"I've been coming here for the past six years to hang with my sweetheart," I tell Bobbie, "and I never tire of it. I know most of the staff and many of the regulars."

I spot Todd, my favorite manager. I'm dying to ask him about his love life. He met a Swiss woman over the Internet. He told me that they were crazy about each other.

I introduce Todd and Bobbie.

"Can I buy you a drink?" he asks.

I order tea and Bobbie has a cranberry juice. "We were a little over-served with top-of-the-line Ripple at a fundraiser," I explain. "Hey, I'm dying to know what happened with the Swiss cheese-cake gal?" She'd sent pictures of her pretty face and fabulous "knockers" as Todd called them. "Is she 'the one'?"

You might have thought I'd told him his mother had just died. "Oh, God, Marla." He scrunched up his face. "Way too much cheesecake. This girl was big! I mean *really* big! FAT-FAT."

"You couldn't tell from her pictures before she came all the way from Switzerland to California?" I asked.

"I asked for other shots besides those from the waist up, but she said she'd have some taken to send later—which never happened. I was really looking forward to seeing her. Her cab was gonna swing by the restaurant, and she'd come out to say a quick hello, then we were supposed to meet up for dinner after she unpacked and rested up from the flight. So the cab driver brings her here, and she calls for me. I go out to the patio. Well, she gets out of the cab, and I can*not* believe my eyes!"

"So, did you spend the two weeks with her as planned?"

"No way, she totally misled me. I had to tell her I had come down with a serious infection and that it was contagious. I couldn't see her, how could I? Of course she was upset, but Marla, I just cannot be with a fat woman. Look, I'm forty and not rich, so I don't expect to attract a top model or anything, but one thing I know, I am not attracted to big women. That's not being too picky is it?"

"Well, you can't force yourself to be attracted to someone," I say, feeling genuinely sorry for the both of them.

"Gosh," Bobbie said. "Was she a size four then, or a six?"

"Relationships over the Internet are a problem," I say. "Stick to local women; that's my advice."

Todd points to his earpiece and excuses himself.

"*Huge* in Los Angeles means you're 120 pounds, right?" Bobbie says.

"Oh, no, Bobbie. Anything over 110 is unacceptable."

Affirmations

All the animals in the world are safe from cruelty.

I have a full head of slow-motion hair.

I am often invited to Hollywood parties with the A-list stars.

Whether my clothes come from Kmart or DKNY, I am still totally hot-looking.

Nothing chinks my rainbow.

But I Look So Young for My Age

N ow I really am sick. I knew I shouldn't have drunk so much wine and then stayed up till two talking with Bobbie. Adolfo is off on a private gig, so I drive her downtown to the train station, drive back home, and crawl into bed. Adolfo keeps calling to see how I'm doing. When he comes home that afternoon, he has trouble accepting the fact that I am still sick. He panics a bit.

He is standing at the foot of the bed. "Aren't you better yet, mi amor?"

"Better? How can I be better? I've had a total of forty-seven minutes of sleep!"

His hopeful expression falls, and he walks out of the room. He reemerges a few minutes later with a spoonful of honey. "Here, eat this." He holds it in front of my mouth.

"I don't want that. I just brushed my teeth!"

"Eat it, Marlita. It will give you energy and heal you," he insists.

Knowing that he will not give up, I let him feed me the honey. I try to zone out, but fifteen minutes later Adolfo is back.

"How do you feel now?"

"The same as I did fifteen minutes ago," I say with my eyes closed.

"Here, take this cough syrup," Adolfo says, hovering above me with a spoon and the bottle of syrup.

Knowing that I have no choice in the matter, I let him feed me the cough syrup, but glare at him, thinking about torture techniques I might employ when I'm stronger. Fifteen minutes later he is back. "Did that work? Did the cough syrup help your throat? Are you feeling better now?"

"Mi amor, I know that you're concerned, but I cannot get better in half an hour," I tell him. "I am sick. I have to rest." Inspiration strikes. "How about doing some acupressure on my feet? Hone in on my pressure points. That would help me a lot."

"Sorry." He backs off. "My hands are tired from playing the piano." He goes back to his studio, saving me from finding the strength to strangle him.

Monday, I call in sick to work, even though I'm certain I'll feel guilty all day about it. I rarely call in sick, even if I am; but this time, I have no choice. I drag myself to the doctor, and for two miserable days I'm in bed with a searing sore throat, headache, watery eyes, and hacking cough. I do a little reading but lack the energy to write. My chapter deadline has flown by unmet, but I email the editor who gives me two more days.

Thanks to antibiotics, my symptoms become bearable. I'm still coughing and really should stay in bed for a full week, but I feel so guilty that I drag myself back to the office. I'm too tired to name-drop to Alana about meeting Matt-the-bachelor at the pig party, so that should tell you something.

Between the cascade of spam and the client emails that have piled up, I'm looking at thousands to go through—one reason I hate to miss work. I finally reach my first client email of the day.

Hi, Marla,
 Jonas is an asshole. Call me.
Hugs, Ariana

Phooey. I was trying so hard to connect Ariana with someone terrific. She's a thirty-five-year-old beauty with long dark curls, Andie McDowell brown eyes, and a five-foot-eight body that rivals any supermodel's. And she's thoroughly nice—a rare combination. Jonas is thirty-two, gorgeous, with a perfect smile, tall, and in great shape. He's always had a lot of women after him, but never seems to stay in a relationship for too long. I've had to coach him about his manners on several occasions. He just didn't grow up in the era of opening car doors for ladies or making sure that they got home okay.

I know he invited Ariana to go to a hockey game down in Orange County Monday night. Ariana lives in Brentwood, but she found Jonas so attractive that she agreed to drive through evening commuter traffic, a two-hour drive that often stretches to three, to get to the game.

I get hold of Ariana and apologize for being out for two days. Like a sweetie, she's concerned and kind. "So, what happened on the hockey date?" I ask.

Her sigh is a long one. "When I got there, I couldn't believe the parking cost forty dollars. Jonas promised to reimburse me, though, so I didn't think too much of it. Then I called him on his cell and waited outside the gate for him to come and get me since he had my ticket. He was annoyed because the game had just started, and I was pulling him away to come get me. He didn't want to miss any part of the damn game."

"How romantic," I said.

"Right. And during the game, he went over to chat with some of his friends, leaving me sitting alone for over twenty minutes. At half time, we went to the concession stand to get something to eat, but Jonas said that he was out of cash, and could I pick up the hot dog and beers? Well, I was almost out of cash myself after paying the forty bucks to park, but I went ahead and bought the food. Then Jonas said he had to go to the bathroom, so I went back to our seats. Marla, I didn't see him the rest of the game! I called his cell and left messages and texted him, with no response."

"Get out! Really? Unbelievable!"

"You know what I think this guy's problem is? He doesn't want to give of himself. It makes him totally inconsiderate."

"Just between us, from the feedback I'm getting, he may be the type of guy who wants physical intimacy without emotional intimacy."

"Sounds about right. I ended up making the two-hour drive home, wondering what in the hell happened to him."

"Talk about a date from hell! I'm so sorry about this. I promise you, hon, that I'll find a great guy for you."

I leave a message for Jonas to call me and then go through my list, looking for someone special for Ariana. Ted would be thrilled with her, but she doesn't want to date men in their fifties, even though he's sure he looks young for his age. There's a guy I haven't heard from in a while. Bill is forty-six, divorced for many years, children in college. He's successful, well educated, not overweight, and has most of his hair. And nice. I put that connection in motion.

I finally reach Jonas who says calmly, "I was sitting in my seat the whole time that Ariana was missing. And I never got any messages from her. . . . Oh. I did turn my cell phone off during the game. Oh, well."

"You apparently mentioned you'd pay the forty dollar parking fee, right?"

"Are you kidding me? The tickets cost me $250.00. She can't spring for parking?"

"But you didn't set it up that way. . . . Jonas? I'd like to ask you something. Are you interested in a relationship, as you initially stated, or actually just dating? I do have women who aren't looking for a long-term relationship."

"Yeah, okay. Let's try that direction then."

Right. I have a list of women about whom I know almost nothing. What they might have in common with a man is pretty irrelevant. It's all about the number of referrals. I euphemistically call it my "Girls Just Wanta Have Fun List." And that's all I'm going to say on the matter. Except that on rare occasions, these matches click and do, in fact, lead to marriage.

But Jonas is still a C.D. I send him some names and move on to the next email.

Dear Marla,

I had a date with Angie last night and it was great! You picked an excellent match, thank you very much! We were so engaged in the conversation that our food came and sat on the table and got cold even before we touched it. The conversation was more filling

than the food. I am not joking. We hardly ate half of it because we were so engrossed in the moment. So YES, I definitely want to see her again. She is outstanding! Thank you again for finding this great girl.
Cheers, Matthew

Wow! I love it when that happens. And what a great way to put it, "The conversation was more filling than the food."

The morning goes by fast, catching up, answering emails, and tracking down ladies who have not returned the guys' phone calls. Our recruiters brought in new names, thank goodness, and two of the women I handed out cards to at the pig party have emailed me, as has Dee Dee. So, now I'm interviewing new gals.

I get a call from Ralph, who wants to take me to lunch—a nice treat. He takes me to Fusion, located right across the street from my office. One of the perks of my job is that I often get taken out to fabulous places for lunch—on the client's tab. Natch!

Ralph and I get to the restaurant, and a hostess seats us. To our right is Larry King and to our left is Regis Philbin. They do tend to eat their food one bite at a time like the rest of us.

Ralph and I are cool; we smile and act like seeing stars is no big thing to us. We order a great meal, never once gawking. Well, maybe I did a teensy bit when Ralph was looking at the menu. L. K. smiled at me. My celeb tally for the month is looking good.

Ralph and I get down to the reason for the lunch. Ralph is handsome and young-looking for his fifty-nine years. Of course, not one of my clients has ever said, I'm really quite old-looking for my age. *Au contraire.* Their claims to possessing eternal youth leave me shaking my head in awe at the depth of people's self-delusion. Probably 95 percent of the people that I interview tell me that they think that their apparent youthfulness is deserving of a younger more gorgeous mate. How many times a day do I hear the following:

"People are always mistaking me for much younger than I am."

"People can never believe that I'm forty. I constantly have younger guys after me."

"Even though I am fifty-five, I don't look or act my age."

I even had a guy tell me, "I know that I am eighty-three, but I am a young eighty-three." Now that was a good one!

That said, Ralph is one of those rare men who has kept his hair and stayed trim, making women his own age rail to heaven against the unfairness of an older man looking so much more youthful than most older women. *And* he's extremely wealthy. *And* oh so charming. His problem is that he never had children and still wants them. Badly. And he doesn't just want one child; he wants, in his words, "an heir and a spare." For years, he had a gorgeous and classy girlfriend named Linda, but he broke it off with her because she was in her late forties and couldn't have children. So, he has come to our agency for help in finding a "drop-dead gorgeous, extremely slender blonde in her thirties, with great legs with whom to have two children—all within the next three years."

I promise to do my best.

"Now, Marla, I'm hoping you'll alter company policy and allow me to browse through your photo albums."

Gary has to okay this, and I hold off as long as possible. We don't even send photos of the individual candidates we suggest. The reason is that a flattering photo can cause great disappointment, and an unflattering one almost always deters a man from dating an otherwise fantastic woman. Men are so visual, but we do try to save them from themselves.

I wink at Ralph. "Nice try. I'm sure I can come up with women who'll interest you."

✝

I'm back at the office now, wondering who in the hell I can match up with Ralph, when Alana comes in. "There's a woman in the lobby filling out a questionnaire." She's barely able to tell me without laughing. This isn't a good sign.

"Oh, boy. How bad is it?" I ask.

Alana is blatantly smirking. Three minutes later, she ushers in a woman who looks not one damn day under fifty, introduces her as Cindy, and shoots me a discreet good-luck-you're-gonna-need-it grin. The woman is no doubt wearing her daughter's out-fit, bought at, oh, Contempo, maybe? A long gypsy skirt, a shrug over a low top. You see what I'm getting at?

"Hi, Cindy," I say with a smile. "Nice to meet you. Have a seat." I take her questionnaire and glance over the top sheet at her stats. Under "age," she has written "thirty-eight."

"Oh, I see you are thirty-eight . . ." I wink. ". . . *again*."

In the past, our agency has discussed asking the women for their driver's license, but I just feel that since we need the beau-tiful women that come in, we don't want to scare them off. Some-how I never had the guts to ask them for their ID, knowing that a lot of them would decline or get insulted. But hey, they should be embarrassed about blatantly lying, right?

"And I see you say you are a size two?"

I assess her figure from behind my desk. If she were to just measure one of her legs, it could wear a size two. If she wanted to bring both legs on a date, we're talking double digits.

"It's crazy how the clothing designers have changed the sizes on us, isn't it?" I ask. "Those darn designers are hoping to make us women think that we are thinner than we really are!"

Perfectly comfortable in her prevarication, she says nothing. I start to ask her about going by Cynthia instead of Cindy, but there's no point in trying to coax honesty. I wrap it up pretty quickly since I won't be able to match her. It's sad, though.

+⁺+

The entertainment industry in L.A. attracts wannabes from all over the world, and the competition for getting an agent, act-ing/modeling/music gigs, screen-writing, and other studio jobs is carnivorous. Being young and thin is as essential as being six-teen to get a driver's license. Coping with all this has fostered "earthy" vegans and granola munchers who frequent gyms, yoga studios, and spiritual centers. It also has created an indwelling of insecurity, narcissism, and flakiness.

Women over the age of thirty-five panic and immediately select a fake age to tell people and then rush out to get Botox (which I find to be a miracle, since I use it on occasion), lip implants, breast implants, even cheek and butt implants, and, hell, implants anywhere else plastic surgeons have figured out they can stuff something. Men get those god-awful hair implants and even "chest plate" implants. This is right up there with cig-arette addiction on things you shouldn't get me started on.

+‡+

I get an email from Warren, a client in his fifties who is finally willing to date age-appropriate women as long as their cosmetic surgery and collagen enhancements don't make them look "clownish." This is just too sad. The woman he went out with, Tamara, wants a man like Warren so badly that she stretched her finances to pay for expensive work on herself so she'd look younger, and now that's the only thing standing between them. It's so ironic it's painful. Tamara will be crushed. How much feed-back should I give her?

Dear Tamara,
    Though Warren found you sexy and delightful in many ways . . . sweetie, no more plastic, okay?

No! I just can't say that. I'll wait for her to ask what the hell happened. I'll say Warren confessed he's opposed to noticeable surgical enhancements and Botox or whatever. . . . Uggghhh.

I manage to hang on at work until seven, feeling like my job is to accomplish the impossible. I trudge home to my prescrip-tion bottle. Oh, dear! Has all this stress and sickness made me look older? I check the mirror and am not pleased. I need more Botox. Maybe I should cut my hair.

Adolfo is home and wants me to go to a movie, but I've already missed one deadline with my editor, and I must finish my chap-ter. I write until almost one in the morning.

Affirmations

Um . . . forty-plus is beautiful.

Thank God for antibiotics.

Oh, the hell with it. Zzzzzzz . . .

eight

You're Smooth, but Not That Smooth

B y Thursday morning, I've managed to turn in chapter 4 of *Good Date, Bad Date* and then plug away through a long day at the office. Eager to collapse on my sofa at home at the end of the day, I almost miss the brown cardboard box sitting on the dining table. I gasp. It's from my publishing house. I hold my breath, hoping it is what I've been waiting for. Really, it can only be one thing, but it seems like a celestial fanfare should be sounding a drum roll and trumpet flourish.

My very own first book, *Excuse Me, Your Soul Mate Is Waiting*. At the bottom of the cover, in big red letters, the print confirms it: Marla Martenson. Ten copies. With a book in hand, I twirl around the living room. I am thrilled! Red-headed Marla Martenson from Federal Way, Washington, is a genuine, bona fide, honest-to-God, published author!

My book will appear in bookstores across the country. Also inside the box, along with a personal letter from the publisher, is an itinerary of upcoming radio and TV interviews for the book. My first booking is less than two weeks away on WGN's *Morning News* in Chicago, and the tour winds up in Portland, so I can hop on up to visit Mom in Washington. I'll have to make arrangements at work, but I have some vacation days coming.

How fabulous! It will be so exciting to go back and see all of my friends back East and to be interviewed on the news. All feelings of exhaustion gone, I hoist my book and run into Adolfo's little studio, practically yelling so he can hear me over his earphones.

"Mi amor! Mi amor! Look! It's my book! My very first book! I'm a published author."

"Wow, honey, this is amazing!" He takes off his headphones and examines the book. "It looks fantastic. I am so proud of you. You are my star. Let's celebrate," he says. "This very minute! Not tonight, not tomorrow, not this weekend. This very moment." He fetches a bottle of chilled champagne and two glasses and then pops the cork.

"It's already chilled?" I ask. "When did you put this in the refrigerator?"

"When the delivery man set that box on our doorstep."

"You knew it was from the publisher?" I asked.

"I knew the box had to be your books." He pours the bubbly into the glasses.

"It's my dream come true." I feel like enough mega-wattage to light all of Hollywood is surging through me as I smile at him. "Cheers, mi amor." I clink my glass with his, spilling not champagne but tears of joy.

"Let's go to dinner, anywhere you want," he says. "I have a feeling you are going to be seated with the beautiful people in the front of the restaurant from here on out."

Oh, I love this man. Kiss, kiss. Kiss . . . Kiss . . . Mmmmm-mmm.

We love to go to a Thai place called Galanga, and that is my preference tonight. I love the yellow curry with brown rice, the spicy green beans, and the Pad Thai with baked tofu. Galanga is a cozy little place, and you get to sit wherever you like. Everyone knows you can BYOB since Galanga doesn't have a liquor license. So we always bring a bottle of Cabernet. Every sip intoxicates. Every morsel tastes more delicious than the last. Every smile connects.

Walking home, every step I take feels like a dance. A quarter moon rises over the palm trees off Santa Monica Boulevard. Neon colors dazzle. Lit pools in condo courtyards glow like aquamarine gemstones studding the night. Adolfo feels it too, this magic.

Back at home, I'm too full of food and dreams to focus on

writing, but I dash off a quick email to my editor, gushing over the books. No way am I checking the Double D inbox. A wave of exhaustion hits me. I'm still not over this damn flu bug. Sitting beside Adolfo on the green sofa to watch an interview on LK, I'm instantly comatose.

I wake up to find that Adolfo has carried me to bed. It's early morning and I still feel like my muscles have become dishrags. Emails from back East arrive as early as six, though, so I drag myself to the computer to see if there's any reply from the editor. Yes. Julie is asking me to do some revisions on chapter 4. Uggghhhh. "And we still need chapter five by Monday. Have you made your reservations yet for your tour?"

In the hour and a half before I have to get ready for work, I get the trip lined up, hoping reimbursement will arrive quickly since I couldn't book well in advance, and the flights jack up the credit card debt—which I'm still working on. By taking an afternoon flight out of L.A., I'll only be missing two-and-a-half days of work. Still, I'm going to have to prove to Gary that the clients' concerns will be taken care of in advance or by email. I'm going to have to really hustle to pull this off. And to get *Good Date, Bad Date* written on time.

✝

Soy latte half gone, I'm sitting at my desk at Double D, waiting and waiting for my email to load. On this computer, I usually get about seven hundred spam emails per day. It's crazy.

penelopeaugitcornelius@towardsemplyment.org
re: Help stop premature ejaculation!

Aleximutanrt82@rosternicht.com
re: Your insatiable chick will be full of pleasure da do

juvenalm7@financialgroup.com
re: Viagra (sildenafil) 5 mg x 60 pills 119.95

restrainf69@geesthacht.com
re: fuck you XXX

I have never understood: who is taking the time to write and send this typo-filled, crappy gobbledygook? Finally I get to the emails from my clients.

> Hi Marla,
>   So I met Fred. He was tall, nice, but not my type physically or intellectually. He held my hand, kissed it, made compliments. I told him up front at the end of dinner that I don't feel chemistry with him since we had agreed to be candid. He didn't speak to me in the car the whole way back. Lesson: Never let somebody unknown pick me up from home. Learning from our own mistakes are the best life lessons. Bring on the next ☺ guy please!
> Kisses baby!
> Jacquie

Jacquie's a peach. I immediately send her two more names of men who are interested in her and read on.

> Hi Marla,
>   Yes, Emily's a nice girl . . . if you like Elvira! Also, she likes to talk a lot about herself. That personality style with a loudmouth like me is far from a match!
> Shawn

Yeah. Emily is quite gorgeous, but she's not what these guys are looking for. I can't imagine what the recruiter was thinking. I send Shawn the info on Amy and vice versa. They're both very together people; I think they should click.

> Dear Marla,
>   I met Stan last night. He is a great guy, very cute, a total gentleman. He even brought me flowers! I would totally see him again, if you get any feedback from him, let me know.
> You're the best,
> Mandi

Ooohhh! I just adore it when that happens. This qualifies as a good day at the office.

+‡+

Adolfo is working tonight, and I spend the evening typing away at the computer. Saturday morning, I'm at it again, determined to please my editor. Adolfo is working away in his studio. By about four thirty in the afternoon, I seem to be unable to string a coherent sentence together. My brain cells have gone on strike. My eyes don't want to look at the screen another second. Man, I wish I didn't have to squeeze this work I love so much into the time when most people are relaxing.

I set the computer down and rest my eyes. I've been working on the green sofa rather than at the cramped desk in the corner of our tiny apartment. When I moved in with Adolfo, I ended up getting rid of a lot of my things because of the limited closet space. My "office" is in a corner of the living room. My "desk" is actually a piece of furniture designed to display things. We bought it at Target, and Adolfo—bless him—put it together for me in a mere four hours. The two drawers aren't very big, so I always have papers and office things sitting around, and it drives Adolfo crazy. He agrees with George Carlin: "My stuff is my stuff, but your stuff is shit." He's got a whole room for his stuff. If I had a whole room for an office, half of our squabbles might be eliminated.

His family in Mexico loaded up their coffee tables with so many decorative things that you could barely put a drink down. I try to discourage this, but if I move one of his many knick-knacks, he notices, and I get a lecture. It is promptly put back. Then I get mad and, when he's not looking, move the item again. He then says, "Lucy, you don't know how to decorate!" and I say, "Ricky, you're plum nuts. I am a fabulous decorator with impeccable taste!"

Aside from a peacock blue mosaic ashtray from Iran that belonged to my dad and which is my only memento of his, and which Adolfo always removes from the coffee table and puts on my desk, the sofa is the single household item that is truly mine, and I'm lucky to have it. It took a whole month of pleading and coaxing Adolfo to allow me to move it into the apartment that was first his and now ours. He hesitated because he thought the couch would crowd the living space—it does—although I think he secretly hates the color. And he kinda knows how much fun I'd had on it in Chicago. When some of my Midwest girlfriends visited, they recognized the couch from my Chicago days, and, of course, spilled the beans about what a wild time we had there. Adolfo can't seem to let me live it down—even though he and I have shared our own good times on it.

Adolfo has had a full day of work as well. He pours two glasses of wine. Brings me one and sits on the floor in front of me between my legs with his back to me. We are chatting and relaxing, enjoying the Merlot. I'm rubbing his back, a special treat.

"The only advantage to being sick," I tell him, "was that I finished reading this really good book called *Bitter Is the New Black* by Jen Lancaster. It's a memoir by a woman in Chicago, no less!"

"Oh, yeah?" he says. "Mmmmm. That feels so good. Now a little lower."

I work my thumbs hard into his "traps" and he moans again. "Jen Lancaster didn't exactly plan to become a writer; she was in the corporate world until she lost her job. She started writing a blog about her experiences and her life and wound up getting a book deal. She really didn't want to go back to working in an office, so *her* husband told her that she should just stay home and write full time! I think that's really great! Don't you?"

Adolfo remains silent for a minute and then turns around to glance at me with one eyebrow arched. "Oh, you're smooth. You're really smooth. But not that smooth."

"Oooh!" I'm pretending to pout and stop the massage. "All I want to do is stay home and write full time! I am soooo exhausted working at the agency and doing everything else that I have to do *and* writing!"

"I know, honey." He takes several more sips of wine. "Now is just not the time. You know that. We want to buy a house soon, and I still have financial obligations to my family in Mexico until October, so just be patient. Keep writing and eventually you'll be able to afford to do it full time. You have a great job, and times are tough right now. Who knows what will happen with the economy? Things could get even worse."

"I know; you're right." I sigh. "Don't worry, I was just testing."

✝

I work hard the rest of the weekend. Adolfo wants me to go with him to hear one of his friend's bands perform at a night-club, and I'd love to go, but I don't dare let up. Adolfo is cranky, but I'm determined that my editor won't think I'm unreliable or unprofessional. Finally, at almost three in the morning, I send the files off to Julie and hit the sack.

The radio alarm goes off much too soon, and I want to hurl it.

Ugghh! I feel horrible. I thought my sickness was over, but I have relapsed. I feel achy and have a headache, and I'm a bit nauseous. Maybe I have some rare disease like Crytococcus—Bobbie's cat just had that. She says her cat sleeps at the end of her bed. Maybe she caught it and gave it to me when we were at the pig party, and it's one of those resistant diseases that never goes away. Or maybe I have the swine flu—or cancer. Regardless, I'm positively sick of being sick. Between work and writing and feeling so crappy, I haven't been able to go to the gym for at least a month.

I simply, positively, absolutely must be well for the book tour.

Affirmations

I meet my deadlines.

I am a powerhouse writer.

I have amazing stamina for my book tour.

I am too that smooth.

nine

Cupid, Angels, and the Day from Hell

The doctor can see me if I come in right away, so here I am at his office before work, hoping they'll be quick for once. I'm the only person in the waiting room. I constantly check the time and stare at faded landscape prints that are probably as old as I am. Not that that's old.

I'm ushered into a small, cold examining room to strip, don the horrid paper robe, and break out in blue goose bumps while waiting another fifteen minutes before the doctor makes his appearance. I rarely see the same doctor for long because Gary keeps changing our insurance provider in search of ever-cheaper plans, so I have to go with the increasingly desperate MDs on their list. I call this old guy Doc Speedy because I've never had him to myself for even three full minutes, and that is no exaggeration.

He enters, scans my chart, pops a thermometer in my mouth, gets a phone page, and leaves. I hear him chatting with a patient on the phone. The thermometer beeps, so I take it out and look at it. Eeww, there is someone else's lipstick all over it! This makes me want to hurl!

Doc Speedy returns and looks me over, listens with his stethoscope and is paged yet again. The man leaves and returns a few minutes later with a needle. "Got some Vitamin B venom that should help you feel better," he says. "Which cheek do you want it in?"

Duly injected, I'm off to the lab to give blood and urine samples.

I scurry over before work for the tests, stop in a café to grab a bagel and a cup of coffee, and make it to the office on time. I just have to get through the next nine hours and then I can go home and go back to bed.

My mind is somewhere else as I delete the latest spam, and I'm not emotionally ready for the first email. Even though it is typical, it hits me like a dumped ice bucket.

> Hi Marla,
> Michelle was a fascinating person. I loved talking with her and had a nice time. But unfortunately I was not attracted to her. She is very pretty, had gorgeous green eyes, and her smile lit up the room but she is awfully flat-chested. I hope that does not make me a shallow person, but flat-chested just won't do.
> Jerry

Gee, Jerry, how could I think you're shallow? You're to be commended for not letting Michelle's fascinating personality fool you. Everyone knows that being flat-chested signifies a maladjusted person. How could you possibly be expected to find someone with a gorgeous face attractive if she lacks those two important mounds of chest fat? I'm sure you'll love talking to those far more than to some fascinating woman—even when the mounds are saline and not actual human fat.

See? She just busts out—no pun intended—that inner devil of mine.

Ha! I've got just the girl for him: our new Miss Dee Dee. Her application says she'd been a "stew" for several private jets, and before that, she was a dancer. Right, as in *exotic*. I'm sure Jerry will find her chest genuinely fascinating and easy to talk to.

And then I get real.

> Dear Jerry,
> Oh, I'm so sorry it didn't work out with Michelle. She really liked you and was hoping to see you again. I'm sending you the contact info for a busty blonde to meet this weekend.
> Marla

Actually, because of the chest problem, I may not refer Michelle to any more of my clients. She has maybe a B-cup and refuses—as do I—to correct this appalling deficiency by forking over $5,000 and undergoing several hours of potentially life-threatening surgery to have two bags of potentially harmful saline solution sewn into her chest so some shallow-minded doofus can manage to feel a sexual attraction. I sometimes wonder if these men who just have to have a double-D woman aren't missing a little something in the *cajones*, you know?

Oh, dear, I've accidentally sent both Jerry and Scott the info on Dee Dee. I don't usually do that; however, the odds of both wanting to go out with her at the same time are slim. I've sent Scott several interesting women. Hopefully, he's busy with them.

Next email:

Hi there, Marla,

I don't want you to think that I'm one of those lecherous old farts. Ha-ha. I go to church every Sunday, and I sponsor scholarships for higher Christian education. But I'm also a red-blooded male, and since my wife died, well, if I'm going to bother having another woman in my life, she's got to be exciting. This is why I stress that I require a slim blonde with at least a double D bosom, and preferably, who likes to go to church.

I don't believe in living in sin, so I'm specifying the terms of a prenuptial contract. I'd spring for an allowance, but not one cent over ten thousand dollars a month. Why don't you try starting at five?

Your questionnaires don't cover nearly enough territory, so I've added a few pages of additional considerations.

Blessings on you and yours,
Wynne

Wynne, honey, I think you'd better start some serious praying.

I click open the first attachment to find twenty-six single-spaced pages, detailing the nature of this proposed relationship. The second is a copy of a prenup. What this guy really wants is a Christian prostitute for a span of two years or so, wife in name only. I have to shake my boggled mind. You think you've seen them all, and then along comes a Wynner.

A follow-up email arrives from Gary, reminding me that the Wynner has paid top dollar, and we must fulfill the letter of the contract.

By early afternoon, I've had it with men and their boob obsessions. I will not answer another such email today. I'm a cupid, damn it, not a madam in a brothel. I'm tense because I'm: a) not feeling well and need to be healthy for my trip; b) disgruntled with certain clients; c) longing for more time to write; and d) needing to get ready for the promo tour. I take a deep breath, and then another. I eat a chocolate ganache. Mmmmm. Lovely. I walk over to the small Zen rose quartz and candle garden I've set up on a little table beneath my wall fountain. I light the candles, focus on the delightful clients I've matched up, and run through my affirmations. More deep breaths. There. Much better. I like to think I attracted what comes next. Alana announces that my favorite female client is stopping by.

Ariana waltzes into my office. She's the one who had the miserable basketball date with Jonas and so I fixed her up with Bill.

"Hi sweetie, I was just in the area. I have an audition and thought I would stop by. I have a gift for you." She hands me a book.

"Ooh, what's this?" I ask.

"I thought it looked like something you'd like. Chick lit. I read it; it was cute. It's about a witch, and I know how you love witches."

"You're right. I can't believe you remembered that." I'm delighted with the book, but something more is going on. "All right. Don't keep me in suspense. What's happening?"

"I really like Billy. We've been together every evening since you set us up last week." She bites her lower lip, smiling.

"Out with it!"

"I spent the night at his house out in Manhattan Beach last night. I think he might be *the one.*" Virtually bouncing, she twirls around behind my desk and gives me a hug. "Okay, I have to run. My audition is for an indie film. I'll call you."

Just when I'd begun to think love is an impossible dream.

I get to work on Wynne and astound myself by coming up

with two names. Of course, it's up to me to interview the women and give them some idea what they'd be in for. I work extra hard to update files and add back-up options for clients to keep them busy while I'm gone on my book tour.

After work, I'm feeling a bit better. Maybe that vitamin B shot did something after all. I go out for a quick walk, heat up a frozen Pad Thai dinner, and try to get some writing done, but all I can think about are clients. The writing's not working, and I delete what I've written, but I have an idea.

I head over to Mastro's to work on chapter 5 rewrites and also 6 while listening to Adolfo's wonderful music. He plays both the piano and the keyboards together, and the sound is amazing, very high energy and eclectic. When I was writing my first book, I used to go over to Mastro's after work on Monday nights and sit at the piano with a glass of wine and write. The place gave me inspiration. I can use some of that tonight—except with herb tea instead of wine. Also, I'm going to be in the spotlight in a few days, and Adolfo will be my biggest fan, so I want to be in the footlights for his performances as well. I get situated in a corner and focus on the book, and things start to click.

The week that follows blurs with my intense work at the office to prepare for my absence and then also preparing material for the signing and talk I'll give at Barnes & Noble in L.A., actually the kick-off to my book promotion. I also spend time figuring out what to wear for it and for the trip, and, of course, writing whenever possible. Occasionally sleeping.

The night of the signing, Gary lets me off work early since one of our clients, Brandy, is doing a makeover on me. She's a make-up artist, madly in love with a wonderful man I introduced her to through the agency, and is so grateful, she wants to help me. She has brought all of her makeup to my apartment and proceeds to glamorize my face and even makes my scraggly hair wisps look sexy and layered. It totally rocks!

Adolfo loves the glam look and plants a lip-lock on me before we head down to the Grove in Hollywood, a mall so L.A. it's a tourist attraction. The same people that did the fountains at the Bellagio in Las Vegas designed the pond and dancing fountain. Like parts of Rodeo Drive, the Euro-architecture features marble and mosaics. The Barnes & Noble there is one of my favorite places on earth. Just the smell of that place has me in heaven. Forget diamonds and Jimmy Choos, give me a gift card to Barnes & Noble, and I'm so buried in the stacks, it takes an expedition to find me. So it's a special thrill for me to have my first signing here.

Outside the B & N, an obelisk stands twenty-two feet tall, topped by bronze angels, male and female, soaring an additional eighteen feet in the air with wings spanning ten feet, frolicking ever heavenward. And there, beneath their glorious protection in the City of Angels, hangs a poster with *my* picture on it in the window of Barnes & Noble. It's been there for two weeks. I'm faint, dizzy, and delirious with joy.

"*Dios mio,*" Adolfo says and kisses me again right under the brass angels in front of the bookstore. Inside, a good crowd has arrived, including Bobbie, up from Del Mar. Stacks of my books appear on one of the front tables next to some of my favorite authors, such as Deepak Chopra, John Gray, Wayne Dyer, and Marianne Williamson.

I can barely look at Adolfo as I'm speaking and signing; he's beaming so foolishly, as if I'd just given birth to triplets. *I love you,* I mouth in between signatures.

My girlfriend Aura Imbarus surprises me with a cake with the cover of *Excuse Me, Your Soul Mate Is Waiting* done in frosting. Little roses and lighted candles outline the borders. I'm so overwhelmed that I let the candles burn until the cake nearly catches fire.

Afterward, Adolfo says, "Honey, I'm so proud of you, I give you permission to not clean the house for two weeks!"

"Such a comedian," I say, nuzzling him.

✢✢

The next morning at work, I seem to be in some kind of afterglow daze. It's about twenty-eight hours before I leave for my book promo trip, and I somehow manage to attract a day from hell. I'm in the bathroom at a coffee shop before work. The window is open, making it possible for anyone passing in the street to see me tinkle, so I attempt to close the window. It comes down so fast that it almost cuts off my left thumb. I have a huge gash, and it swells up right away. It hurts like demon torture. What do you want to know? I'll tell you anything. Just make this freaking pain stop.

I bandage myself up using the crummy first-aid kit in the office, and with my sore thumb standing out like it would on a harpist, I meet with four women, all beautiful, interesting, and accomplished, and two new male clients, including Francesco, a handsome Italian real estate developer, only thirty-four years old—very match-able.

As it turns out, the wonders of this day are just getting started. On my lunch break, I'm hiding my thumb, prancing down Rodeo drive in my gold Italian high heels that I purchased last year in Mexico City. I'm looking for some special earrings for the TV interviews, when I miss a step coming out of a store. I lose my balance and fall, badly twisting my ankle.

I'm in agony again as pain slices across my ankle. I imagine tendons ripped off a bone that has snapped as I hobble over to the curb and sit down. I draw a few stares but no offers of assistance. Great. This is perfect. I'll be in a cast on the *Today* show. After a few minutes, the most excruciating pain subsides. Maybe the ankle isn't broken. I stand and finally hobble back to my car. I have to drive to the Agency's Orange County Office, thumb throbbing, foot pain brutal.

From two o'clock on, I'm hopping around on my one good foot while trying to make sure our Orange County clients are in good shape. My right shoulder and neck are now aching from twisting as I turned on my high heels during the fall. I feel like a complete wreck.

That evening, I'm on my way home from Orange County, in pain and exhausted, thinking of everything I need to do for the trip. It's dusk and traffic still crawls along on the 405 freeway, so I decide to get off at an earlier exit. Wrong move. I end up in

Manhattan Beach and have absolutely no idea how to get home. The sky is getting darker.

I call Adolfo on my cell phone. "Hola, Ricky, honey," I say, hoping my sweet husband can help me sort my way out of the maze. I'm trying for humor to stay brave and not cry.

"Hola, mi amor. Where are you, Lucy? You must be lost."

I start crying. "I am! I'm in Manhattan Beach!"

"Manhattan Beach? Ay, Marlita. You have no sense of direction. Stop and ask someone where you are and how you get here from there."

"Gee, I'm glad I phoned you," I hiss.

"Honey, it's just that I'm worried about you. It's too dark to be in an unknown part of town. You need to get home."

"No kidding. I haven't packed yet. I'm exhausted. Every time I try a new street, I'm going the wrong way."

"Stop somewhere right now and ask someone for help."

"Aargh! Glad I called. I just *never* would have figured that out myself." For the next hour, I grope my way home, foot swollen, thumb aching.

My adoring husband groans upon seeing me limp into the apartment, but he has hot soup waiting. I explain about the fall on Rodeo Drive in my gold shoes.

"So what about your hand?" he asks. "I know you didn't hurt it vacuuming. Or doing the dishes or—"

"Enough, wiseass," I say.

"Tell me, Lucy . . ."

I go over the whole dang day.

He says, "If your ankle isn't better by morning, you'll have to cancel the trip."

"No flippin' way, José," I tell him. "I'd go if had to hobble around on an old lady's cane!"

I hear my email chime. Hoping to see a word of encouragement from the publisher about the book tour, I limp over to the computer and find that I do, in fact, have a note from my editor.

> Marla, you assured me you'd have chapter six in before you
> left. I'm still waiting, dear girl. I also want seven by our original tar-

get date. Since you only have three shows, maybe you'll have a lot of time to write. You're hot right now, so we've got to strike while the iron is too. Good luck on the tour. I'll be watching. Julie

Affirmations

I am a high energy person.

My dynamite talks blow my audiences away.

I get a lot of writing done on my trip.

I'm hot and striking while the iron is, too.

ten

"A Toast to Your Success . . ."

Next day at work, Gary shows up, even though it's Wednesday. I'm fully dosed with extra-strength Motrin, but dull pain still saps my concentration as we go over virtually every current male client before he's satisfied that I'm entitled to take two and a half days of vacation time.

"I'm paying you to work full-time, Marla," he says, running his fingers through his wavy jet-black hair. "I insist that you give this job your first priority. There are plenty of people eager to replace you."

A chunk of mental ice slides down my spine. "Is there anything you feel I've left undone?"

"That's not the point."

"Of course, this job comes first," I say quickly, and it's true. But how I wish it didn't need to be.

I leave work at noon with Adolfo, who drives me to the airport for my 2:10 flight to O'Hare. We're both a bit wistful about not seeing each other for four-and-a-half days. He gives me a once-over in my chic black trousers, a low-cut black tank with a gold and silver studded cross on the front that I got on Hollywood Boulevard, and a black button-down pin-striped shirt, the top four buttons left fashionably open. He thinks I look too sexy for strangers.

"Hasta la vista, baby." He holds me and plants a thorough goodbye kiss on my lips.

I should respond more, but I hurry off to the terminal lounge at LAX, relying on my open-toed flats to ease the pain in my ankle, now wrapped in an Ace bandage—as is my hand. I'm doing a high speed limp-wobble.

Once airborne, I open my laptop to get some writing done on the four-hour flight, but I'm so excited that I make little progress with chapter 6. I'm thinking how much I love Chicago. I miss rollerblading by the lake, walking through Lincoln Park to the zoo, going to the museums, strolling down Michigan Avenue, people-watching while sitting in the square at the Water Tower, seeing the Navy Pier at Halloween. I miss walking everywhere; I miss the big fat snowflakes in the winter and the blossoms on the trees in the spring. I miss the cafés and incredible restaurants, and I most especially miss my fabulous friends.

My girlfriend Rita, who is like my big sister, picks me up at O'Hare. She's a redhead with a lipstick-ad-beautiful smile. She lives downtown right on Michigan Avenue in a condo with a view of the lake and Navy Pier. I adore staying with her and having a guest bedroom and bathroom all to myself.

I'm tired from the flight and my hand and foot are both throbbing. I'm looking forward to a cozy supper with Rita and then a good night's sleep. I'll get up early to write before my interview to make up for the ineffective hours on the plane. She has another idea, however.

"Remember that documentary about haunted places in Chicago you told me about? I took a chance on booking a ghost tour tonight!"

This is positively irresistible. She and I meet her friend Jim at the Rock-n-Roll McDonald's on Clark street, catch the "ghost bus"—an old school bus painted black—and tour famously gruesome sights. We have a ball and snap pictures on Jim's digital camera that actually contain ghostly balls of light and even faces we didn't see at all while on the tour.

Amazing. I'm going to get a camera and try this at home.

Back at Rita's apartment, I'm exhausted, but she and I have a deep discussion about the supernatural as I ice my hand and foot. It's around one before I finally turn in. When I get up after only five hours of sleep, there is no time to write. Groggily, I walk into the living room and gaze a moment out the window at the beauty of Lake Michigan. Across the tops of the buildings, I see the John Hancock building, Bloomingdale's, and the Drake Hotel. I look out across the lake to Navy Pier and to the Planetarium. I'd love to stand there all day, but I have to hurry.

The humidity has dorkified my hair, and with my bad hand, I can't do much with it. I pull it into a low ponytail, leaving a few wisps, hoping my gold, double-hoop earrings and mustard-yellow knit top from my favorite store, Anthropologie, will compensate. I hail a cab since I have to go north about seven miles to WGN. Once there, I wait in the green room, watching the screens until I'm called. Then, I step before the cameras of the *Chicago Morning News*. Somehow, I'm not nervous with the three anchors, two guys and a woman, all of us laughing and having a great time.

After the show, I simply can't be in Chicago and not say hello to my friend Glen. Back in the nineties—both of us young and living paycheck to paycheck—we worked together at Voilá, a French bistro in The Loop. Walking up Rush Street to meet him, I spot my old friend, author Brad Thor. Actually, Brad encouraged me to write. I love how you just run into people you know in Chicago, something that rarely happens in Los Angeles since everyone is in their cars. We both start running, arms outstretched like we're in a movie, and embrace. It's so good to see him. Now we're both authors, although Brad is a *New York Times* bestseller. I'm so thrilled for him. We vow to stay in touch.

Inside Starbucks, I find Glen easily.

"Marla, great to see you."

We drink our lattes, and he asks about my bandaged hand and foot. They both still hurt, but the swelling has gone down a bit. Inevitably, we reminisce about our crazy times at Voilá, when everyone wanted their check at the same time so that they could get to the theatre.

"We did get to see some great productions though," I say.

The manager of the Schubert Theater occasionally gave the restaurant free tickets, the only perk to the job. We got to see *Rent, Chicago,* and *Stomp* that way. Glen used to convince me to smoke with him out on the loading dock during breaks.

He starts to laugh. "Hey, you want to go out and have a smoke right now for old times?"

"Do you have any?"

"Any smokes? Does the Pope wear a funny hat in church?"

We walk outside and up Rush toward Lincoln Park. He lights me a cigarette. I'm soooo not a smoker, but for friendship's sake, I just don't inhale as we chat away. I have really missed my Chicago friends. It's one of those moments where you ask yourself: Is this where I belong? Am I just in the wrong place in L.A.? Is that why my creative energies are so fragmented?

Back at Starbucks, I get in a good hour of work on my chapter—but I've lost my momentum. Before leaving for the airport, I check in with Adolfo via cell phone—the neighbors miss me, he teases, as if he didn't. And then I'm flying on to NYC.

Arriving at my hotel around ten that evening, I find a Korean translation of *Excuse Me, Your Soul Mate Is Waiting,* sent by my publisher to mention during the interview on the *Today* show in the morning. A note accompanies it: *Looking forward to your next chapters. PS. Break a leg!*

They haven't cut me any slack. I'm almost done with chapter 6 but have only a rough outline of 7 and pages of files to go through to choose the best material. I'm just too tired to write tonight. I pick up the cheerful yellow book with the cute red heart that looks like my masterpiece but with unintelligible writing on it. Korean? How fun.

Next morning, the interview goes well, but isn't quite as relaxed as with WGN's anchors. They make a word play on Soul Mate and Seoul-mate. So, aren't I officially a hotshot of some kind now?

Immediately after the show, I pick up my luggage at the hotel and shuttle to the airport. In, out, zip, zap, slam, bam. The next morning, Saturday, I have to tape a show in Portland. I limp down the aisle of the jumbo jet and a man sitting next to my assigned seat. It's one of those days when I suffer from PMMS: People Make Me Sick, a carryover from my restaurant days. I buckle up next to the very fat man in the window seat whose belly is spilling over into my space and who smells like stale coffee. All I need is Steve Martin in the other seat, and we'd have a movie sequel to *Planes, Trains, and Automobiles*. I try to work on my laptop, but the man keeps ordering drinks which keep getting passed over my keyboard. Very tough to concentrate.

Flippin' A. The guy has ordered a fourth drink, which spills on me, barely missing my laptop. I should do a few quick affirmations on patience, but instead I repeat: Red Bull and vodka *will* come out of my white jeans.

✝✝

At last, I'm in my room at the Embassy Suites in Portland. I have a few hours to write and finish chapter 6 before my morning taping. I breeze through the Portland interview in the morning and then catch yet another flight. I'd planned on driving to Seattle, but my foot is sending shooting pains up my leg, possibly from being so cramped all of yesterday when I sat next to the fat man. Pulling my baggage around has reopened the gash on my hand. So I fly into Seattle.

After landing, I haul my luggage off the carousel and drag it—hand bleeding under stress—outside to wait for Mom and her best friend, Marilyn, to pick me up. I have to stand near a dozen people lined up against the wall getting their nicotine fix after the flight. I choke in their gray clouds. At least the pace will slow here, and I can finally rest, nurse my wounds, and write.

"Marla! Marla! Marla! Over here, honey, over here!"

I spot my mom hanging out of the passenger window of the car flailing her arms. She and Marilyn pull up to the curb. Thank God Marilyn helps me, the near cripple, load my two bags in the trunk.

"How about lunch at Akasaka on Pacific Coast Highway?" Mom asks. "Marilyn and I have been holding out till you got here."

I do have to eat, and each time I've come to visit, Mom takes me to my favorite Japanese restaurant. Mr. Lee, the Korean owner, is making sushi.

"Marla!" he calls. "So good to see you! You big movie star now?"

"Not exactly." I tell him about the TV and radio shows. "I have something to show you." I pull the Korean translation of *Excuse Me, Your Soul Mate Is Waiting* out of my bag and hand it to him. "Cool huh?"

"Ohhh!" he says, studying the Korean print. "Mr. Lee very, very impressed. I have very famous friend!" He sees to it that the three of us feast on California rolls, miso soup, spider rolls, and rice.

After lunch, I'm thinking we'll go to Mom's, and I'll unpack and get some writing done.

"Let's go visit your book at Barnes & Noble's," Mom says. "Marilyn wants to buy a copy for her niece."

It's just across the street, so we go over and find the self-help section. They just have three copies, situated between books entitled *How to be More Orgasmic* and *Tickle His Pickle: Your Hands-On Guide to Penis Pleasing.*

"Oh my God! Can you believe that title?" I say.

"Need a book on penis pleasing, Marilyn?" my mother asks her friend.

"Not so much," she says, "but being more orgasmic might be fun."

We laugh. Finally, we head home to my mother's community of manufactured homes for seniors. It would make a perfect setting for an episode of *Murder, She Wrote.* The residents refer to it as The Park. Everyone keeps their yards immaculate and blooming with flowers. At Halloween, pumpkins and pots of rust-colored mums sit on porch steps. At Christmastime, the lighted trees and reindeer displays draw people from all over town. Denizens of The Park always help neighbors who can't do something for themselves—even if it's yard work.

I finally get to work that afternoon and make a good start on chapter 7, trying to ignore the gorgeous day and some sort of high excitement going on in The Park.

"You gotta come see this," Mom calls. "Grab a lawn chair."

It's about three thirty and I'm on a roll. "In a bit!" I call.

I see constant motion in my peripheral vision and finally look out the window to see everyone in The Park walking around, gesturing and pointing, carrying umbrellas and pitchers of iced tea.

I can't imagine what could possibly be happening to cause such a to-do. Has the bingo kitty reached a whopping hundred dollars? Cutthroat shuffleboard?

Further work is impossible. I must have an answer. I sigh and head outdoors, following the sound of a hundred people talking at once, along with great warping sounds and booms and huge motors at work. Up the street, they are putting in a new mobile home. A huge truck pulls it slowly into the cul-de-sac. This is a spectator event that surpasses golf-cart drag-racing. But on a Saturday afternoon?

"It was supposed to have arrived yesterday morning," Mom says.

Everyone, and I do mean everyone, seems to know my colorful mother. They call her by her name, Donna Reed—not the film and TV actress—but mostly they refer to her as the "park angel," possibly because she invites them one and all to her home for wine, or maybe because even at seventy-one she can still get back up on her own after stooping down to pull weeds from the garden.

I learn that folks keep some kind of score around here, awarding more "points" for being a widow over being a divorcee or a spinster. Mom didn't bother telling them she was a divorcee before becoming a widow, and her secret's safe with me. Mom has also earned points for never having had knee surgery.

Makes sense. Why not be queen of the hop for having good knees?

"Mom," I ask, "do you still go outside when it rains and do a little rain dance?"

"I do," she answers, "and I still walk under a full moon backwards so as not to lose sight of it."

Mom is a real character, and I love her for it. She is my best friend in all the world. My only complaint is that she is and has been a heavy smoker most of her life and has no plans to quit.

"It's a miracle I'm alive after growing up on so much second-hand smoke," I tell her.

"You weren't brought up on smoke," she says. "You were brought up on Cap'n' Crunch."

The mobile-home process eats up two hours before the movers realize they have put it in backward. They will have to return Monday to take it back out and put it in right. What a fiasco. In unison, all the seniors boo.

✝

I write that evening after dinner and then all Sunday morning, but I refuse to cancel today's outing to Gig Harbor to have lunch with my cousin Rosie. Both my foot and my hand are better, so I'm driving. We have to cross the Narrows Bridge, and I'm hoping that together, Mom and I can find it. I'd packed my TomTom GPS, which she'd given me for Christmas, knowing how I'm always getting lost. However, when I unpacked, I discovered the TomTom had been removed from the zippered pouch on the side of my suitcase. Obviously the baggage handlers at SFA, Sticky Fingers Airlines, had swiped it.

After the Narrows Bridge, I miss the exit, drive twenty minutes going the wrong way, and we almost give up.

"The reason I get lost so much," I tell her, "is because I grew up with smokers, and so that part of my brain suffered from second-hand smoke."

She shakes her head. "I see now that other parts of your brain obviously suffered as well."

We both laugh.

We finally arrive, and Rosie comes running out. We embrace. I haven't seen her in a couple of years. She has recently finished months of chemo for cancer, always keeping the most amazing positive attitude. Her hair is short and silver, having just started to grow back. She looks very chic. Her house has a view of the water and is surrounded by trees and beautiful flowers. It is peaceful and relaxing, and I breathe in the smell of pines.

I point out two houses for sale on this street. "I need to tell Adolfo that we must buy one of them, so that I can live the writer's life up here." As soon as I say this, I long for it to come true.

"Oh, Marla," Mom says. "What a positively wonderful idea."

"It is, isn't it!" How refreshing it would be to live among down-to-earth people who are not concerned whether they are a size zero or a two, or obsessed with breasts—people who are perfectly comfortable having a few lines on their faces. Another moment of longing hits me. I'm yearning for a home that is part of a community with nooks of quiet where Adolfo and I can connect with our muses.

Rosie has cut fresh flowers and set up guacamole and chips in the living room where we see family photos, which include their five kids, their kids' kids, and even several kids of kids of kids—a big close family who all support each other. I only have my mom and Adolfo. And it's not like I need a child, per se. I have Adolfo!

Still . . .

It's been a great day but it's not over, and I've had little time to rest or write. Mom is throwing a cocktail party for me this evening with twenty-five friends and neighbors coming to get their copies of my book signed. The potato salad is made, the fruit plate is arranged, the beer and wine chilled. Shelly arrives early, and we chat and giggle while I'm making mimosas. The main crowd arrives. It's so nice to see so many old friends. To them, I *am* a celebrity, and they love keeping up on my life in Hollywood.

Adolfo calls and says hello to Mom, Shelly, and Marilyn. I step into the quieter bedroom to tell him about the wonderful houses on Rosie's street in Gig Harbor with the beautiful views of Puget Sound.

He doesn't say anything for a minute. "How do musicians do up there?"

Oh, right. There's that. And he'd be so far from his family in Mexico. His life is in L.A. "Well, I just meant how nice when we have lots of money to have a vacation home here. . . ."

"Right," he says.

I can tell this has upset him a little. "I love you, mi amor," I say.

"Me too. Have fun." He sounds a little lonely.

"Can't wait to see you tomorrow."

I click off and return to the party as Mom is thanking everyone for coming, for being who they are, and for supporting me. She asks me to say a few words.

Aaaaahh! What I am supposed to say? First, I echo Mom's gratitude and then plug the next book. "Feel free to act as crazy as you like while I'm here. It will only give me more material for my writing. I also want to show you what my mom gave me as a gift yesterday." I hold up a T-shirt that says, "Be careful or I will put you in my novel!"

Big laughs. Shelly clinks the side of her glass to draw attention, and then raises it. "I propose a toast to Marla, who lives the life of high glamour and then gets to write about it and then talks about it on TV! You rock!"

"You go girl!" someone says.

People cheer and finish their drinks, and I join them, determined to feel as happy as they imagine I'm feeling.

Affirmations

I am a TV personality.

I am an actual hot shot.

My editor loves my work.

I own a townhouse in Chicago and a vacation house in Gig Harbor.

eleven

"If Ya Think I'm Sexy . . ."

By four thirty Monday morning, I'm dressed for work in my mustard knit top and gold double-hoop earrings, and I hop into a shuttle to catch a 6:50 flight out of Seattle. Far from rested during my stay in Federal Way, I grab a few winks on the plane and connect with Adolfo at 9:20.

"Ricky Ricardo Taxi Service," he says.

It's wonderful to see Adolfo's handsome face again, and we catch up on things as he contends with Monday morning L.A. traffic. I get a call on my cell phone from my editor who explains to me the printer's timeframe to accommodate advance reviews and publicity and catalog positioning and how we don't have endorsements for the back cover yet, and I still haven't turned in my work. She sounds really nervous, and I absolutely hate it that she might not be thinking of me as a dependable writer. I try to emphasize the hectic but successful tour.

"Yes, yes, good job, but we're getting down to the wire on this."

"You can count on me. I'm turning in chapter 6 and a rough chapter 7 today."

Adolfo is frowning and giving me circular wrap-it-up gestures while I respond with helpless shrugs. He drops me off at work, settling for a quick smooch. He has to work tonight, so he won't get home until around one, by which time I'll be so soundly asleep, he'll wonder if I'm still alive.

I arrive only fifteen minutes late for work. Alana is covering for me and has my computer all booted up.

"I saw your WGN interview online," she gushes. "And I watched you on the *Today* show too! Wow, Marla! You're sooooo big time!"

Mm-hmm. So, now let the royalties roll in. I give her a hug. "How was your weekend?"

"Well . . ." She pulls something out of her bottom desk drawer, hides it behind her back, and dashes into my office. She places a bottle of red wine on my desk. "I was in wine country!"

"Napa?"

"Yep, and I got you a bottle of wine—think of me when you and Adolfo have a romantic evening! But don't let anyone else see it; I only bought one for you."

"How sweet! Thank you." I look at the label. "Ooh, this one looks good! I love Cabernets. So Arthur took you to wine country for a romantic weekend?"

"Oh, yeah. We've been dating for three months now."

"And?"

She gives me a sheepish grin. "Well, let's just say we didn't leave the bed and breakfast except the one time we went wine tasting and I bought your wine."

"Ooh la la! I like it."

The phone rings at her desk, sending us both back to work. I check my inbox. It's official. Two gazillion and eight emails. When I get to an email from Francesco, I open it eagerly. Over the weekend, he's dated all three of the women I introduced him to and liked them, but:

> Marla, my problem is that I find all beautiful women fascinating. I love women. My family wants me to marry and give them grandchildren. I'm ready to move into this stage of my life, but I don't know how to choose one fresh lovely creature over another. Select only one kind of wine for the rest of my life? This is difficult. Yet I know I must. I rely on your expertise.
> Cordially yours,
> Francesco

Can't choose just one wine? That's not a problem if you happen to be a grape. Since women are not actually consumables, though, we have here the age-old dilemma.

> Hi, Francesco,
> I think you're right to date many women through our service. I feel certain that at some point, one will linger in your heart a bit longer than the others. I'll be sending you new names later today.
> Marla

Marcus is my second problem of the day. I had originally referred him to Rita, and then two more just in case he got antsy during my four-and-a-half-day absence. All three girls have outgoing personalities and are gorgeous—their faces, hair, and their figures.

> Dear Marla,
> I met with Kirsten for dinner, and Rita and I went on a total of three dates. I enjoyed the time we spent together, and I think you're calibrating well on the personality front, but we need to thin them up a bit.
> Thanks for your help,
> Marcus

Thin them up? What? Like they're trying out for *The Biggest Loser*? I pull up Kirsten and Rita's files on my computer screen and call Alana back into the office. "Take a look at these two," I say.

"Wow!" She leans in closer to the photos, clicking on one and then the other. She looks at me, reads my face. "Don't tell me some dork is finding fault!"

"Marcus."

"One of the Manhattan Beach guys."

I nod.

She studies them again, using the zoom feature. "He doesn't like the way Rita uses a contrasting lip-liner?"

I shake my head.

"He probably thinks Kristen's hair is too short."

"Nope."

"Are they my height then?"

"One is five five, the other five seven." Petite Alana knows that 99 percent of our guys say they won't date a woman under five three. "He thinks they're both too fat."

She peers at the photo again. "Is this one of those rare men who doesn't want a double D?"

"I don't think that's it. Honestly Alana, he's just plain crazy. I have also seen these women personally, and they are slim! No one is thin enough for these guys! What is the deal?"

I rant on about appreciating the whole woman. "So many women walk through these doors and they have everything a normal guy could ever dream of. It's just crazy they get turned down."

"Hey, you sound like you're ready for a glass of that wine now!"

"Oh, good idea! It may only be ten o'clock in Beverly Hills, but it's five o'clock somewhere, right?"

We laugh it all off and get back to work. I decide to try matching Marcus with Michelle—whom Jerry found "flat-chested." She is not, of course, but she is a tiny bit slimmer than Kristen and Rita.

Let's see. Oh, goodie! Stan and Mandi have officially "gone exclusive," as have Ariana and Billy. Shawn and Amy had a second date. Yay! Matthew and Angie are still cooking after a fifth date. Well look at this: Joseph (no big butts) and Sandy Puffy-dress are on their third date.

Jerry sent an email saying essentially, "now that's what I'm talking about" after dating Miss Dee Dee. But then—oh no! Scott sent an email saying the same thing. They're both dating her. Hopefully this is a passing fancy. Dee Dee wrote me the following:

> Hey Mar, both Scott and Jerry were real sweat. If Scott would of [sic] taken me to a nicer place, we would of [sic] had more fun. I'll just tell him that sounds boring next time he wants to go some place cheep [sic]. Jerry got us in at Spago.

I've had clients reject women because of their spelling, but neither Jerry nor Scott seemed to notice any problems in this area. At least, they're all happy—for now. As are Sonia and Barry. The next email is from fifty-nine-year-old Mr. Heir-and-a-Spare. He's rejecting all three women I sent him. One because her stubby fingers suggest that she might gain weight during pregnancy; another because he thinks a thirty-six-year-old is too old to start a family. He complains of having little in common with any of them.

This is going to be tough. What he wants is a Jacquie or a Cheryl, but neither will date men over forty-five. Our older men often think that they don't need a woman to be a companion, but they're disappointed to find that they have little to talk about with younger women. They don't want that to be true, however, so they'll say our agency just doesn't have a nice enough selection to choose from. I call Denise and Greta to describe Ralph and his desire for a family, and, to my surprise, they agree to let me give him their contact info.

Break time at last.

I forego a much-needed trip to 'Bucks for a latte and use the fifteen minutes to send files from my flash drive of chapters 6 and 7 to my editor. The rest of my morning is taken up with meeting new clients and answering calls.

By one, I'm starving and limp over to Whole Foods to get something to eat. I'm on Dayton and Rodeo and look across the street and see a man in black jeans, a black shirt with the sleeves rolled up, a wine-red tie, and an English bowler hat. He's strutting toward a camera shop. I recognize the man's gait: It's my all time idol, Rod Stewart!

I often see celebrities walking around in L.A., but I hadn't seen Rod Stewart since my West Hollywood waitressing days. I watch as he enters the camera shop and decide to mosey on over. First though, I dig out my cell phone and call my mom. She doesn't pick up, so I leave her a message that I've just spotted Rod Stewart.

I wander into the shop, and just as I enter, Rod-baby passes me on the way back out. We are inches away from each other. I am hoping that he will look at me, and when he does, I will say "hello."

But he doesn't. He just walks on by.

As I enter the camera shop, I hear someone call out, "Raaaah-hhd Stewart!"

To this, Mr. Stewart is very cordial and shakes the man's hand. Then the idol moves on to where his driver awaits him. *Darn, I should have said something.*

✝̤

I've been in love with Rod Stewart since I was fifteen years old. The walls of my bedroom were plastered with his posters. In 1978, my family moved to Tehran, Iran, for six months because of my father's work. I carried my precious posters across the Atlantic and plastered Rod all over my Persian bedroom.

I'm inspecting cameras, but I'm flooded with memories of the time I met him in person—swoon!—when I was working as a cashier in the famous French restaurant, L'Orangerie, in West Hollywood, which was often featured on *Lifestyles of the Rich and Famous.* I met stars like George Burns, Merv Griffin, Catherine Deneuve, Frank Sinatra, Gene Wilder—the list goes on and on. I always checked the reservation book, though, specifically looking to see if Rod might be coming in. The day his assistant called to make a reservation for him and his then girlfriend, Kelly Emberg, I was so excited, I couldn't breathe right.

On the night he came in, I made sure I looked really good—sexy enough to meet my idol. And, I made sure that I was up at the front desk when he came in. Then things started happening. The maître d', Jean-Philippe, took Rod's coat and large Louis Vuitton wallet from him. He handed the wallet to me for safe keeping at my cash register. I rushed back caressing *Rod Stewart's* wallet! I decided that I would write him a love note, and include my phone number, and slip it inside. Just as I started writing, Jean-Philippe came to get the wallet back. Dang!

I grabbed my purse and ran to bathroom, brushed my hair again, put on more lipstick, pushed up my A-cup boobs, squirted on perfume, waltzed into the dining room, and stood only a few feet away from Rod's table. I pretended to assess the room, hoping he'd notice, and then went back to my station.

"You should have seen Rod checking you out," Jean-Philippe said.

"He was?" I asked. "Rod Stewart checking me out?!"

Emboldened by Rod's reported interest, I made one more tour through the dining room. His date, Kelly, had gone to the ladies room, so I walked over to his table, and though I could barely breathe, cooed, "Hello, Mr. Stewart. What a pleasure to have you dine with us. How was dinner?"

"Oh, it was great, love. Say, Jean-Philippe sent me this dessert, but I am so stuffed, I can't even think of eating it. Would you like it?"

Rod Stewart was offering me his dessert? I thought I would die right there.

"Oh, how nice of you to offer, but I just couldn't!" I told him, wanting only to jump in his lap and ravish his very being.

"Hello," Kelly said, taking her seat.

I bid farewell and scurried back to my post, making one final tour past his table about twenty minutes later while they were having coffee. Imagine my surprise to notice that Kelly was crying and Rod was talking to her very seriously in a low voice and pointing his finger at her.

"Oh, goody," I thought, maybe they are breaking up, and I will have a chance—but how will he find me?

Oh, my! All those years have passed, and I'm still infatuated with him—along with a billion other fans. Damn, it sure would have been nice to talk to him.

✝✝

The camera salesman has been jabbering away. Surprisingly, he carries inexpensive cameras as well as top of the line ones, and since I'd wanted a camera, I go ahead and get one. Because of my dalliance at the camera shop, I don't have time to go to Whole Foods, so I head back to the snack-bar just down from the office building where Double D occupies a fourth of the sixth floor. The kiosk and cart are owned by a Korean couple. I decide on a peanut butter Clif bar, and while reaching for my wallet, I find the Korean translation of *Excuse Me, Your Soul Mate Is*

Waiting still in my oversize travel bag. At the register, I show it to Mr. Kim, the owner.

"Mr. Kim, look, I wrote a book, and it has been translated into Korean," I say proudly. "I have heard that self-help books are very popular in Korea."

"Oh yes, very popular. You have friend, gave you Korean book?"

I shake my head. "No, this is my book. I wrote this."

He motions to his wife, "Oh, trans-ah-lated, ah, very good, very good." He bows and hands it back to me.

I still don't know if he's understood me. I tear into my Clif Bar and return to work where an email awaits.

Dear Marla,
    I met with Nancy on Friday. The pitch I got when I joined was that you set us up with 8s, 9s, and 10s. I have mentioned to you I am fine with an 8 or a 9, it's what I usually date. In my eyes she was a 6, 6.5 tops. Can't—and won't—do. Feedback?
Phil.

Ooohhh, I'd like to give him some feedback all right! You usually date 8s and 9s in your dreams, mister. I look again at Nancy's picture. Well . . . maybe she could use a nose-job, but really that's all that's holding her back. Bright, well educated, funny. A very pretty brunette. Size four. I call Nancy and ask for her evaluation of Phil.

"Oh, Marla, he was so into his car. He drives a red convertible Infinity, and actually brags about his speeding tickets. He may be in his forties, but a big part of him is still in high school. We were totally bored with each other."

Sometimes when people don't click immediately, they can't see anything appealing in the other person. I thank her and try to pair Phil up with Natasha who "goes ape-shit" over expensive sports cars. I have a feeling about Phil and Natasha, though. Natasha is an earthy woman, with high, Slavic cheekbones. She's a size six except for her massive help-me-I've-fallen-over-and-can't-get-up bust-line. A surprising number of men find her unclassy. She's just too much woman for some guys, I guess. She makes raunchy jokes like needing kneepads to compensate some guy properly who's done her a favor.

Marla, this pairing just might work, I tell myself.

+‡+

At home, I wolf down some carbs and check my email. My editor only has a few changes for chapter 6—yay!—but has a lot to say about chapter 7. There's no way I can work on anything tonight, though. Adolfo has brought my suitcase in from the car, but I'm too tired to even unpack. Sleeping mask in place, my head hits the pillow. I'm out.

It's after midnight when Adolfo comes home from Mastro's, kissing me awake. It's been a week since we last made love, and I try to wake up a bit. I pull my sleeping mask off. He talks a little about being excited that Sheryl Crow was at the restaurant bar tonight. He's a big fan. Well, it's a name-dropping moment, right?

"Guess who I saw today? Rod Stewart!" I tell the story. "I love him! He looked so good!"

"Well, did you talk to him?" Adolfo asks.

"No, I was going to say 'hello,' but he didn't even look at me."

"Well, of course he didn't look at you. You're old and wrinkly!" Adolfo says. "And Rod is old! He has wrinkles, too."

I'm not fully awake. "No he doesn't, he looks amazing," I say in defense of Rod. "I saw his face, and he is as sexy as ever, really!"

"He is old! In his sixties . . ."

"So? And if he is old, I don't care; we all get older."

The stinger finally penetrates the gray pudding of my exhausted brain. Did my husband just say that I am old and wrinkly?

I yank my sleeping mask back over my eyes and am not talking to him the rest of the night. And no sex either! I turn my back to his side of the bed.

Affirmations

I am young, sexy, and wrinkle free.

I am soooo big time.

Other people's (Adolfo's) negative opinions slide off me.

My love for Rod Stewart is eternal.

twelve

Kiss My Botox

I tiptoe out of the apartment to leave early for work. Adolfo is still sleeping, and despite my affirmations, I am hurt about the "old and wrinkly" comment he made last night. It's bad enough that I have to hear that women over thirty-five are "old" on a daily basis at work, but from my own husband? I don't think so!

Even stopping for a vanilla soy latte, a venti today, I'm an hour-and-a-half early at Double D. I'm working on chapter 7, but I can't quite concentrate. For some sympathy and soothing, I email Bobbie and complain about Adolfo's comments. Within moments she replies.

> Marla,
>
> God bless you married gals. 24-7, you put up with more than I would! Speaking of marriage as a challenge, look what I found in a 1950s magazine—and by the way, DO NOT SHOW THESE TO RICKY! He might want to hold you to this list! Not only that, but he'll frame it. Anyway, things could be worse:
>
> ### Things to Make Your Man Happy
>
> - Listen to him. You may have a dozen important things to tell him, but the moment of his arrival is not the time. Let him talk first; remember, his topics of conversation are more important than yours.
>
> - Never complain if he comes home late or goes out to dinner or other places of entertainment without you, or

even if he stays out all night. Instead, try to understand his world of pressure and his very real need to relax.

- Make him comfortable. Have a cool or warm drink ready for him.

- Don't question his judgment. Remember, he is the master of the house and as such will always exercise his will with fairness and truthfulness. You have no right to question him.

A good wife always knows her place.
Bobbie

Wow. Thanks, very quaint! Where can I get a 1950s wife? I need one! I'm sure not going to be anything close to a "good wife" tonight! I'm still burning mad at Adolfo. My cell phone is ringing, and I see it's from him. I'm not answering it! Well, Adolfo has hung up, leaving no message. Ahh, but there he is, calling again. I'll send an update. Bye!

I'm so tempted to pick up the phone, but then I think of the paragraph I reworked in chapter 6. I stress not ruining chances for good communication by talking when the emotions are too volatile. Let anger cool. Such wise counsel. I turn off my cell phone. I try to do some writing, working off my flash drive, but I imagine things I want to yell at Adolfo. Fortunately, just before we open our doors for business, the flower service arrives. The decorator has specified certain color schemes, but today's is pretty classic. A bountiful bouquet of pale pink roses is brought into my office, replacing the lacy hydrangeas that had started to droop. Other roses grace the reception counter and the sales office. The whole office's airy, leafy potted plants are watered and groomed. This calms me a bit, and I get to work.

After tiring my index finger from deleting dozens of spam ads, I find that Lewis has sent in his evaluation of his date with Monique.

Hi, Marla,
I met Monique last night, had dinner, and listened to how much her ex disagrees with the way she handles their son. And I agree

with him, not her, but I kept my opinions to myself. She went on and on about her unbelievably intelligent son, who must sit in the back of the room with dividers around him b/c he has ADD so bad. And then I heard more than I wanted to know about her last relationship. She doesn't like to go swimming (b/c her hair gets wet) and does not want to wear a bike helmet (so tandem bike riding with me through Europe is out of the question). She only stays in 5 star hotels. I don't think the Queen of England could figure out a way to wear more diamonds, yet she has no income to speak of. On a first date she's wearing a dress that allows her breasts to hang out across the table. Other than that, I picked a great bottle of wine, and it got me though the drama.

Hope you are good.

Lewis

Monique's lack of boundaries is clearly an issue, but I didn't realize she was so non-outdoors-y. She likes tennis and so does Lewis, so I thought they had that going.

I seem to remember that Cass likes to ride bikes. I pull up her chart. Yes. She's biked along the south rim of the Grand Canyon and places like Martha's Vineyard. I contact her and describe Lewis. She's interested, and I give her contact info to Lewis. Fingers crossed.

Dear Marla,

I want to tell you something very interesting. I didn't tell you this when I met you because I wanted to see how I liked the service, but now I feel like I should let you in on a secret. I'm thrilled to have you as my matchmaker because before I ever knew that this matchmaking company existed, my cousin insisted that I call a psychic who lives on the East Coast and consult with her about my love life. I told her absolutely not, I was not interested. But she badgered me and insisted on it. I finally broke down. The psychic told me that I would indeed meet my match, and it was going to be facilitated by a person with the letters M A R in her name that would help me. When I met you and saw that both your first and last name begins with the letters M A R, well, I was in shock. So this is very exciting for me, and I'm so happy that you are helping me find my soul mate.

Nate

What a story. I love it. I ask Nate if the psychic gave him a specific name of a girl, and he says that she actually did: Kimberly.

I have a gorgeous gal named Kimberly in Orange County that is just the right age, sweet, down-to-earth, and successful. I will go to great lengths for someone who tells me they want to meet a soul mate. I give Kimberly a call and connect right away. That's one of the perks of this job. People are usually eager for my calls and take them right away. I don't tell Kimberly about the psychic stuff, but she is interested in meeting Nate.

Dear Nate,

Well, guess what, I have a fabulous match for you. Her name is indeed Kimberly. She lives in Orange County and she wants to meet you. She is thirty-one, five feet-five inches, blonde hair, sparkling blue eyes, great smile. Never married, no kids. She is a marketing manager for an advertising firm. She is family-oriented, outgoing, well traveled and cultured, down to earth, easy to talk to; loves theatre, film, music, fine dining, red wine, hiking, yoga, basketball games, Pilates, reading, learning about new cultures and people; she likes to cook and entertain. I think you should give her a call right now! I am so excited about this. Keep me posted.

Marla

I'm thinking my morning is about over when Alana opens one of the etched glass double doors to my office. "Hey, lady," she says, "You wanna see some sexy pic-tchas?" Smirk, smirk.

I follow her to her desk in the reception area. She opens up an email attachment, and I look at a photo of a guy with no shirt; oiled, leathery tan skin, flexing his muscles. "Meet Doug."

The man is ostensibly at a party, beer in hand but gripping it in such a way that it shows off the biceps. He looks a bit purple-faced from sucking in his gut and rather cocksure that he's irresistible to women.

"Whoo wee, what a bod, what a catch! Think he'd call a woman shallow if she fell for him because of his body?"

"Not him!" Alana closes the attachment and clicks on another. "You'll love this one. Heeeeeeere's Jill."

A woman has sent us a photo of her ass in a thong.

"I bet you can't wait to match her up!"

"She should be perfect for Doug."

"Totally."

We get all kinds of strange submissions from all over the country, and sometimes the world, from people wanting us to match them up. At least it provides some entertainment to our day!

+¦+

Luisa, one of our gorgeous recruiters, pops into the office. Italian from Argentina, Luisa has the most gorgeous long, shiny mane of coal-black hair I have ever seen, not to mention emerald green eyes. I can't believe she hasn't been snatched up by one of the millionaires in town yet. "Hey, Marla, I've got a place for cheap Botox. I'm gonna go on my lunch break. You wanta come?"

Old and wrinkled. Old and wrinkled. Old and wrinkled.

"Actually, yes, that would be fabulous," I tell her. "My wrinkles are getting out of control, especially on my forehead!"

I've decided to get Botox about once every year or so. It's too expensive to go any more often than that. This will be my third time.

Luisa and I drive down Santa Monica Boulevard about two miles to Century City and are waiting patiently for the doctor to call us in. This doctor is a dermatologist, and there are sensuous pictures of women's youthful skin and slim bodies decorating his waiting room. Brochures offer a variety of services, and the air smells of herbal infusions.

"Last year when Adolfo found out I was going to get Botox, he tried to talk me out of it," I tell Luisa. "'Just leave the cracks!' he said. 'You are beautiful, you don't need it. I love you with or without the cracks.'" I don't tell her what he said last night.

"He probably just doesn't want you to spend the money," Luisa says.

"Yeah."

"I consider Botox one of the basic food groups," she says, "so I subscribe to putting it in my body, just not via the digestive system."

"I know that what I spend on Botox should be going into our savings account for a house or to my retirement account, instead of being pumped into my forehead, but hey, I am doing TV interviews for my books, and I meet with high-level clients and work in Beverly Hills. It makes me feel good to look fresh and youthful."

"Absolutely, you don't have to convince me," Luisa says.

"Now breast implants, lip implants, or liposuction; I think that's going a bit too far."

"Definitely. Well, I'd consider a little lipo here and there, but not in lieu of serious weight control. But don't you love it when women say, 'I'm getting breast implants for me, not for anyone else'?"

"Right, like if they lived out in the wilderness with no contact with the human species, they'd still want the implants."

"Yeah, and what about if all the guys on the planet were blind?" Luisa says. "Would they still get the implants?"

"Remember the gal we worked with a few years ago? Grace? She got D-cup implants and started wearing really skimpy, low cut tops. Her cleavage was all you could see when she was approaching. Yet, she would get upset when men stared at her chest when she talked to them. When I asked her why she got the implants and wore revealing clothing if she didn't want people to look at them, her response was, 'The men are supposed to just take a quick glance when I am not looking.'"

Luisa laughs. "Like, I shove 'em up in your face, and you better pretend I'm not."

The Botox procedure causes a few winces and feels a bit thick at first. I look a little odd, but nothing to gawk at. The past couple of times I got Botox, my eyelids drooped so much that I could barely apply eye shadow, so for nearly ten days I walked around really self-conscious because I felt half naked. Another little unwanted side effect the first time around was that two deep lines appeared temporarily, one above each eyebrow. My loving husband, whom I can always count on for giving me his brutally honest appraisal, asked, "You trying out for the Joker's role, Lucy, honey?" God bless him. What would I do without him helping me to stay humble? His comment last night, though, crossed a boundary.

I plough through the rest of the day and then drive home to confront him. I know he'll be there, but I've never turned off my cell phone before. How much drama will I have to face?

Affirmations

Botox is in perfect harmony with my body.

I meet my publishing deadlines.

I excel at bringing the right people together.

I am loved, wrinkled forehead or smooth.

thirteen

Goddess Plan

"Hola, mi amor," I say as I step inside the apartment to see Adolfo standing in wait, glowering.

He starts to bark at me, but then he relaxes, runs his hand through his hair. "Marla, we shouldn't fight." His voice is husky with emotion. "Let's not argue anymore."

"I agree," I say, unable the keep the archness out of my tone. "But I didn't realize that you found me to be so old and wrinkly!"

"I didn't mean it! I love the way you look. You are gorgeous and not old!" He blinks about six times rapidly, and I know he's having every bit as hard a time with this as I've been having. "I just didn't like it that you are lusting over someone else."

"What!" *Someone else? Oh, right. Rod, baby.* "Honey, I'm not lusting over anyone except you. Rod Stewart is my favorite singer and has been since I was fifteen, but you know, it's not like I'd leave you for him."

"Well, why didn't you say so? I know he is your idol, but you made it sound like you are in love with him. What if I told you that I am lusting over Sheryl Crow?"

Ouch. That *would* hurt. But I don't want to concede the point. "I didn't say I was *lusting* over Rod Stewart."

"You had stars in your eyes, *mi estrella,* when you were talking about him. And if I was Rod Stewart, and I saw such stars, I'd think you wanted my body, and I'd take you up on it."

"Oh, for goodness sake. I was excited, so I told you about it because you are my best friend, but I guess I can't say anything like that."

"Divorce happens," he says gravely, "too fast in this town. Maybe you noticed? I don't want that to happen—"

"Oh, ya big galoot!" I plant a long mooshy one and then pull away. "Anyway, Rod only likes blondes, and I'm about twenty years too old for him."

"Very funny!" He's bleary-eyed with tenderness. "You know I love you."

"Yeah. I love you, too."

His gaze leaves my eyes and travels upward. "Ay, ay, ay! You got more Botox, Lucy?"

"Well . . ." I admit I'm milking this. "When Ricky Ricardo tells me I'm old and—"

"*Por Dios!* Let's open a nice bottle of wine and pretend you just got back from your trip and walked into my arms."

Unfortunately, I have to cut our special evening a bit shorter than what Adolfo has in mind, because, of course, I must write, write, write. And when I do that, I sometimes also munch, munch, munch.

✢

By Wednesday evening after work, I feel like a corpulent slug. I haven't been going to the gym because of being sick, traveling, and writing. Adolfo is at Mastro's. I'm going to get a workout tonight. I am.

My gym on Sunset Boulevard in West Hollywood provides the towels, shampoo, conditioner, hair driers, body lotion, Q-Tips, and tampons. Everyone is so in shape that I really should get my bodkin fabulous-looking before I set foot inside. They offer amazing classes like Ayurvedic yoga, budokon, belly dancing, and bell ball boot camp. The gym also has a café that serves fresh juices and sandwiches and a boutique where you can buy the latest pricey workout clothes. Upstairs, the spa offers bikini waxing, dreamy treatments like a lemon sugar body polish, a body soufflé smoothie, or basic massage. My favorite part of the gym is the steam room. It's my special treat after a hard workout—but I can't go that far tonight, naturally.

I do my machines and weights and then actually mentally

embellish a chapter while I pump away on the elliptical. The young woman on the machine next to me is a knock-out, and she's not wearing any kind of ring on her left hand. I force myself to keep at it as long as she does so that we can get off at the same time. This stretches my elliptical session to forty-five minutes and just about kills me.

"Whew!" I say to her as I step down the second she stops pedaling. "That felt great!"

She barely glances at me as she almost nods, recalibrates her settings, and keeps going.

Well, sayonara, sweetie. When I joined, I figured that the pricey membership would pay for itself since I would be able to recruit bevies of beautiful women, but I didn't realize how snobby these super-fit creatures can be. I have yet to get even a smile returned to me in passing, let alone find a chance to strike up a conversation. They just seem to glide by with their size zero bodies in their $250 yoga pants. Jessica Alba was once pedaling on the stationary bike right next to me, and she actually said hello. I should find a less expensive gym, but I'm so spoiled, I just can't give it up.

I look longingly at the steam room and pass it by. Feeling great, but starved, I load up on Pad Thai noodles and tofu at home and then sit down on the green sofa with my laptop. I've only slept a total of twelve hours in the last two nights, so I barely have my files open before my personal batteries run out of juice. I'm asleep when Adolfo comes home. I sleepwalk to bed and crash.

Next morning, I have a vague memory of him being fussy, but when I try to rouse him, he's in deep REM. I get in a few hours of work while I'm fresh.

✝

Ha! I'm hot. I'm on a roll. Blue-streaking. Groovin' with the muse.

Huh?

Adolfo hovers over me. "I said, you never have time for me anymore." He rubs my neck, massages my shoulders, lifts my hair, and kisses the back of my neck.

"I just need to finish this page, honey. Hold that thought?"
He mutters in Spanish. "I'm going to take a cold shower!"

"Honey . . ." I say absently.

"Never mind." The bathroom door slams. The shower goes on.
Now where was I going with that paragraph?

+‡+

It's now eight thirty Monday morning, and I'm finally emailing chapter 7 to my editor before getting ready for work. I was up
at five, even after tapping the keys all weekend long doing
rewrites. I couldn't go out when Adolfo wanted to yesterday, and
he's not happy about it. Chapter 8 is due tomorrow, so tonight
will be another hump.

I'm standing in front of the bathroom mirror and assessing
the Botox job. Pretty damn good, I must say. The next time I run
into Rod Stewart, he is definitely going to look at me. Though
my eyelids had drooped a bit, it only took a few days for this nasty
little side-effect to disappear. Now my forehead is not only back
to normal, it is smooth, and there are no crow's feet at my eyes.
I like what I see in the mirror. This doctor is good! At least the top
half of my face looks about twenty-five now; the other half looks,
well, forty.

Monday means that Gary will be in the office, so I have to pay
extra attention to my hair. Gary has a thing about women's hair
and demands that Alana and I wear ours down. No glorious rolls
or buns, even if held in place with bejeweled pins and combs.
No ponytails or braids.

I have problem hair. It's thin, dry, frizzy, scraggly, and see-
through, so I like to wear it up. Gary acknowledges that while
wearing one's hair pulled back is chic on a woman, he doesn't
want us to look chic. Even though the clients aren't going to be
dating us, he wants us to look "hot"—which, according to him,
is only achieved when a woman's hair is "down and loose." Of
course, how could I expect Gary to understand what it is like
having thin hair when his is so thick? I don't know how he gets
a comb through it. Gary is actually pretty attractive, though on
the short side. I actually tower over him in my heels.

My husband is also radically opinionated about how I wear my hair. While he likes it up, he says that any woman, regardless of her age, and no matter how smart or beautiful she is, who wears her hair short is "dike-like," and, therefore, a "turn off."

Every time I see a woman with short hair who looks absolutely stunning, I, of course, point her out. I'd like my hair "dike-like," but while I might be able to help Adolfo change his biased view, there is not much I can do to influence my boss.

So I wear my hair shoulder length for my Adolfo, and "down and loose" for my boss.

Hair down, new Botox working, I'm set to face Gary and the weekend feedback. I sort through it, adding to profiles, getting ideas for better matches. The majority had a nice time on their dates with people I recommended, but found them too something and not enough something else. Francesco had a nice time. Lovely date. Who's next? he asks. I'm starting to get nervous that I'll run out of sweet young things for him.

Some had a not-so-nice time:

Hi Marla,

Do you have any new hotties for me? The guy I just went out with, Howard, pitched an absolute fit about my having a dog. Marla, I have no kids, no STDs, no drug/drinking problems, no debt—actually investments. He said single people shouldn't have dogs, and it makes them pitiful! Say what? Weird.
Cathy

Dear Cathy,

I'd choose a dog over a guy like that any day! See attachments for two new hotties.
Marla

This is my second strange feedback on Howard, and I file him in my PNJ file. It's my code for Possible Nut Job. Now, I deal with hundreds of clients, so I have need for classifications. A single rich guy dating a few women does not. And yet:

Hi Marla,

I arranged to get together with Liz over dinner and then talked with her on the phone. It's unlikely we'd be a match. I certainly wouldn't call her a 9 or even an 8 or 7, though she has an attractive body. As to her Enneagram type, remember that I specified a preference for a 2, 6, or 9. Liz is clearly a 3, with whom I'm least compatible.

As to her Myers-Briggs personality type, she's again, quite oppositional. ESFJs make a very incompatible partner for me. I do best with the ISTPs of the feminine world. I myself, as I believe I mentioned am an ISTJ and tend to butt heads with women who are also in that J category. I'd think it would be very simple and efficient to employ these categories to increase the likelihood of compatibility.

So, what now? Is there hope? Or should we be talking about rescinding the contract and charging me some fee for services rendered to date?

Let me know your thoughts.

Thanks,

Greg

Whoo boy. I think this guy was one of the clients whose complaints got Charlotte fired. He's paid top dollar, so I don't dare disappoint him. I take a tedious look into the Enneagram and Myers-Briggs categories, and begin to see what he's after. It doesn't require a personality inventory to get there. He wants a gorgeous woman with a degree from a top university who will make a submissive 1950s wife without sounding like that's what he's after. I'm going to have to give this some serious thought.

Some bloggers say that profiles like the Myers-Briggs work really well while others say they are total hooey. "They stuff spontaneity and chemistry into a narrow pigeon hole." Several couples believe their particular Myers-Briggs personality type represents the crème de la crème of humanity, a superior race.

It seems to me that one of the most complicated issues on earth is for men and women to understand what makes the other happy. The guys feel women don't have it right, and women feel that men don't have it right. I place blame on outrageous expectations. Most male clients feel that if they have money, that's all they need to bring to the table. So if he's out of shape and not all that good looking or well mannered, well the girl should overlook those things because "He who has the gold, rules." This sets up a shitty attitude in response from women. I see it constantly. Many women feel that if they put up with a guy they consider to be a 5, 6, or 7, that he'd better pay off. They'll trade their beauty and sex for a so-so guy who'll buy them the good life. And yet, the rich boys are often stunned that they've attracted a gold-digger and shocked that they're not loved for themselves alone.

And everyone bitches. The men resent women who expect to be showered with expensive gifts, travel, and entertainment. The women resent the men who seem to care only about their looks. Blah blah blah.

Women have their own style of maddening shortcomings.

Dear Marla,

I flew into town for three days just to date my three referrals. I had dinner reservations at La Dolce Vita. Karly arrived an hour late, so we missed dinner and had to settle for an appetizer at the bar. No follow-up response. Greta was supposed to go to the Elton John concert and sounded delighted with that on the phone. She pulled a no-show. Rita joined me at Spago, but I have heard no response, let alone a courtesy thank-you. Am I too much of a gentleman?

Steve

I compliment Steve for remaining a gentleman, arrange for a hotel comp at the Beverly Wilshire, and introduce him to three women who are more reliable. Then I email Karly, Rita, and Greta asking for explanations. Greta claimed she got her wires crossed and will apologize. Karly responds that she just texted him. Further inquiry reveals the following text message: THX SRY C ya. (Thanks, sorry, see ya.)

WCIS? (What can I say?) I only tolerate these girls because they're stunning. And they know it. I need to keep them interested.

I send them emails with a few pointers in etiquette standards, reminding them that texting is too impersonal and sometimes arrives much later than when they think it might. Every day, I spend hours upon hours tracking down women who haven't returned phone calls from their matches. Like, just call the damn guy, already, ladies. If he took you to dinner, and if he paid the dinner tab, call him and thank him—even if he creeped you out. If you never want to see him again, tell him you're going to be out of reach for a few months while you treat your STD. Say something! Just make the damn phone call.

That afternoon, I get an email from Ralph. In his rush to find his future heirs' perfect mother, he has rejected Christina, but is seeing Denise a second time. Actually, I don't see any reason why that pairing wouldn't work.

Phil sent me an email expressing his dismay at meeting a woman like Natasha.

> . . . She's just not what I had in mind, but she jumped at the chance to go to the Malibu car show this weekend when nobody else wanted to go with me, so I guess I'll give it one more shot.
> Phil

He probably never laughed as much in his life as when he was with her. I knew he'd find some excuse to go out with her again, whether there was a car show or not.

Matthew and Angie have seen each other four times; they seem to click.

My brain is swimming. Must have vanilla soy latte now!

I walk down to Teuscher's chocolate shop. They have a little window that faces the sidewalk so that people can order specialty coffees and pastries to go. Most of the customers are people who work in the area, so I see a lot of the same faces standing in line waiting for their grande chai lattes or double shots of espresso.

While waiting for my latte, a woman sitting at one of the three tables on the sidewalk starts chatting with me. Probably in her early thirties, she has a nice smile, but is average-looking with mousy brown hair. In her baggy sundress, she looks to be about fifteen pounds overweight.

"Do you work in the area?" she asks me.

"Yes, a few blocks over," I tell her pointing in the direction of my office.

"Do you work at Atlas?" she asks. Atlas is a big time talent agency nearby.

"No, actually I am a professional matchmaker." The minute that sentence comes out of my mouth I regret it! Men may come to our matchmaking agency randomly—if they can write the check, they're in—but women, of course, are carefully hand-selected.

"Oh, wow," Ms. Sundress says. "I'd love to be matched up. Do you have a card?"

I can't possibly tell her she's not what our clients are looking for. I waffle. "No, I don't have any cards with me. But if you give me your email, I can send you some information."

She thrusts a scrap of paper into my hand. Luckily, my latte is ready, so I grab it and dash back to the office, rehearsing my answers for the next such awkward moment.

"What do you do?" Ms. Size Eight asks.

"I'm independently wealthy." Or, "I work for the IRS." Or, "I'm a writer." I decide this to be the perfect answer, until I imagine her next question.

"What do you write about?" she would ask.

"Relationships," I would have to say. "Dating and how to find your soul mate."

"Interesting." The inevitable question occurs to her. "What makes you qualified to write on that subject? Are you a psychologist or something?"

Gah! "No, I am a professional matchmaker."

"Ooohh . . . can you match me up?"

By the time I'm back to the office, I've decided what to do with Greg, the personality profiler. I email Cheryl, whom I'd taken off my main list for being too picky. She has this lowered gaze that is both sultry and innocent at the same time. What seems like a passive personality is actually merely languid. She's a purring cat without claws. Every man who's asked her out has wanted more, but she just slips out the back somehow. She's a catalog model, but she graduated from UCLA. I pull up her file and see she's twenty-eight. Just had a birthday—not getting any younger. I also contact Kendra, a gorgeous Asian girl with a slight accent who works as a translator for Pacific Rim corporations. And, I risk a new girl I haven't referred before: Tate, a recently divorced airline stewardess who went to Berkeley but didn't graduate. She may be a little too outgoing for him.

To each of the girls, I describe Greg as forty-three, divorced, no kids; still has hair, fit, five eleven; rather nice-looking. Loves international travel in his corporate jet and wants a companion whose schedule is flexible enough to accommodate him. Your mission, should you accept it, is to come across as smart but not too; seem be a doormat without making it obvious; make it appear that he has all the great ideas.

No, I don't put that last part in about the mission. And they know the code: "rather nice looking" means not nearly as ugly as some of the guys you've been fixed up with. By the end of the day, I've heard back from all three *femme fatales,* and they agree to have their files sent to him. Let him dare bitch about these women. Ha! He's dealing with a full-on goddess assault. He won't know what hit him. Damn, I'm good.

It's seven o'clock, and I shut down the Double D. I've been working since five this morning. And chapter 8 is due tomorrow.

Affirmations

I have all the time and energy I need for friends, exercise, writing, and for mi amor.

I have a full head of gorgeous, healthy hair.

Chapter 8 dazzles my editor.

I am chi-chi matchmaker.

Darling, José Eber You're Not

At two on Monday morning, I email chapter 8 to my editor, then sleep till eight forty-five. I wake up happy I don't have the deadline hanging over my head, but I'm feeling sick again. No matter. I fix my hair loose and long and get myself to work.

I drive down to our agency's San Diego office, stay overnight at Bobbie's, and get in another workday in San Diego. By Tuesday evening, I've received my rewrite notes on chapter 8, and Bobbie, as an author herself, agrees to go over them with me. As a result of her questions, I come up with some great changes.

On Thursday, I drive to and from Orange County through brutal traffic—both ways. I still just haven't recovered from being so sick before my book tour. What if I have chronic fatigue syndrome? I book an appointment with Doc Speedy for my Friday lunch hour.

At the office Friday morning, I check emails. I lot of people seem to be on second dates with their latest contacts. Ah, here's one from Mr. Personality Profile (who helped get Charlotte fired) commenting on one of the goddesses.

Hi, Marla,

You have certainly surprised me. I have two dates on the calendar, and I've already taken Tate out for dinner. I see that my suggestions on personality profiling have helped you make much

better decisions. I suspect that Tate leans toward the E more than I'm comfortable with, but she is lively. I normally wouldn't date a stewardess, but we had our Berkeley days in common—although mine were a bit less recent! I'm leaving the door open, as I look forward to my next two dates.
Greg

Great. And with the printed copy of this chipper email, I seal the contract. He can't weasel around and blame any failures on the agency now. I feel a twinge that I have probably set him up for some heartbreak, but as a moderate C.D., he asked for it. And here is Tate's response.

Hi, Marla,
Greg is an interesting guy, and I thanked him for a very nice evening. He didn't flinch when I suggested we eat at Koi. That place is fabulous. I had their miso-bronzed black cod, and we saw Demi and Ashton! I doubt that I could ever have feelings for Greg. I left things open though.
Tate

Open means in case none of the other matches offer any sizzle. I'll be especially eager to hear about goddess number two. Next email is from Scott.

Dear Marla,
Dee Dee's got me hopping all over town, but I think she's falling for me. I'm a bit worried that she dates other fellows still. —SCL

No, no, no! Scott is the one who is falling for this gal. And I scroll down to find Dee Dee's feedback.

Hey Mar!
Scot took me to dinner at Grace and Frida. Very cool. I like his dimples. And Jerry takes me to French resterants [sic]. Don't tell them I still see Daryl tho. K? (The old guy I was with at Mastro's. We kinda got engaged, but I still want to date.)
Dee Dee

I wonder if the air rushing through this woman's brain cavity makes a screaming sound when she moves quickly. I scroll around and find Jerry's feedback.

Hi, Marla,

Do you think it's too soon to offer Dee Dee a ring? I'm pretty sure she's hot for me. We had a very romantic night at Chateau Marmont. You know that hotel up on Sunset Boulevard that copied a Loire Valley castle and has all those pictures of old movie stars? Please advise.

Jerry

Oh, no! This is turning into a nightmare. I hustle around to find some new names, contact the women to get their approval, and then send emails to both Scott and Jerry, strongly suggesting that they keep playing the field. I tell them that Dee Dee has indicated she loves dating several guys at once, hoping they'll infer that she's what I call a multiple serial dater—which is PC for you know what. Keep those options open, guys, I tell them. Most of my clients don't like a lot of competition.

And finally, an email I've been expecting nervously from the man willing to pay a monthly allowance of between five and ten thousand dollars to a nice churchy, busty, slim, blonde wife:

Dear Marla,

Well, I never thought I'd be dating a woman with a Russian Orthodox faith, but so far Sofia and I are getting on just fine. I haven't even contacted the other two gals yet. Thanks.

Wynne

What d'ya know? Actually, I thought Sofia would be his last choice. Isn't that a hoot?

✝

"I'll be right with you, honey," Doc Speedy says as he whizzes by the open door of the little room I'm in. He finally comes in with my chart, looks at my throat, listens to my lungs, pokes the gut. "Anything different in your routine? Are you stressed or under severe pressure?" he asks.

I spill out my life like he's a shrink and add, "I still feel terrible. My throat is a bit sore, and I just feel like I am on the verge of coming down with something all the time. I have no energy to take my morning walk, let alone work out."

The doc removes his glasses, folds them, and puts them in his coat pocket, as if about to deliver a serious you've-got-six-months-to-live talk. "I'm going to give you a kick in the pants," he says holding up a yellow box. "Now, Provogil is effective, perfectly safe, and kind of a fun drug. You'll probably think it's a placebo. But it *will* do something. Take 'em and call me next week."

A perfectly safe drug, huh? Is there such a thing? "How about I just take a vitamin B shot instead?"

He finally gives in and jabs me again with the "B venom."

"So, you have no idea what's wrong with me then?" I ask.

"Yes, you're right. I don't."

+ͦ+

I get a good night's rest that night, hoping for the strength to pound the keyboard over the weekend. My editor wants chapter 9 by the end of the week. But it's the last chapter. I'll be done with my second book. And it's an easy chapter on dating journals. I've booked a massage at my new favorite place on Hollywood Boulevard to help restore my energy level for the final push.

Saturday morning, I walk into the cool lobby of Thai Sabai and am escorted down a hallway of little elevated rooms behind curtains. Inside one of them, I find a matt on the floor with an orchid on the pillow and three black stones on the pad where my feet go. I undress down to my thong, put on the light cotton shorts and halter top provided, and lie down on the cool sheet. In comes the masseuse. Edie kneads and pummels my body until I am floating on a cloud.

+ͦ+

"Ricky, I'm home!" I, the new, young, sexy, healthy woman, shout as I close the front door. He hugs me and gives me a kiss. "I'm so glad you are feeling better."

"I'm in great shape to really get busy and finish the book this weekend."

He cuddles me up again. "But of course you have made some time for me today."

Well, no. Time away from writing now will mean more late nights during the week. "Um . . . what did you want to do?"

"Let's go to the gym!"

"Whoa!" I sit down on the green sofa. "I don't know if I feel that good. Actually, I'm a bit tired now. I was just going to go for a short walk before getting down to work."

"Oh, come on," he coaxes. "Just a short workout."

"Honey, I love hanging out with you, but I don't particularly like going to the gym with you."

"What's that suppose to mean?"

"Well, you think you have to train me when we go. I've worked out for years and like to do my own routine. You push me too hard. Especially the abs. It's torture!"

"It's the only way. I see how you work out. So wimpy. You'll never get your abs in shape the way you do it."

"Oh, I know how to do it, Ricky!"

We get to the gym and put our stuff in the locker rooms and meet back in front of the machines.

"Come on, let's go over here and work your abs a little," Adolfo says.

"Noooooo!" I whine. "I've been sick. I'm still tired, and I really don't think it's a good idea to do anything too strenuous; so please go away!"

Adolfo drags me toward the dreaded ab machine anyway and instructs me to get on. "Just a few," he promises.

Oh, right, like I believe that. I realize he's not going to give up, though, so I reluctantly get on and start counting. I do fifteen and hope I am done.

Adolfo manages to get me to do about seventy-five altogether, along with leg and butt exercises. I escape to do fifteen minutes of cardio and a bit on my arms, and I hit the sauna.

I love Adolfo. Of course I do. It's just that even my own parents didn't micromanage my life like this. I think of Dee Dee and how she uses her body to get exactly what she wants out of life. She knows how to work the C.D.s of the world. She micromanages with her boobs. I wonder if she judges me the way I judge her. She probably thinks *I'm* the fool. If Scott or Jerry or the old guy she's "kinda" engaged to tried to push her to do something she didn't want to do, she'd just say *adios*. And they know it. And she knows they know it. Yet they would love her—at least for a while—and she would probably *not* truly return the love of any of these men that she controls. She acts like she's happy, but I wonder.

✝

It still feels like summer in Southern California, but actually, it's mid-September. After a week of basically working two jobs, getting too little sleep, I'm feeling surprisingly okay by Friday morning, especially now that I've turned in my last chapter of *Good Date, Bad Date*. I want to celebrate, but I have a disgusting event to go to this evening and . . . just look at my hair!

"I really need a haircut," I say to Adolfo. This comment is a huge mistake.

Adolfo's throat is tired from singing the night before, and my hair is a matter that requires intense discussion, which makes him cranky. I protest and plead, but he insists on styling my hair and puts oil in it. He combs it through and works it with his hands like he's José Eber. Unfortunately, he is not, and upon seeing his creation in the mirror, tears of frustration and horror at my appearance well up and spill over. I hyperventilate.

"Marlita, your hair looks fantastic, leave it like this."

"Are you kidding me? It's awful! You don't know how to style hair. I can't leave the house like this." I grab a tissue and blow my nose.

"What do you mean? Look again, I did a great job. It's so sexy!"

"You are really something you know? Stick to song-writing. You could never make it as a hairdresser. I just want to cut my hair off. Actually, I would just looooove to shave my head!"

He puffs up, angrily. "I don't care how thin, scraggly, or dry your hair is, as long as it's not short! I *hate* short hair on a woman!"

How can he be like this to me? After more tears, I think he feels a little guilty, so he hugs me.

"Let's compromise," he says. "I don't want you to be unhappy."

"Okay, then let me show you want I *want*." I show him some shorter styles in magazines.

He jabbers rapidly in Spanish, which I can't quite understand, ending with, *"Verdad?"* which means, "Isn't that right?"

I agree, but I'm not sure to what. So, all seems to be well, but my face is puffy, and I feel drained. Why is love such a *many-splendored-thing* again?

Well, off to the love ranch.

✛̤

"If you do this right," Gary says at work that morning, "This one event can completely solve our problem of not having enough women in the Orange County database. Get us fifteen phone numbers tonight!"

In his dreams. I'm dreading "The Taste of Newport"—an annual pain in the ass. About a hundred restaurants from Newport Beach set up booths with food and wine. Gary requires that we go and round up as many attractive, single, skinny women as possible.

"But Gary, every year we go and only end up with about four or five ladies who actually come in and join," I plead. "And they are usually *not* 9s or 10s. Can't you just send the recruiters? Why do the matchmakers have to go?"

"Because you know precisely what our male clients want, Marla. It's a big event. I'm requiring you to go. I insist. Wear a little black dress and heels."

Arrgghhh! I hate it. I hate it. I triple hate it.

You know how you can always spot the folks pushing religious pamphlets by the way they dress? That's what a black cocktail dress is like at this shindig. Most hot young babes wear hip-hugger jeans, crop tops, and flip-flops. You see a lot of T-shirts and tennis shoes, too.

I light candles in my zen garden and breathe deeply.

Affirmations

I am young, healthy, sexy, and energetic.

I am slim, toned, trim, and at my perfect weight with six-pack abs.

I speak clearly, eloquently, and assertively when I convey my wishes to Adolfo.

My completed manuscript sprouts wings and flies into bookstores everywhere.

fifteen

One Percent of the Population

L uisa comes to the office at four thirty so that we can drive to the Newport event together. I refuse to wear a black cocktail dress and hobble around on spike heels all night, so I change into a sexy wrap-around sundress and flats. My hair is pulled back in a ponytail, and I feel like a rebel. I am in no mood for anyone telling me how to wear my hair right now.

We crawl down the 405 in Friday traffic at five in the afternoon. Brutal.

I whine to Luisa about Adolfo's attitude toward short hair. Since she is from Argentina, she understands, better than do I, the hair thing with Latin men.

"How many Mexican women do you see walking around with short hair? Latin men are obsessed with long hair!"

We arrive at The Taste of Newport and park. Gary only reimburses us for the outrageous twenty-five dollar entrance fee. Eventually.

"Damn, can you believe the food and drinks aren't included?" Luisa says.

We hook up with Amanda, an Orange County recruiter, a gorgeous brunette in her twenties with the figure of a runway model and long, curly dark hair.

"Let's eat first," says Luisa. "I'm starving."

"Try their pot-stickers," Amanda says. "They're to die for!"

We head to the wine booth—first things first—and I buy a glass of Chardonnay. Luisa prefers Merlot. We also load up on pot-stickers, expertly balance our food and wine on our clip boards, trying to not be too conspicuous as we assess the face, midriff, tits, and ass of every young woman we pass. We are to approach each attractive woman we see, asking her if she is interested in joining the service. This is a fairly intrusive procedure. In fact, last year we almost got kicked out because we were seen as more or less invading the event and accosting attendees.

"Is it just me, or does it seem like all the attractive women are on the arms of men?"

"Imagine that," Luisa says.

"Yeah, it's going to be a long night." Fifteen hits? Not a chance in hell! For one thing, the type of women we recruit represents one percent of the world's female population. There aren't that many 10s at this whole event. Last year we were so exhausted and disgusted that we starting approaching 7s just to fill up our clipboard.

"How are you going to manage walking around all night on concrete in those four-inch spikes," I ask Amanda.

"Painfully," she concedes. "Very painfully."

Last year I promised myself that it was my last year to work this event, but here I am, walking around with a list of interview questions. Of course Gary attends the events to make sure that we're doing our jobs. He demands that we stay for the entire event—even if we've met our quota of finding, as Bobbie calls it, "fresh meat" for our male clients.

In my rebellion against the black cocktail dress, I wore a dress that exposes even more bare skin—something I now regret. It has been dark since seven, and the cool ocean breeze has picked up. I'm shivering as I watch scantily clad young women vie for attention from guys in button-down shirts over T-shirts, drinking beer.

I spot a hot-looking brunette in a black mini skirt. I'm guessing she's forty. I point her out to Luisa who runs over and asks her if she happens to be single. Luisa's look of rejection as she walks away conveys the answer.

We continue along, scanning the crowd for 10s, but we're already noticing 7s. I spot a booth selling pink champagne.

"Ooh, let's get a glass!" I whip out my card. "My treat, ladies. Three glasses please."

"Hey, if we wait here for the women to drink enough, they'll gladly hand us their phone numbers," says Amanda.

"Good thinking," I say, "but tomorrow they won't remember speaking to us and that they signed up to go out with short, fat, bald men."

"Don't forget rich. Rich. Rich-rich," says Amanda.

We make our way over to three ladies sitting at one of the white plastic tables and start chatting with them, giving them our spiel. The dark-haired one on the left shoves a diamond-laden finger on her left hand at us. The blonde in the middle announces that she is married, and the petite Asian on the right explains that she is in the middle of a divorce.

"Oh brother," I remark. "This is hopeless."

"Marla, look," Luisa says, pointing to two very beautiful women. We get closer and realize they are already on our lists. We recruited them at this event last year. We chat a while and move on, desperate for names and numbers, cruising the bar circuit again. Amanda leaves after signing four women.

"I'm cold, and my feet are killing me. Can we go home yet?" Luisa begs.

"I've got five names and numbers. How many do you have?" I ask.

"Six, but three of them are not that pretty."

"It'll have to do. I haven't seen Gary for a half hour. Let's bolt. This will be our last year to do this, no matter what the consequences," I vow.

Finally, feeling fluish and coughing from being out in the cold, I'm at the apartment and in bed at twelve thirty in the morning. Adolfo walks in, home from playing at Mastro's. He stands at the foot of the bed, looking handsome in his black suit and white shirt.

"Honey, I was thinking tonight while playing the piano. I have changed my mind about your hair. I want you to grow it long."

"Good night, Ricky," I say as I pull my sleeping mask down over my eyes. It's either that or throw things at him.

✝︎

I'm at the beauty salon the next day, Saturday, dealing with what puts *me* in the same category with a mere 1 or 2 percent of the human population: having red hair. As a young person, I was teased endlessly. Kids called me "carrot top," to which I needed some sort of reply, or else they'd think they'd gotten to me, which meant that the goading would continue. I was forced to come up with stupid responses: "Carrot tops are green; don't you know anything!"

Or they would yell, "The redhead is de-ead; the redhead is de-ead," thinking it was cute just because it rhymed. Some kids would even pull at my hair. I hated all the persecution, but when I'd go home crying, Mom—also a redhead—would say simply, "Others are jealous that they don't have special red hair and you do."

I've come to think of being a redhead as an attitude as much as it is a physical state; a special privilege, a gift of nature to signify creativity and uniqueness. I suppose Adolfo's obsession with being in charge of how it looks stirs up—in addition to fear of being controlled—deep-rooted stuff about loss of love going back to my childhood.

I'm at Fantastic Sam's, but I used to get my hair cut and colored in Beverly Hills, until Adolfo convinced me to try Mimi—a woman he knew who is just as good as the Beverly Hills hairdressers but at a fraction of the cost. And, of course, by my going to Mimi's, Adolfo thinks he can better monitor how I wear my hair.

I'm excited about going to lunch with him today because we're celebrating the completion of my second book at the famous restaurant, Mr. Chow, where the paparazzi circle and hover, constantly poised near the front door to click away at whatever celebrity is dining inside. However, I'm very nervous about what Adolfo is going to say when he sees how short my hair is now. Nor is he going to like the new color tint, but I just love it.

I rehearse my defense all the way home from the hairdressers:

Adolfo: "What the hell did you do to your hair, Marla? It's too short and bright red."

Marla: "It is? I didn't notice, let me go see." No. Maybe: "Oh, I know; I hate it too. I told her not this short! And I don't know what she did to the color! Thankfully the tint will wash out and my hair will grow out. Honey, please don't make me feel any worse than I already do!"

I get home, turn the key in the lock ever so quietly, take my shoes off, and walk gingerly and quickly into the bathroom. Oooooh, I just love my new cut and color. I dart back into the kitchen while Adolfo is in his studio playing the piano. He finally comes out.

"Hey, why didn't you tell me that you were home, honey? I didn't even hear you come in."

"Oh, well, you were practicing." I lean my head into the cupboard, pretending to search for something to prolong the confrontation.

"You're snacking before going to *Chow's?*"

I shut the cupboard and brace for the worst.

"Wow, your hair looks great, honey. Mimi really did a good job."

But . . . ? I wait for the next line. Nothing. Ha! I breathe a deep relaxing sigh. This proves miracles do happen.

+‡+

It is Sunday afternoon, and I am tossing my gorgeous hair at Starbucks on La Brea and Santa Monica. I can look out the window and see the Hollywood sign. An obese, middle-aged man comes in, wearing maroon-colored sweats, a huge silver "Go Raiders" T-shirt, and big yellowish slippers with Winnie the Pooh heads. The guy with him makes an equally stunning fashion statement: green-plaid mini skirt, a pink boa, and two-inch red heels. It's just another day in "Holly-weird."

This Starbucks is in an outdoor shopping center, catering to computer users—which is one reason I'm here with my laptop. Another reason is to get out of our tiny apartment. Adolfo is fussing over the fact that I keep returning my father's Iranian ashtray to the coffee table, alongside all the doodads from Mexico. The ashtray's lovely peacock color draws the eye, but Adolfo puts it

back on my desk shelf because "we don't smoke." I'm not allowed
to have one dang four-inch ashtray that means something to me
on his flipping coffee table. So . . . Starbucks.

I take my vanilla soy latte and blend in with the other hip-
sters working on the next great American novel. Adolfo and I
will be going to Mexico for a wedding, and I need to make sure
my clients are in good shape before I can leave. I haven't asked
Gary yet for the remainder of my vacation time. He's not going
to be happy. To get a head start, I open the Double D emails.

Dear Marla,
    I ended the relationship with Carrie on Saturday night. She is
a wonderful girl, just not the right one for me. And after as long
as we went out, I simply wasn't interested in moving to the next
level with her, sorry. I'd appreciate your forwarding me more
matches as soon as possible. Thanks.
All the best,
Thomas

Carrie? Carrie? Oh, yeah. Oh, no! Carrie is a doll. I thought
they were quite well matched. These splits, after long-term exclu-
sivity, are quite disappointing. I won't answer today, but I'll have
some names for him on Monday and contact Carrie to see if she
wants to continue with us. Here's an email from one of the
women Francesco is seeing:

Dear Marla,
    Francesco is fantastic. He's taken me to amazing Italian restau-
rants. He even took me to see *Nights in Rodanthe.* Whoo! Very inspiring, if you know what I mean. Has he said anything about me? I'm
so going after him.
Karly

Well, well. Karly, infamous for her terse text messages, has
communicated in a whole paragraph. I shouldn't say this, but I
hope Karly isn't the one he chooses, singular sensation that she
is. Since she has real competition, she needs to take it slow. I
draft the email I'll send tomorrow, telling her there hasn't been

any specific feedback, but that Francesco is enjoying the dating process immensely, and I'm sure that includes her.

I'm guessing "inspiring" meant so turned on, she banged her brains loose. Women are positively throwing themselves at this guy. And he knows what they want. Italian restaurants and a chick flick? I need to issue a cardiac warning with his referrals: possible heartbreaker.

Affirmations

I am loved and safe from cardiac misadventures.

Writing provides me with all the income I need.

This is positively my last year working "Taste of Newport," this I vow to heaven.

I wear my hair the way I like it.

 *sixteen*

Two Life Lines

At work Monday, I send Gary the email telling him of Adolfo's brother's wedding in Mexico and requesting the rest of my vacation time. Then I line up with my Cupid energy to make the best matches, so there will be fewer complaints to deal with in these intense two weeks before the trip. I turn my wall fountain on and light the zen candles. Fresh pink and white orchids look lovely against my chocolate wall.

I begin with the emails.

> Hi Marla,
>
> I met Drew. He is a total sweetheart, but not for me. He seemed really nervous and brought me a cute bracelet and showed me a whole photo album of all the celebrities that he has met through his company—50 pages. Can you please tell him that I'm not interested as I'm sure he is going to be Myspacing me soon. Also, he asked for details about my past relationships, and I said that you're never supposed to talk about this kind of thing on a first date! I told him I am sure you wrote that in your book . . . and he was like, yeah she did . . . but she didn't say anything about just asking about them . . .
>
> I am meeting Andy tomorrow. I kinda like those Southern boys.
> Xoxo
> Naomi ☺

I wish her luck with the nipple guy. Drew claimed he used to date a Victoria's Secret model and had high expectations, but that must have been, oh, fifteen years ago? He's gotten quite a few rejections, so maybe he's more realistic now. I get busy and find some new names for him.

Samantha, a gal we signed on recently, hoping she might be good to line up with some of our pickier clients writes:

> Marla,
>   I do hope to meet someone who is serious about having a future with me. My last three dates told me how hot I am, but they're not that well off or serious about marriage. I would like a very wealthy gentleman, your top 2%. I am willing to adapt to fit that special gentleman's needs and wants.
>   By the way, I got hair extensions. What a difference. I will send you a photo.
> Samantha

I want to send her an email that says, to get in the top 2 percent, you're going to need more than hair extensions, girlfriend! But I just tell her I'll see what I can do. I forward her info to Anthony, a very wealthy guy indeed, maybe in the top 10 percent of our clients.

I sneak in a little private business and quickly send an email to one of my clients whose best friend is best friends with Dr. Phil. I am trying to get blurbs for *Good Date, Bad Date,* which is now scheduled for a spring release. I need well-known people to give me endorsements. I've always loved Dr. Phil with his no-nonsense attitude and his "How's that workin' for ya?" line. Anyhow, my client already gave my book proposal to his friend, who gave it to Dr. Phil, and now I'm shooting off an email to see if my client has heard anything. Then I quickly log on to my private email.

Oooh, a note from my publisher, subject line: *I think you will like this.* I open it up. There is an attachment. Woweeeeee! It is the new book cover. I absolutely love it! It is a man and a woman embraced in a kiss. The style is like the old-fashioned comic books. The title *Good Date, Bad Date* is in black above a couple's heads. A circle in red holds the subtitle of the book, *The Matchmaker's Guide to Where the Boys Are—And How to Get Them.*

At the bottom is my name, Maria Martenson, author of *Excuse Me, Your Soul Mate Is Waiting.*

Maria? Oh brother. I shoot off an email back to Jim at the publishing house.

Hi Jim!
    Wow, I just love love love love the cover! Thanks a million. Although ... they did spell my name wrong.
Xoxo, Marla

Later in the day, I get a response:

Dear Marla,
    Glad you like the cover. Why don't you just change your name to Maria so that we don't have to fiddle with the cover?
Jim

I sure hope he's just kidding.

Gary calls me in to discuss my vacation time. "Going into the holidays is our busiest time of year, Marla," he says.

I point out that I'm working Charlotte's people as well as mine, yet I'm on top of it, and I'm putting in extra hours so that everyone will have multiple contacts while I'm gone.

He frowns at me, trying to find a flaw in my reasoning. "Let's make those extra hours official then. You work until eight every evening until you leave."

What? "But Gary, I've earned this vacation time. You're talking over ten office hours. At the very least that should give me a bonus vacation day."

He squints at me. "Do you want this job to be waiting here for you when you get back, Marla?"

The word I'm thinking starts with an "a"—you follow?

⁺⁺

It's the Friday morning before our flight to Mexico. I feel confident that things are under control, and I'm tempted to simply turn on the automatic reply that says I'll be away from the office until Monday, October 13. Oh, here's an email from Francesco. I can't resist. I've now referred fifteen women to him, including Tate, whose is name the subject of the email. I was impressed with the way Tate charmed Greg, the picky personality profiler. She was gracious with him, even though he didn't really interest her. She has a lovely face and natural figure, but I'm nervous that Francesco, with his Italian family and their vineyards in Tuscany, is going to consider a stewardess to be beneath him.

Dear Marla,

I've taken Tate to an elegant restaurant, out for a picnic and walk on the beach, and out to Antelope Valley to look over a small winery and to hike. During all of these outings, she took pictures, and when I looked at them, I could hardly believe what she captured in me. She makes me, a crass capitalist, look like a poet and a visionary. I am, at long last, captivated. You were right. I want to try "going exclusive" with her.

In great appreciation,

Francesco

How fabulous. Oh, I hope this works. This makes me think of how love sees the best in the beloved. And this, in turn, makes me think of my Adolfo, seeing me as a writer when I had lost sight of this vital part of myself. I have high hopes for this vacation to Mexico. We so need the stress-free time together.

Not long after this, I get an email from Karly.

Marla,

Francesco hasn't called me in almost two weeks. I'm going nuts here. As you know, I flipped for him on our first date. We saw each other two or three times a week for three weeks, and he seemed really into me. Know what I mean? I left a message, the other day, but he didn't return it. Has he offered any explanation as to why he isn't happy with me? Has he left the country? He'd better not be abandoning me. I'm a week late, ya know? Please help me.

Karly

Nooooooo.

This isn't right. Now I think I know what she meant when she said, "I'm so going after him." I've got to think. Nobody's in the sales office, so I go in and turn on the big fountain to watch the water sheeting over stone and pooling at the bottom. My inner devil wants to send Karly a text message: SRY, GL, C Ya. (Sorry, good luck, see ya.) But what if she really is pregnant?

My God, I don't want to be thinking about this now. I close my eyes, breathe deeply, and envision a positive outcome. Twenty minutes go by as I do brain damage trying to decide what I should do. I make a decision. Back in my office, I send Karly an automatic reply. Then I email Francesco, telling him as much, and that though I'm pleased to hear about his relationship with Tate, a situation has arisen with Karly. If he contacts her soon, I say, she won't think it was my idea, which might make a solution easier. I wish him good luck.

Alana and Luisa cover for me, and I bolt out of there at four that afternoon.

+¦+

At long last! Adolfo and I are heading to Mexico City for his younger brother's wedding. My mother, our friend Marvin who is like family to us, and a married couple who have been dear friends for years, Tony and Monica, will fly to Mexico together. We will stay in the city for a few days and then all fly to Puerto Vallarta for a week.

At the airport, I walk alongside the moving walkway as my mom and Adolfo step onto it. Adolfo trips but catches himself before taking a spill. He looks over at me and gives me a dirty look and starts cussing me out in Spanish.

"What did I do? I'm not even anywhere near you!" I say.

My mom is behind him. "Yeah, what did she do?"

"It was your energy, you made me trip!" he says.

Oh, that is a good one! Ricky Ricardo blames me for *everything* and I mean *everything*! I jokingly tell people that he even blames me for 9/11. We're obviously still in bicker mode.

Airborne, I catch myself thinking of clients like Francesco, but I deliberately banish them from my vacation. Adolfo falls asleep, and I allow myself to hope that the marriage and happiness of his brother will put him in a more romantic mood.

At forty-six, Alberto met Veronica, an attractive, feisty, and intelligent lawyer in her mid-thirties, and the two fell in love on their very first date—just like Adolfo and I did. The similarities don't end there. Alberto and Veronica's wedding will take place on the same day as our anniversary, October fourth, in Mexico City.

Six years ago, forty friends and relatives came to witness Adolfo's and my simple ceremony. I felt utterly beautiful that day in my simple yet elegant princess cut floor-length gown with thin straps, bought off-the-rack in a boutique at the Beverly Center for $180. It blushed slightly in a pink so pale it was almost white, and silk roses clustered just at my lower back. I wore my hair in a French twist with tiny silk roses. It rained at the end of our reception, which I was told meant good luck. I know Veronica will feel as happy as I did.

I give Adolfo's hand a little squeeze, and he wakes up enough to squeeze it back.

In Mexico City, Monica, Tony, and Marvin are all staying at a hotel, and my mom is staying with Adolfo and me at the rented home his brother has been living in with their parents, Sergio and Dionisia. After being single for so many years and looking after mom and dad, Alberto finally found love just months before his father passed away. Then, one year later, his mother died, as well. At least they both got to know Veronica.

The living room is filled with antique furniture that has been in the Bringas family for some thirty years. A tiny sitting room holds a loveseat where they sat side by side every afternoon, enjoying a cocktail and listening to classical music. I feel sorry for Alberto that his parents will not be standing by his side at his wedding.

But he will keep this beautiful home with its memories and its three floors of living space, its walls adorned with beautiful old paintings, a few statues, and one-of-a-kind lamps gracing the halls and brightening the corners. Adolfo has been paying $1,500 a month for the rent for many years, which was a lot of stress on him and the reason that we've not been able to buy a house of our own. But now Alberto and Veronica are paying the rent, freeing us up to start house hunting.

Alberto has neglected his parakeet named Gasparin, and I hit the pet store for toys to relieve the bird's boredom. A sweet blue and black parakeet looks so much like a pet parakeet I had as a child, I know it is the just the right mate for Gasparin. I take the bird back to the house and introduce him to his new room-mate—along with fresh birdseed, a bigger water dispenser, and toys. "Gasparin, meet Pierre," I say.

Every time Pierre tries to come close, Gasparin pecks his face and squawks.

"Why is Gasparin acting like they're married?" Adolfo asks.

Ha-ha.

A few months later I will learn that Gasparin has become Gasparina because she has laid an egg!

✝✝

Sunday afternoon, dressed and looking splendid, we all gather in front of the house for photos before going to the church. Adolfo's cousins and longtime friends have arrived. We are all wedding-day happy when Alberto, looking dashing in his tuxedo, approaches, holding a framed photograph of his parents.

"Mom and dad will be with us today, too," he says tearfully.

My heart just breaks. The whole situation is bittersweet, but perhaps God had the timing perfectly planned so that Alberto wouldn't be alone after his parents passed on. I think we all feel their presence in spirit.

Of the five Bringas children, four live close by. Only Adolfo left Mexico, traveling to the United States to tour with a rock band in 1980. Though he never returned to live in Mexico, it was Adolfo who provided the financial support for his parents during their final eight years. I love seeing his devotion to his family. He is such a caretaker, protector, and provider.

The men quietly move to take a place near their wives, and the spirit of love seems to rule this moment. And then in unison, Adolfo's brothers and sister go to Alberto, and simply hold one another.

Blotting their tears, the group proceeds to the church and gathers in the courtyard to greet other family members and friends. Dozens of shutters click as the bride arrives, glowing and lovely.

Adolfo and I are the *madrinos*—godparents—of the wedding, so we stand behind the bride and groom and are in charge of the *lasso*. After the bride and groom have exchanged their vows, the madrinos loop a long rosary in a figure eight around the necks of the couple, symbolizing the union and protection of marriage.

The reception follows, under a tent in the garden behind the church. Round tables flank both sides of a long dance floor, a three-piece band, and singer at one end. They're really good, but Adolfo and our friend Jorge will be jumping in to sing a few songs, too. A waiter comes by often with margaritas, and the food is *muy deliciosa*. I meet or reconnect with people I only get to see once or twice a year. Bless them! They all want to know about my book. We turn our attention to the stage, where Adolfo has taken over, and is dedicating a song to the new Señor and Señora Bringas. It is one that he wrote and Veronica's favorite. She asked him to sing it tonight.

Everyone dances as the rain pours down and a small river gushes off one side of the tent onto the grass. Veronica and Alberto are starting off their marriage with a sign of good luck. Adolfo holds me tight during a slow dance, and I'm feeling the grand magnificence of life in this moment.

Except for the cigarette smoke. To avoid Mom and Jorge's toxic haze, I go sit at another table next to one of Adolfo's long time friends, José.

He looks at me a bit mysteriously and says, "Marla, I think that you are a good person. I want to read your palm."

"Oh, you read palms? Okay, here." I thrust out my hand, palm up.

"Oh, my!" He puts a hand to his chest and gasps. "You have two life lines."

"Oh, good," I say. "If I were single, I'd only need one. Being married, I need two."

"You have been feeling some anxiety and stress, but you have energy galore now. Am I right?"

"Oh, you'd better believe it, José. I'm percolating!" Now that I'm away from work and finished with my book; and once I get rid of my chronic fatigue and cough. "My work often makes impossible demands on me," I admit.

"Do not worry." He takes another look at my hand and quickly jolts back, grinning. "Exciting things are going to be happening in your life very soon."

I thank José, who is quite drunk, but I choose to take his predictions as profoundly accurate prophecy.

✝✝

After the wedding, Mom, Marvin, Tony, Monica, Adolfo, and I fly on to Puerto Vallarta for a few days at the Marriott Resort and Spa—key word: spa. This is all about relaxing, swimming, lying by the pool—under an umbrella with half my weight on in sunscreen, eating well, and being pampered. I plan to get rid of this cough and fatigue once and for all.

Aside from a ruined $120 bathing suit from Saks Fifth Avenue in Beverly Hills—wah!—and an argument about replacing it with a bikini—Adolfo wants me to get one, but I remind him that on our Acapulco honeymoon, I wore a bikini swimming in the ocean, whereupon Adolfo pointed out that my left breast was hanging out, and that everyone on the beach was getting a grand view— we enjoy life in the chaise lounges. I mentally calculate how many massages I can afford—after my quota of daily margaritas!

Glorioso! Fabuloso! Fantastico!

On our last day, we hire a driver, and our group tours the town and continues out past the touristy restaurants and gift shops, past the cathedral, and up the winding cobblestone streets. We reach a place called Mama Lucia, where a tall, thin, dark-skinned man with a generous mouth full of very crooked teeth tells how his family makes tequila. After a stop at the gift shop, we're back in the minivan and off to catch a boat.

Before casting off, Adolfo buys a bucket full of ice and bottles of cold beer and then sees a local woman selling a beautiful brown sundress with sparkly dragonflies. He gets that look on his face that lets me know he's picturing it on me and then buys it.

"For you, my angel."

"Gracias, mi amor, I love it." And I do. This trip has worked wonders between us.

The magic continues as we ride along in the boat, the ocean breeze refreshing us. The view of the Sierra Madre's lush mountain greenery and the multi-colored homes nestled among the palms has us all snapping photos. Charming and beautiful. Twenty-minutes into the ride, we arrive at a small beach with a lounge and a restaurant right on the sand under a tent. We pull up chairs and help ourselves to cold beers from the bucket and loll. I decide to go for a swim and wade out into the water where the others are already swimming. A few other boats are anchored nearby. Adolfo puts in our order for lunch.

"You want enchiladas?" he yells to me. I give him a thumbs-up and wade into the ocean.

Paradiso.

It isn't until I'm at the airport returning home that I notice a souvenir from the day: a huge blister on the inside of my left ankle that continues in a red strip that wraps around to the other side of my foot. More blisters are forming as I inspect it. My ankle is stinging. Sunburn? I was so careful with waterproof sunscreen, and I was mostly under the umbrella. Must I pay for all the glorious excess of sun, food, and drink?

You know that saying, I need a vacation to recover from my vacation? So terribly true. And tomorrow's Monday. Where's that second life when you need it? That gift of more time that my own hand foretells? When do I get to cash in on that?

Affirmations

I love and am loved inside a loving family circle.

I am relaxed and in perfect health.

I take many wonderful vacations.

I am uniquely blessed with two life lines.

Back at the Double D Ranch

I arrive at the office with an ice bag for my blistered and now swollen ankle. Heels are out of the question, so I'm in capris and slip-on sandals. I'm a little early so that I can get a head start on deleting the spam. When Alana comes in, I hobble over to hug her and give her the earrings I bought her in Puerta Vallarta, which she loves. She hands me a stack of mail.

"This is the thanks I get?"

"Sorry." She grins and shrugs. "Good to have you back!"

I pretend to stagger even more under the weight of the mail. "*Great* to be back."

Finally, I get to my client email. There is nothing from Francesco, and I'm tempted to email him and find out what's happening. Oh, here's one from Phil. Let's see how he's doing with the red-hot momma, Natasha.

Hi, Marla,

Well, enough is enough. I've been seeing Natasha. It's been a wild and crazy ride. Yeah, it was fun, but I told her last night that we're just not a match. I really want someone with a little more class.

Phil

Okay. Fine. I arrange for three women for him to contact: Jacquie, Carrie, and Jen—who likes German sports cars. Jacquie and Carrie are both pretty, charming, busty, and classy. I doubt if they'll actually go out with Phil, but you never know. He's got a big mustache which most women don't like. But these names should keep him busy for a while.

Now let's see how the personality profiler made out with the femme fatale.

Dear Marla,

Well, Cheryl is quite something. I certainly couldn't ask for a more beautiful young woman. But, she doesn't have a lot to say. Still, the way she listens, it's like she soaks in what I'm saying. She's a classic type 9 on the Enneagram, and, amazingly, an ISTP as well. I'm frankly stunned that you found such a creature. I'm rather smitten even though the evening was very quiet. And I'm a bit stung that she hasn't returned my last two calls. Doesn't she realize that what I have to offer doesn't come along every day? What more could she possibly want? I'm not overweight. You know what? The hell with her. Have you heard feedback from her about me?
Greg

My, my, my, my. I knew this would happen, of course, but I'm feeling a bit guilty. I messed with his heart in giving him Cheryl. I wonder if Cheryl sent any feedback. Ah, here it is:

Hi, Marla,

Well, another guy in mid-life crisis. Tell him to stop fricking analyzing everything. For a while I tried to see myself traveling in his jet all over the world. I just have no interest in being with him, talking with him, or seeing him, let alone having sex with him. Sorry.
Cheryl

Dear Greg,

Cheryl thought you were appealing and interesting, but she didn't feel the necessary spice that would make it work for her. Since you asked, she did mention a tendency to analyze things too much—FYI. I feel confident that you'll have better luck with Kendra, who sounded very enthusiastic about meeting you. I suggest you call and make a date right away. It's always good to have something to look forward to.
Marla

Since I can't walk, Alana goes and gets a soy vanilla latte for me, and I use my break time to check personal email. Here's one from my publisher telling me that they have changed the cover of my new book. It is now a man and a woman facing each other sitting on a pair of red lips. He explains that the major bookstores feel that the first cover was a bit outdated. "Sleep on it and I am sure that you will love it as much as we do," he writes.

I really liked that first cover. Oh well, until I am rich and famous, I guess I have to accede to the creative powers at the publishing house.

I still haven't heard from Francesco, or Tate, or Karly, so I risk replying to Karly's initial bombshell.

Dear Karly,
    I'm sorry that your email arrived when I was out of town. Has anything been resolved? How may I help you?
Marla

Before lunch, I get the following reply:

Dear Marla,
    I am, in fact, expecting, and Francesco is the father. Fortunately, he called me, and I told him the news. At first he was upset with me, but then he agreed to marry me. I ask him why he seemed so unhappy about becoming a father and having a great wife who is crazy about him. He said we'd have to marry in haste, and he wanted a huge wedding. His family is traditional and this will bring him embarrassment. I admitted I'd love a big family wedding too. I asked him if he'd marry me if I wasn't, you know, preggers. He went on and on about what a great wife and mom I'd make. So I scheduled an abortion, and he'll be there to see me through it. Then he says we'll start fresh. These things happen, right? Now we'll have all the time in the world to plan our wedding.
Karly

I'm shaking my head; bad vibes all over this one. I'd bet money that she trapped him, and doesn't really care about having a child, and I'd bet the same amount that she's about to walk into *his* trap. I send her an email, hoping for the best, and then

I'm butting the hell out. I don't trust myself to say anything that wouldn't later bring a lawsuit to the dating service, or at least the wrath of Gary down upon me. Harrowing situations like this are one more reason I hold onto my love for Adolfo.

†‡

By Wednesday, my ankle hasn't improved, so I go to see Doc Speedy on my lunch break. I feel like I am keeping him in business single-handedly with all of my ailments. Unfortunately, he has no idea what the blisters are all about. He tells me to apply some Neosporin on the blisters to keep them from getting infected and then pats me on the shoulder. "Nothing serious, my dear. You'll live."

Thanking him for this good news, I hobble out in pain.

On Thursday, I drive to our La Jolla office for a few appointments with clients, and afterward, I drive to Bobbie's house in Del Mar. She's invited me to go with her to an art exhibit held in a mansion in Rancho Santa Fe. The artist is none other than actress Jane Seymour.

I had no idea Jane was an artist, so I'm looking forward to seeing her work. I Googled her and found out that she has created a greeting card series to support her charities. One of her watercolors was featured on a Discover card and raised $25,000 for the Make-A-Wish Foundation. She also was asked to design a special edition champagne bottle for Korbel and an Escada scarf. She is also an author, a jewelry designer with a line available at Kay Jewelers, and a celebrity ambassador for the nonprofit organization Childhelp.

Interestingly, while in Spain on a film shoot, she had an allergic reaction to an antibiotic that almost killed her and thereby led to an out-of-body experience, one in which she claims to have seen the "white light" and, from the corner of the room, the doctors trying to resuscitate her. It was a life-altering experience for her. She wrote that she realized that when you die, the only thing you leave behind is the work you have accomplished.

It's food for thought, that's for sure.

✢

"What's wrong?" Bobbie asks when she sees me. "Why are you limping?"

I pull up my pant leg and show her my wounds. "I don't understand what happened."

"Ooooh. Jellyfish sting. Been there, done that; got mine in Hawaii," she says matter-of-factly as we climb into her car. We head toward Rancho Santa Fe.

"Wow, that's a perfectly logical explanation," I tell her. "I knew it couldn't be sunburn. I didn't even feel a thing when it happened though. It appeared the day after I swam in the ocean."

"Maybe you need a new doctor—one with clean thermometers."

As we drive past the Del Mar Racetrack and then the Fairbanks polo grounds, I tell Bobbie about a client I think she should date. At first she refuses, but I beg her to help me out and she agrees to give it a go.

"Thanks, girlfriend! I can log this party as working hours for Double D now, especially if I pass out a few cards."

We drive through an area where homes in the exclusive community appear to be eight to ten thousand square feet.

"When does a house become a mansion?" I ask.

"Above four thousand square feet, it becomes a starter castle. Six thousand to twelve thousand, it's a McMansion. Above that, it's a big-ass palace," she says.

"For real?" I ask. "Well, without the big-ass part?"

She laughs. "Probably some truth in there somewhere."

"How do these people afford such splendor?" I ask.

"I've heard realtors call it 'affluenza.' Let's hope it's contagious."

"Right. I'd have to sell an s-load of books to be able to live in this neighborhood."

She grins at me for not swearing.

We park, approach the manse, and walk in. It is elegance beyond the classiest hotel I've ever been in. Artwork hangs everywhere; beautiful and well-dressed people chat and browse, all holding tall crystal flutes of fizzing champagne. We meander from room to room, each wall flowing with incredible paintings of flowers, self-portraits, hearts, and ocean views—all ranging in price from $5,000 for a simple flower to $23,000 for a portrait or landscape scene. We'll just be looking, thank you very much.

Bobbie spots Jane. She has met her before, so we go over to say hello and wait patiently as Jane chats with an older woman whose face is pulled so tight, she looks like a bass.

"Hi Jane, nice to see you again," Bobbie finally says. "This is my friend Marla Martenson."

I feel like bowing at her feet, a lowly ant compared to her accomplishments and talent. She looks stunning in a red cocktail dress, chestnut hair flowing down her back. I compliment her on her necklace and matching ring, an open heart in diamonds.

"Thank you," she says sweetly. "These are from a jewelry line I designed."

By now I'm thinking maybe she created the planet.

The laden kitchen counters offer baked brie with walnuts and figs, finger sandwiches, carved roast beef, fresh fruit, three kinds of quiche, and then a dessert table that heaven couldn't possibly surpass. I can't resist a half slice of chocolate espresso truffle cake. When I sneak back for the other half, I meet a pretty young blonde, eying the goodies. Her plate has a few veggies and a single slice of beef. We joke about choosing *one* indulgence to last the week.

"Love your bag," I say of her quilted Prada—$995.00, unless she got it online.

We chat a bit more and exchange cards. I give out another card over by the pink champagne.

Bobbie and I mingle, drink, eat, and enjoy a fabulous evening.

✢

On the two-hour ride home from Del Mar to Los Angeles, I contemplate Jane and her success. Not only is she very accomplished in her career, but she also has a husband and children. She has boys to take to school, soccer games, and outings with friends. I barely manage working at the office, writing, working out, spending time with Adolfo, seeing friends, and laundry. Imagine if I had kids? I'd have a nervous breakdown. How on earth does she do it all?

I must find a way to be more productive. The author of the book *No More Mondays,* Dan Miller, posts on his blog that watching television remains the single most common and most time-consuming leisure activity among Americans. Both men and women average 2.6 viewing hours per day. That's 18.2 hours a week, 78.8 hours a month, or 949 hours a year!

I start calculating. If I gave up watching TV and wrote during that time, I would most likely have finished a few more books by now. But I can't live without my Oprah, Larry King, Nancy Grace, plus the discovery channel's documentaries, and the HBO and Showtime series that I like. Still, a page a day is nonetheless a book a year. I can do that. I will see it as a labor of love, a path I choose—one that will change my life.

Affirmations

Thank God Adolfo and I have each other.

I am young, slim, fit, and so healthy, especially my ankle.

I get paid to work at fabulous parties.

I write and sell an s-load of books.

eighteen

Women of Leisure

've gained another pound, and so I swam at the gym twice over the weekend. I can't do any other form of exercise because I still can't put my full weight on my ankle. Swimming makes me ravenous, and Adolfo fixed a Mexican dinner Sunday. I justified it since I'd done such virtuous exercise. Monday morning, however, that pound is still a part of me. I put on a slimming black dress to wear to the office.

At work, I check emails, beginning with Marcus's, who likes super slim women and is still dating Michelle. Shawn and ultracool Amy are going to try going exclusive, but they sound a little hesitant. Joseph (no big butts) and Sandy Puffydress aren't dating any longer. I find some quick options for each. Here's one that makes my day: Lewis and Cass are going biking through the redwoods next weekend. Two emails that put knots in my stomach: Scott and Jerry are clinging to the hope of going exclusive with Dee Dee. I guess that woman makes them feel like total studs. I send them each another email reminding them that she has no intention of going exclusive.

Next is Neil's email. Maybe 20 percent of our male clients are actually really nice, down-to-earth guys who want an equally nice mate. How refreshing on a Monday morning to hear from Neil.

Dear Marla,
    Allie was pleasant enough, but 100% academic and although the conversation was interesting at times, I don't want to date

academics. She is quite pretty but far too curvy for me, and to be honest I did not enjoy the date. On top of that, the place she picked, Stella, was very pretentious, not my style at all! She also decided that we should order champagne and two different wines to compliment the 6 courses. The evening cost me $550, which is money I would rather have given to UNICEF.

Where is that simple "girl next door" with a good heart for me? Thanks, Neil

Ouch! Poor Neil. That is totally out of line for a first date. He lives in Orange County, so he didn't know that Stella is one of the most expensive restaurants in Los Angeles. I place a little green dollar sign by Allie's name, and contact two real sweethearts. Nancy—who found Phil too "high school"—and Cathy with the dog, both 8s and with adorable personalities.

And then:

Dear Marla,

I met Samantha for a coffee date, and knew she wasn't my type, but I thought surely our charts must match up or we wouldn't be paired. Interestingly, she told me that some of the guys she has met from your service have told her that she is a breath of fresh air compared to some of the airheads they had met. So I brought her along to a fundraising event for one of my causes, which she said she strongly supported. As to humanitarian interests, hers were minimal at best. I would expect that women I meet who are in their mid-thirties and up should be rather accomplished or at least stable in their life circumstances. I can't figure out how Samantha supports herself. And there's something weird about her hair. I don't think it was a wig, but ... oh, well. If she's typical of the type of women that your service has to offer, then perhaps my signing up was a big mistake.

Anthony

My neck hurts. And my shoulders and arms. I need a break. I can't really explain to Anthony that the two guys who supposedly called Samantha "a breath of fresh air" were complimenting her before declining to date her again. I'll deal with him when I get back. I head to The Coffee Bean around the block for a vanilla soy latte where I notice a woman with a sensational body ahead of me. Long dark hair cascades down her back. She is talking on her cell phone. Her jeans are unique with pockets situated very low. They fit just right. A peek at the brand on the tag reveals they are Ming Jeans. I've never heard of that brand. I'd ask her where she got them if she wasn't on the phone. I hear her voice and suddenly realize, as she turns sideways, that this gorgeous creature is Penelope Cruz! I pick up my latte and head back to the office.

In the lobby, a young woman is just finishing up filling out a questionnaire. I take her back to my office with me. She is a tall blonde, wears heavy make-up and perfume, is dressed in designer jeans and a crisp white shirt open at the neck to give a good glimpse of her D cup breasts. Chandelier earrings weight her ears, and four-inch strappy gold sandals keep her on her toes. Gold bracelets jangle at her wrist, and she's carrying a smart, new Gucci clutch. She must be Russian. I glance down at her questionnaire. Svetlana. Bingo.

She settles into one of the two oversized leather armchairs across from my desk. She has a lovely smile and a rather heavy accent. She hands me some professionally done photos and explains that she is an actress and has come to L.A. from St. Petersburg because she is dedicated to her craft and is determined to make it as an actress here.

"I am not interested in being someone's girlfriend," she informs me.

I look up from her profile. "Oh? What do you mean Svetlana? The men here are all looking for a wife or at least a long-term relationship. That's what we're all about."

She looks at me intently. "I don't have time for that. My whole life is my acting career. I don't want a guy who expects me to spend a lot of time with him. I need a rich man to pay for my bills and classes." She samples a Godiva from the crystal dish on my desk.

I fake a smile, hoping that blood won't shoot out of my eyeballs.

"Why would any guy be interested in a situation like that? What's in it for him?"

She shrugs. Her phone rings. She digs around in her purse for what seems like about two minutes, finds it, and finally turns it off. "Well, that is what I want. I am not giving up my dream to waste time with a guy. I have acting class five nights a week and auditions in the day. I have no income, so I need to meet someone right away." She helps herself to a truffle and drops a wrapped cordial into her purse.

"Honestly, Svetlana, I probably won't have anyone who would be interested in that type of an arrangement." I usher her out of the office before she can mooch any more candy. "But I wish you luck."

I try to be civil, but gads, the nerve of some people.

There is a puzzling phenomenon here in Beverly Hills that I have yet to figure out. Many women apparently have fabulous lifestyles, but don't really seem to work. Los Angeles is an expensive city. Even with a husband to share expenses with, I have to work my butt off just to help pay rent for a small apartment, bills, and have some money left for savings and a bit of fun. When you ask these women of leisure what they do for a living, they are either "taking a break from working," "changing careers," "thinking of going back to school," or, "I'm and actress and a model," or they give some vague answer like, "I have a website." And that means? What exactly? We never quite know. Of course, when I Google them, there are maybe a couple of small credits from years ago—at best.

Samantha falls into this woman-of-leisure category, and I think I've misjudged Anthony. Sometimes, when I see the Scotts and Jerrys of my client list, I think all men want is a Dee Dee. Men say all the time they want women with brains and accomplishment, but when you give them such a person, they accuse her of being a motor mouth or not pretty enough. Anthony may be one guy who really means it when he says he wants a woman of substance. I'm going to take a chance and introduce him to two women I met at the pig party, lively Donna who works for CBS and pretty Heather with the slow-motion hair and the gay date. Turns out she's a storefront lawyer for a 501C3 association of charities. I've been saving these two for someone special. I work my magic with the young women, and Anthony expresses an interest in meeting both of them.

Tuesday brings a variation on a theme: Arthur—not Alana's Arthur. Arthur is the other guy who got Charlotte fired. He's been out of the country and is now back. He's decided to make things really clear as to what he's looking for, and Gary assured him we'd handle his requests in person at his home.

So we drive down to Laguna Beach for a ten thirty appointment with Arthur, who is fifty-three, average-looking, extremely successful, cultured, and lives in a gorgeous home with an ocean view. I wish Adolfo were here to see this and dream of such a home with me.

Arthur hands me an eight-page summary called, "Life Partner Search," which he insists we read over and discuss in mind-numbing detail together. One of his main requirements:

* *Either does not have kids, or they are already of driving age and independent. Motherhood experience preferred for reciprocal understanding of my parenting responsibility and passion.*

He rants about the entitled class of Newport Beach "Range Rover Lunch Ladies who suffer 'relentless expectation syndrome'"—as if he didn't have it himself.

Another essential:

* *She respects her father and his love for his daughter is eternally unconditional. Very important that she does not suffer abandonment issues.*

Here's an item with three stars:

*** *She is smart and pretty—and she learned how to leverage both of these qualities to advance her career.*

Arthur also wants to be able to pick out her history:

* *If formerly married, the marriage most likely broke up over financial concerns that led to other behaviors that destroyed the relationship.*

Arthur's future woman must not simply like to ski and be organized. She must be:

* *Solid recreational snow skier . . . not afraid to get a little cold once in a while, especially if the snow is epic.*
* *Organizational skills: She maintains a daily calendar and keeps her commitments.*

And on and on. I return to L.A. after lunch and storm into my office. "Alana!" I call as I pass her, "You've got to take a look at this client's list!" She knows Arthur was instrumental in getting Charlotte fired. "This guy has to be in dreamland to think that I will find all of these traits in one person or that I could even screen someone for each and every trait. Just scan it so you don't throw up."

"Oh dear God," she replies after a few seconds. "At least the list isn't as long as Wynne's."

"But it's way more demanding. He insists he's not looking for a supermodel, because intelligence and class are more important to him than looks."

"And if we believe that, we are TSTL," Alana says on her way out. Too Stupid To Live.

Right. Still, after misjudging Anthony, I stupidly take Arthur at his word. I carefully evaluate the questionnaires and amaze myself by matching the guy up with a very attractive, highly intelligent, successful doctor. She is willing to give Arthur a shot, and I send off the contact info right away—with no photo, as is our policy.

I take off my left shoe to stretch my foot. It has been ten days since my jellyfish sting, and I'm only today able to wear nice shoes, walk comfortably, and exercise. I didn't work out much when I was trying to meet my writing deadlines, and I pigged out in Mexico. So I have gained a full eight pounds from my ideal weight of 120, which was already ten pounds heavier than what is acceptable here in Beverly Hills. Oddly, much of it has gone to my chest. Standing in front of the mirror in my bedroom last night, I assessed my new body. It has exploded into a full C cup, and in my new Very Sexy Bra by Victoria's Secret, my girls look like Ds! I'm going to be wearing a lot of black until I shed some weight. Today's black dress has a lower neckline than some, and the clients have been making comments—like Clarence.

He's here for his Tuesday afternoon appointment, a VIP client for years, who gets to see my photo books with a synopsis of each female client every couple of months. I sit with him, and he asks me questions about the ones he likes. Clarence is fifty-five but doesn't want to date anyone over thirty-eight and doesn't bother pretending that he's not just looking for a pretty face and nice bod. He and I feel very comfortable with each other.

"Now are you sure this gal is fine with my age?" he'll ask.

"Oh, yes, she likes old farts," I tease.

He is sitting across from me flipping through the books while we make small talk. "Wow, it says this gal has double Ds. I think it looks a bit too much," he says.

"Yeah, I know; it seems like most of the women in the service are enhanced."

"Well, I notice that you got implants recently," he says pointing at my chest.

"No, Clarence," I laugh. I explain the weight gain. "I would never get implants. A lot of my friends are wondering what happened. My mother is now a triple D! I guess it's hereditary."

"Well, your husband must like that."

"He's telling me to thank my mom for the genes."

"Okay, here's my list Marla. Go through it and pick the ones that you think are good for me."

Right.

Actually, despite the attention, I don't like how my clothes fit now. I much prefer the gamine look of a flapper. Of course, Adolfo couldn't be more thrilled.

"Don't you lose a pound!" he pleads. "You were too skinny when I met you. You are so hot and sexy now!" Watching me walk down the hall to the elevator, he carries on. "Wow, what an ass! Nice body! Incredible!"

This feels pretty good, since at five-feet-six, and 128 pounds, I would be too fat for most of my male clients. Thank God I'm not single in this town.

Wow! I've been visualizing and affirming looking young and sexy. The Botox and haircut do make me look younger, and then here's my hubby willing to swear in court as to my new sex appeal! Funny how that works.

Hmmm. I'm going to have to be very clear about what I affirm.

+¦+

The next morning, Wednesday, I'm greeted with an angry email (addressed to Gary, cc'd to me) from Arthur. He found a photo of our attractive doctor online by Googling her. However, the photo isn't flattering. He's furious, asking Gary how dare I try to set him up with someone like this?

> Marla is pulling the same crap as Charlotte did. This woman is not attractive enough, and that is not what I paid thousands of dollars to meet.

He insists on seeing photos of all prospects first, or the deal is off.

Wait. I think I get it now. Arthur, aren't you just another C.D. who wants a Dee Dee but won't admit it—even to yourself? That would make you as shallow as the next guy, and we simply can't have that, now, can we. By all means, dress up your fantasies with your complicated list of high standards, so you can impress the hell out of yourself.

There will be no pleasing this client.

Gary sends me an email telling me to make this priority one, "even if you have to hit the streets of Rodeo Drive to recruit."

Gag me.

Affirmations

I am young, slim, healthy, and sexy. And my clothes fit right.

I balance my leisure with meaningful work.

I live in a spacious home with a fabulous view.

As my palm foretells, something exciting will happen very soon.

nineteen

Butterflies

I nspiration hits on my lunch break. How about overly curvy academic Allie? I know she likes to ski. If I could tell her how Arthur feels about the Newport ladies, maybe she'll not insist on a five hundred dollar restaurant as she did with Neil. She's probably younger than what Arthur wants, but she might buy me some time.

Later in the week, something so exciting happens that I don't get upset that Adolfo has moved the peacock ashtray off the coffee table and back to my desk. We're approved to buy a house, and now that the market is down, there are so many foreclosures in California that property values have fallen. It is exciting but also scary. Adolfo is nervous.

"What if we buy a house and then lose our jobs?"

"Well, then we would just go out and get another one. We need to get in the game; it's now or never," I say.

Driving to the Realtor's office Saturday, we are like someone new to the dating service, listing all the main features we think we must have: hardwood floors, at least three bedrooms and two baths, and a location on a nice tree-lined quiet street somewhere in North Hollywood, Sherman Oaks, or Burbank. Of course a pool would be nice. Oh, and please, no carpets. The stains, constant vacuuming and steam-cleaning—it's just too much.

Our Realtor, Linda, is a beautiful, petite young woman from Orange County and determined to help us find our dream home, except that she doesn't know her way around too well. I'll have to find out if she's single, because she's just the type of woman many of my shorter male clients are looking for.

"Love your purse," I say of her stylish Miu Miu bag.

We climb into her SUV and head over to Alcove Street in North Hollywood. The photo looks fabulous: A three bedroom contemporary home with palm trees in its large front yard. The price has apparently dropped by $175,000.

"It looks like a resort," I say, and Adolfo agrees.

Bring All Offers, the brochure says. Freshly painted with hardwood floors, AC, granite counter tops, pool, 2-car detached garage, and many more features that make my pulse speed up. This is going to be easy.

After we've been driving for twenty minutes through some nice neighborhoods, Adolfo says, "Seems like we're going the opposite direction from where we started."

Linda plugs in the address on her GPS. "Right, I'm following the recommended directions, but it looks like there's a much shorter way."

As we park in front of the place, my jaw drops, and I hold up the photo to compare it to reality. The palm trees are actually not even on this property.

"The photographer must have been lying prostrate in the yard across the street," I say.

"Hey, we'd be living next door to Sanford and Son," Adolfo says of the adjacent yard's dry dirt, scraggly brown shrubs, and piled refuse, complete with an empty grocery cart. Faded brown paint is peeling off the shutters that hang at odd angles on the house. A dazed, bedraggled man comes to the doorway, looks us over, and nods.

I manage to close my mouth, which has been hanging open.

"How's it going?" Adolfo calls. He casually steers us back to the SUV, speaking under his breath. "The guy's either waiting for his Welfare check or his dealer."

"Or both. On to the next location." I say, confident our dream home awaits.

We drive the shorter route out of the area along graffiti-covered concrete walls. "My God, this neighborhood is next to gang turf. No wonder they gave 'recommended' directions."

A leathery tan guy is sitting on a corner, begging. His sign says, "Saving for a hooker."

Ya gotta laugh. At least he's honest. Linda drives us over to Encino where we step inside an empty house.

"What a difference," Adolfo says.

The two thousand-square-foot house sits on a huge lot. Three bedrooms offer plenty of closet space. The large dining room has a fireplace in it, and the living room is gigantic, with a wall of windows that look out to the gorgeous pool and Jacuzzi—and it's situated in a wonderful neighborhood. Drawbacks: the carpet needs to be ripped out, flooring needs a lot of work, the walls need painting, and we'd need to buy new appliances.

"Encino is quite a drive to Hollywood or Beverly Hills," Adolfo says.

We aren't too happy about having to go to the other side of the hill. Hollywood is where all the action is.

Linda says, "This place just went on the market, and it'll be gone by Monday. If you're interested, you'd better put in an offer right away."

✝✝

Adolfo likes to take me to breakfast on Sunday mornings to La Conversation in West Hollywood. It's the most charming little place, decorated to make you think you woke up in Paris. Cool Hollywood types with their Chihuahuas and Boston terriers sit at the outside tables and pretend they're big-shots. Some are, of course; I once saw Nicole Ritchie waiting for a table.

Adolfo and I go straight to the tiny bar in the back near the cappuccino machine and grab two stools. We put in our order and turn our attention to real estate, chatting on and on about pros and cons. I definitely have buying fever, but not for the Encino house.

"I think we should keep looking," I say.

"Are you sure?"

"I'm sure. Let's go back out next Saturday. I bet we can find a place in Burbank."

It's a buyers' market, we say. We can find the perfect place. I sound like one of my clients, holding out for a perfect mate.

Back at home, I go online, planning to look for real estate listings, but I check my personal email first. One came in from Bobbie, with the subject line: *Last Night's Date.* I make a cup of tea to sip while I savor her story.

Hi Girlfriend!

Hey, thank you for lining me up with the new guy who lives in Cabo—and Brazil and Klosters, Switzerland, and—how many damn homes does he have anyway?

So, here's a review on George-baby:

The knock on my door: My reaction:"Wow! A cool guy!" He's a distinguished, successful businessman who speaks five languages. We eventually walked to his car, a dirty van with bird shit all over it! I was about to say,"Oh, let's take my car," but he had the door open; whereupon I was greeted with a mess inside, too.

Then the eloquent apology,"Sorry for the bird shit on the car."

I guess he didn't think that arriving in a car like that makes the statement: You're not special enough to wash the car for. So I'm thinking as we're driving out of my neighborhood, *Please God, don't let my neighbors see me in this crap-mobile!*

We arrive at the restaurant, and who arrives in the car just before us? the *mayor* (a dear friend) and his wife. I duck until the attendant opens my door, and then hustle over to the restaurant door while George-baby deals with the valet. At the door, I hug and greet the major and his wife, and they go inside.

At our table, George says,"Now, I just want to be upfront and honest with you about the fact that I'm married, and my wife and I have a fifteen-year-old daughter, and my wife and I agree not to divorce because she says she just wants a 'time out' from the marriage to think things over. I didn't see this coming, and I thought she and I were very happy. I'm hoping she'll snap out of it, and she probably will because frankly, she doesn't know what she wants, and my friends say just have yourself a nice time while she is deciding, and so . . ."

Now at this moment, I'm thinking, I showered, shaved my legs, put on my best perfume, and I do look terrific tonight, and well, I could be home petting my cat!

In short, George is looking for an affair.

He had the nerve to ask me to please be open-minded and to see that his "arrangement" with the Mrs. wasn't a deterrent to his intentions of finding a woman to hang out with.

Since he asked me for my thoughts, I asked him to be open-minded and consider my position:

1) I couldn't introduce him to my friends, because I'd be embarrassed to admit to dating a married man, something I find disgusting in any case.

2) Sleeping with him would be pointless for similar reasons.

3) If I fell in love with him without the option of marriage, I'd have to be sneaking around since his wife owns a home in La Jolla, etc. etc. So in this small community, she'd find out about me, and my name would be mud.

Our dinner was out of this world awesome, and I enjoyed our discussions, very much. We walked around the restaurant after dinner, and I was definitely attracted to him. I knew I just needed to end the evening, though.

So we had the attendant bring up the car, the one with the bird shit! Other than that, he was a nice guy. Moving on!

Bobbie

Holy cow! I knew George's divorce wasn't finalized, but I had no idea that he was hoping to reconcile with his wife. I feel so bad for putting Bobbie through that. Ugh!

Note to self: Start getting together a male guide of how to prepare for a date, meaning a clean car for starters—*after* the divorce is final.

+⁀+

I'm online throughout the week, looking for more home listings. Work goes fairly smoothly, except for Arthur, who actually liked Allie a lot until she revealed her true seasonal colors: harvest gold-digger and spring greenbacks. I managed to find someone else to pacify him for another week or so.

By Friday, I've heard nothing from Francesco, Tate, or Karly. I don't really see a positive outcome here. When clients have a horrendous negative outcome, they start wanting to blame as many people as possible other than themselves, and that is often the dating service. If that happened, Gary would fire me fast, and then we couldn't get a house. Blade-winged butterflies are frantically flapping around in my stomach. *Okay, Marla, just* stop. *You're attracting disaster.* La, la, la, la, la. No rainbow chinks. Everything is fine in this moment. Breathe.

"Marla, you have a delivery," calls Alana from the front desk. "Flowers!"

Flowers? Ooohhh. Butterflies flutter off into the sunshine. I scurry up to the front. They are gorgeous, all white roses and lilies in a short square vase. I read the card.

Marla,
  We both thank you very much for the introduction.
  You are amazing! We are off to Vegas tonight. I'll give
  you details next week.
Jack and Carmella

I am amazing! "Wow! I just matched them up a few days ago. They really must have hit it off. How great is that," I remark to Alana. "Two of our clients are falling in love!"

I rush back to my office and shoot off an email to Jack thanking him and asking for details when he gets back. Thank goodness for something positive to cap the week off. How silly to worry over made-up scenarios.

†

The next morning we're going out again for the day with our realtor, Linda. She has five houses lined up for us to see. I'm so excited. Adolfo is acting all cool and collected, continuing on with his assumption that we could be losing our jobs soon, a made-up scenario. I wish I could get him to envision a positive outcome. What good does pessimism do? What are his negative vibes attracting?

"We have to be cautious," he says. "Do you know how many people out there have lost their jobs?"

"Si, mi amor, I know, but that doesn't mean that we will lose our jobs. You have to start changing your language. Words have power and you are putting out negative energy to the universe."

He shakes his head. "I am just being realistic; you're in fantasy land!"

"Well, I refuse to affirm that we are anything but prosperous, abundant, and secure."

We arrive at the location in the North Hollywood area where we are meeting Linda. It's very hot today, even though it's early November. Fires are blazing north of us in Sylmar. Many people have lost their homes. Montecito, part of Santa Barbara, has been burning as well. It is so tragic.

We climb into her Range Rover, and the first house we see is too much of a fixer-upper.

"On to the next location," Adolfo says.

I take one look inside the next house. "Oh, I am in heaven!" I coo. "This is it for me." I'm smiling blissfully at the three-bedroom home, built in 1950, located on a cul-de-sac named Craner Place.

I picture myself dancing on the gorgeous hardwood floors, lazing by the fireplace in the living room, writing in my own office. I smell the fresh paint. The tiles in the kitchen and bathrooms are in great condition. This house is positively charming.

Out in the backyard, an orange butterfly visits a gardenia bush that still has a bloom or two on it. I'm enchanted—certain it's a sign. Adolfo takes a peek over the fence and notices that the neighbor's yard is messy. There are also little tea lights hanging over the patio. We can hear a radio playing as well.

"I'm worried about the neighbors," says Adolfo. "It looks like rednecks live here. I'm sure that they have parties out here every weekend. And they seem loud; I can hear a radio or TV."

"What are you talking about?" I try to keep my voice level. "You cannot make an assumption like that. We live in a city. We're going to hear sounds occasionally."

He starts walking back into the house. "We can't risk it."

I *want* this house. A wad of ferocity builds up in me, but that will get me nowhere. I swallow the raw emotion for the moment, back off, and try a new tactic. "Honey," I plead, "I love this house. Let's go knock on the neighbor's door and introduce ourselves, and that way we can see just what type of people they seem to be."

"Good idea," says Linda.

We approach the front door and knock but there is no answer. The gate is cracked open, so we push through. A middle-aged man appears to be putting in a Jacuzzi.

"Hello!" I shout. "Do you live here?"

"Yes, I do," he says in a friendly manner. The man is wearing a dirty white T-shirt and tight spandex shorts—providing a generous view of his package. Dusty from head to toe, he sets down his shovel and wipes his brow.

I explain that we're house-hunting and want to know what he thinks of the neighborhood. I'm focusing carefully on his face.

"I'm Brad," he says. "Come take a look at the pond I'm building for some turtles I rescued."

Turns out that Brad has twenty turtles and is on the call list at PetSmart. If anyone drops off a turtle, the store calls Brad, and he adopts it. I spot three turtles sunning themselves on a rock.

"That's Big Joe, Marcus, and Tippy," Brad explains proudly. He tells us that he has lived here for five years and loves it. "The neighborhood is great, very safe and quiet," he says. "And the guy across the street is cool. He makes cabinets for movie stars' homes. And you'll find the location very convenient—close to Costco and IKEA; the airport is only a mile and a half away, but you don't hear the planes because they go in the other direction."

Linda thanks the man and we bid him farewell.

"You see," I tell Adolfo in the car. "The radio was on while he worked in the yard. He's not a redneck, and he likes it quiet, too. I *love* this house. I think we should put in an offer."

"Hold on. Let's look at the other houses on the list first," my killjoy husband says.

"Okay, fine, but my mind's made up. I love this one!"

The next house looks charming from the front: rose bushes and a little wooden bench under a maple tree, the street's quiet and pretty. We go inside. Right away, I hate the kitchen. All the walls need to be painted. The back yard is big but ugly with a horrid concrete driveway running along the side.

Adolfo, however, falls in love with the largest of the three bedrooms because it would make a perfect studio, and he could put a sound booth in the corner. I tell him that I don't like the house.

He tries to convince me, and I'm getting agitated because I'm in love with the Craner house.

"I won't live here! I hate it!" I pout. I stamp my foot.

For this, I get a lecture in Spanish not to argue in front of Linda. He's right. I have to keep cool. I plead my case about the Craner house again.

"Yeah, but that neighbor's eccentric. And we have to consider the noise from the airplanes," Adolfo says.

"What? The turtle man is very nice, and he said that you *don't* hear the noise from the airplanes. Ugh!" I'm so frustrated I could scream myself into orbit, but I take a deep breath. "Let's go see the next place."

The next house has an amazing backyard. There is a nice wooden deck just off the master bedroom. It would be perfect for sunny breakfasts. The lush grass invites bare feet, and a huge tree off to one side promises shade in the afternoons. I wonder why we're seeing the back first? Oh. The inside of the house is hideous: filthy wall-to-wall carpet; walls needing paint and/or scraping; ugly blinds; the kitchen cabinets outdated; odd mantel over the fireplace. Another fixer-upper—for which we'd have no extra money. A house has to be ready to move into.

Linda has another appointment out in Rancho Cucamonga. We thank her, promise to discuss things, and get back to her in the morning. I. Want. That. Craner house.

Affirmations

My fears flutter away like butterflies.

I am amazing.

The perfect house is waiting for us—and Adolfo and I agree on it.

Everything is working out for our highest good.

 twenty

Baggage

've prayed and meditated and thought. I guess the house on Craner isn't the right house if Adolfo doesn't feel the same way. I must be very careful about not trying to convince him of anything.

If we move into a place and anything at all goes wrong with it, it will be my fault. I can imagine him saying, "I didn't want to move in here in the first place, but you convinced me. I told you this wasn't the right house!" It has happened to me in other situations. I went to buy a couch once with my ex. We went to a really nice furniture store in Culver City, and I picked a beautiful sofa and matching armchair, the upholstery a tapestry of muted colors. I asked him repeatedly if he liked it.

"Are you sure? You like it, right?"

"*Oui, oui,* I really like it," he said.

"Are you sure? Because it's expensive, and I want to make sure that you like it, too."

"*Oui, bien sur,* I like it. Let's get it." He was insistent.

We only had the sofa for a few months, and it wasn't even paid off yet when he told me that he wanted to get rid of it.

"I never liked this sofa," he stated. "You are the one who picked it out."

"But you said that you liked it. I asked you over and over to make sure."

"I just said that I liked it to make you happy. Why do I have to live with the same sofa for the rest of my life?" he yelled.

"But it isn't even paid for yet," I screamed back.

So, the last thing I want is to repeat that scenario over a house!

+‡+

I'm wearing the brown dress with sparkly dragonflies that Adolfo bought me in Puerta Vallarta. We're on our way to church where I'll trying to get my head in the right place over this house issue. The service reinforces my hope and positive outlook; but afterward, I meet a friend and soothe myself with two vegan hot dogs. Now I feel fat.

I weigh myself at home, and study the numbers that come up. Maybe the scale is a bit off. I refer to a book called *Outsmarting the Midlife Fat Cell.* The probing questions in the first paragraph make me squirm, asking if my mirror shows why lying on my bed trying to button my jeans isn't working. Does my scale support the mirror's message? Do I rationalize that my scales are being overly sensitive in calibrating four pounds in one week?

Uhhh, yep that would be me. According to the book, lower hormone levels and slower metabolism at midlife cause bodies to go into overdrive to cram calories into abdominal baggage to provide a natural source of estrogen, now waning in the ovaries.

Yikes! Battlefield ahead! All uphill for miles.

+‡+

It's another Monday morning. I woke up dreaming I was living in the Craner house, and it felt like home. Then as I drove to work, I thought of Karly and wondered if she'd had an abortion or not. And I'm not looking forward to the Monday morning too-this-too-that-not-enough-something-way-too-much-something-else emails. I need coffee. I don't care what my fat cells will do with it; I'm craving a vanilla soy latte and that's that. I head over to Teuscher's Chocolate Shop, admiring the store windows that are already decked out for Christmas. Thanksgiving is still almost two weeks away. I approach the window at Teucher's and get in line. *Ooh, they now have eggnog lattes.* I usually try to restrain myself, since the calorie count is no doubt in the triple digits and would most likely find a permanent home in my giant midlife midriff fat cells. Today though, an eggnog latte practically qualifies as medicinal therapy.

At work, fresh pink poinsettias look fabulous against my chocolate wall. Fountain on. New pink zen candles lit. Breathe deep. Sip latte. Ahhhh.

I open my email. Oh this is wonderful; the day starts out with good news.

> Marla,
>
> I don't know where to start. I thought that Julie was one of the most incredible human beings I have ever met. She was incredibly sweet. I had no idea that a girl who looks like her can also have a great personality and intellect. I wasn't going to go through with this but I am glad I did. I was still depressed that Lucy turned me down, but after meeting Julie, I have a new attitude. She is just the sweetest and most precious thing ever! I am hoping she will give me a second date. Please call her to ask her how she felt. Have a great day.
> Damon

And? Here's Julie's feedback. Yes! It's mutual. This is terrific. Next. Here's Arthur. I'm shocked, *shocked!* that he's dissatisfied with another woman. No one is good looking enough for him, and I am sending him our most attractive ladies above thirty-five. Can't believe he stresses how looks are secondary and then this is his chief complaint.

Ooh, here's an email from Jack, the guy who sent me the flowers for introducing him to Carmella. This should be good news.

> Marla
>
> Well, unfortunately Carmella is not for me. We really hit it off and she is unbelievably beautiful, that is for sure, but when we were in Vegas, we went into a store and she picked up a $1,200 purse, handed it to me and *told* me to buy it for her. I told her that I don't operate that way and that she is high maintenance. I don't think she liked it, because she copped an attitude for the rest of the trip, which really ruined things. I am really not looking for someone so spoiled. Thanks and talk to you soon.
> Jack

Now, I appreciate a great handbag as much as any woman, but this is ridiculous. What a shame. They would have made a stunning couple. Then I notice an email from Carmella.

Dear Marla,
  Well, it's over between me and Jack. We went to Vegas and I thought we were having a good time, but then he had to go and call me "high maintenance."
  There is no need for him to call me names.
Carmella

Dear Carmella,
  Here is some invaluable advice: Even if a man is extremely wealthy, if a woman starts asking for expensive gifts from the get-go, he will either think that she is only interested in him for what he can buy her or that if they were married, she will drain his bank account, or both.
  Once you are in an exclusive relationship with a successful man, he will most likely spoil you, but not within the first week of meeting.
Marla

Dear Marla,
  Unless he lives under a rock, he'd have to know just by looking at me that I like nice things. He could see my clothes, my expensive watch.
  Have the rules of the game changed?
Carmella

Unbelievable. She thinks this is a game. I guess her idea of "winning" is how many designer bags she can squeeze out of these guys.

+¦+

The next day, Alana pops into my office. "Umm, there is a lady in the lobby filling out paperwork, and she has five big Hefty bags full of purses with her."

"Why?" I ask.

"Well, she says that they are gifts for us. She's a purse designer."

Gary whizzes into my office. "Marla, get that woman out of the lobby, she looks homeless with all of those Hefty bags out there. I have an important meeting with a prospective client in five minutes, and I can't have him see that. Plus, she's what? A 5? We can't use her, so do a quick interview and send her on her way."

I walk out to the lobby and see a woman with short, bleached-blonde hair sitting on the couch with a clipboard, earnestly filling out the paperwork. She is heavily made up and is wearing a black mini skirt, despite being about fifteen pounds too heavy to carry it off. She looks up at me with a big smile as I introduce myself.

"Oh, so nice to meet you," she says in a heavy Russian accent. "I am Olga. I brought you handbags. They are samples from last season. I am designer. I hope you like."

"How thoughtful. Let's just get these out of the lobby, shall we?" I pick up three of the bags and Olga follows me into my office with the other two. "Have a seat, Olga," I say stuffing the bags under my desk. "That is so sweet of you to bring these, I will look at them later." I glance over her questionnaire and tell her how we work. Then she cuts in with a long story about her last relationship. She goes on and on.

I see Gary standing outside my doorway off to the side. He is making a motion with his hand across his throat. *Cut it off. Now!*

I somehow manage to end the interview and send her on her way with a promise that I'll call her if I get anyone that I think she would be compatible with. Alana runs into my office.

"Let me see those purses," she says as she tears open one of the Hefty bags.

I take a few bags out and display them on my desk. There is an unfortunate taxicab-yellow patent leather bag the size of a closet, as well as the same style in bright blue, green, and white. There are also a few leather bags in gold and silver with metal studs at the top and down the sides, and a couple of purple and green bags with fringe hanging down the front.

"Well, no wonder she was so generous bringing us five bags full. I doubt she could've unloaded these babies anywhere," I say.

"What are we going to do with all these?"

"Hey Gary, wouldn't your wife like some new handbags?" I chuckle and then stop. Did I attract this? I *have* been admiring designer bags. Maybe the universe has a sense of humor?

Affirmations

The perfect house is manifesting in our lives now.

I am one of the lucky ones who gives and gets love.

My midriff is free of midlife fat cells.

I am free of excess baggage.

I Am Not Obsessed!

Today, Adolfo and I are set to see Linda again to look at more houses. All week I've been looking up listings and emailing Linda the info.

"You are going to drive that woman crazy!" Adolfo tells me.

"Actually, I'm helping her with her job."

"You are obsessed! Stop wasting your time on the Internet. You have other things to do."

"I am not obsessed! We are looking for a house, and I am excited about it. You should be happy that I am taking such an interest in this."

"Okay, mi amor. I just don't want you wasting your time when you should be writing or doing other things," he tells me.

Wasting my time? Does he know something I don't?

We meet Linda in North Hollywood on a street called Clifton that is located very near the Craner house.

"I have fifteen houses for you to see today. Are you up for it?" She asks.

We both nod excitedly. This feels like the day we'll find our dream house. Linda has the patience of three saints; she really cares that we find the right place.

Huge power lines tower a couple of blocks from the first place we visit, but the neighborhood is quiet, and the house is gorgeous inside: Pergo laminate floors, granite countertops, recessed lighting, a fireplace, a gorgeous chandelier in the dining room, and a sparkling pool in the backyard. There are three bedrooms and two baths, but the square footage is low, not that much bigger than our apartment.

We consider a house in Van Nuys with bad carpeting but a great backyard. We could redo the kitchen cabinets, paint the place, tear the carpet out, and deal with the rest later. We adore the walk-in closet in the master bedroom, and I pick out which room would be my office. The neighborhood is fabulous, and we're ready to tell Linda that we want to put in an offer on it when the aggressive sound of big barking dogs makes us jump out of our skin. Two German shepherds raging in their dog run right next to the master bedroom window. Deal-breaker. Adolfo and I look at each other, our hearts, formerly cruising, now sinking. Next!

By five o'clock we have seen all fifteen homes. Our heads are spinning. We are astonished at how some people live: yards full of dead weeds, paint chipping off the walls, debris, an old broken-down filthy sofa or a shopping cart left carelessly in the front yard. In our price range, this is the situation more often than not. We either didn't bother going inside, or we walked in the door and walked right back out again. We take one more look at the little house on Clifton, still concerned about the size despite its charm. Most of the houses we've seen either need a lot of work, or if they are move-in ready and we love the house, the location is shitty. Sometimes literally.

It's getting chilly, and I didn't bring a sweater with me. We bid our goodbyes to Linda and head back to Hollywood. On the ride home, I wonder if I could be a Valley Girl. We are so spoiled in our beautiful neighborhood that is close to everything we've become accustomed to: work, friends, our favorite hangouts, wonderful restaurants, Runyon Canyon where I like to hike, the Catholic church we like to go to, our usual mani/pedi spot, our dry cleaners, hair salon, gym. Since we can't afford to buy a house in the Hollywood area, though, we have to make compromises. I hate that.

+¦+

At work the next day, I finally hear news of Francesco and Karly—from Tate.

Dear Marla,

I'm in such grief, I can barely make myself type this email. Francesco and I both felt that love-at-first-sight rush with each other. I was happier than I've ever been. Over the weekend, he finally confessed to me what has been going on. That little idiot he was dating before he met me lied to him about birth control and deliberately got pregnant. Then Francesco conned her that he was going to marry her and wanted a big wedding if she'd get an abortion. He stayed with her throughout the procedure and then dropped her. He told me he respected me enough to want to tell me the truth. Marla . . . I just can't handle it.

Yes, Karly was a horrible bitch to start a human life just so she could marry a handsome rich man. But Francesco's cold-blooded manipulation of her? He's really upset with me for not seeing his side in all this—that he did it because after meeting me, he knew he didn't want a life with Karly. He didn't do anything worse than what she did, I guess, but, it's just so cold. I don't know what else he's capable of. Two lies don't add up to truth. I pretty much ended things with him. I dread trying to act happy during the coming holidays.

Marla, this has upset me so deeply that I don't want to meet any more men through the agency, so please take my name off your list. Thank you for your time and effort on my behalf.
Tate

Dear God. This is devastating. I feel horrible for all three of them. Not getting the right house is nothing compared to something like this. It makes me fall-on-my-knees grateful for Adolfo's love and honesty.

†‡

Wednesday is the day before Thanksgiving, and after work, I get a statement from my publisher. Book sales are brisk and they've decided on a second printing of *Excuse Me.* This puts me into a holiday mood.

Adolfo comes home with the grocery items I asked for. For last year's Thanksgiving gathering, I tried to make vegan cupcakes and ended up giving the whole batch to our neighbor's dog since they were basically inedible. One year, I tried to make macaroni and vegan cheese and blew up the blender. Adolfo is always telling me that I am not domestic. I intend to show him that I'm so domestic, I deserve a new kitchen that can accommodate my true talents. I'm not only baking pumpkin cupcakes with chocolate frosting—okay, the cupcakes are from a mix and the frosting is from a can—but I've also bought little gingerbread-men molds. Hmmm, I see that Adolfo bought German chocolate instead of a gingerbread mix. This should still work, and everyone will ooh and ahh and be very impressed—or at least relieved I haven't bought something weird. The baking goes well, and I feel semivictorious until I slice my right index finger on the metal edge of the Saran wrap box and scream. Blood gushes onto the counter. Adolfo comes running out of his studio.

"What happened, Marlita? What did you do now?" He sees the blood. "You need a maid."

"No! You don't understand. If I didn't have to work so much, I would be totally domestic—cooking and cleaning like crazy. I am a wonderful cook. And I can bake, believe me, I can!" Tears stream down my face. I feel like I might not get a new house if I'm not certifiably domestic.

"You are a writer!" he says. "Not a housewife, and that's fine with me." He hands me a Band-Aid.

"But I *am* domestic," I cry, tears of frustration rolling down my cheeks.

I'm not, of course.

♣

Thanksgiving Day is gorgeous, and I'm dressed for a power walk before our afternoon gathering. Adolfo is concentrating on his music, so I head out the door, wearing a pedometer to spur me to walk at least two and a half miles. We live on a hill, so I'll get aerobic bun-tightening. My real purpose is to visit a dream house on Stanley Street that is for sale. I'm in love with this four-bedroom 1920s bungalow that includes a guesthouse and all the features I admire. Adolfo and I toured its open house a few months ago. The price is only a million dollars beyond our range.

I have been saying my affirmations and also put a picture of the house on my vision board, but so far, I haven't manifested the money to buy it. I walk by the house about once a week to see if it's still for sale. Here's my fantasy: I win the lotto, secretly buy the house, fly Mom down here, and take her and Adolfo out to lunch. Then I drive us all over to the house, pull up in the driveway, and shout, "We're home!"

I approach the house. The flyers are still there but now there's also a sign that says, "For Lease." So, they haven't been able to sell it at that outrageous price. Interesting.

The house we're going to today will deepen my longing for a beautiful home. Dinner will be at my aunt's fiancé's daughter's place in Beverly Hills, the home of Lorna and Mitch. What a treat not to have to drive to Orange County to my aunt's where we'd normally spend the afternoon. She's the one I stayed with when Dad was in the hospital. I'm excited to see my cousins Jodi and Wendy as well, my only family in California.

I decide to wear one of my favorite tops, one bought in Beverly Hills for more than I have ever spent on a top before. Deep red with a v-neck, it features red jewels running under the bust and up the sides. The sleeves are slit open with optional ties.

"You're wearing that porno top to Thanksgiving?" Adolfo asks.

We argue about this, and I decide I look fat.

"No! No! You look amazing," Adolfo says. "You are not fat! Go ahead and wear the porno top, really."

"Quit calling it the porno top! I'm not wearing it. Out of my way." I rifle through the closet, looking for something else to wear.

"No. I am sorry. It looks great. Wear it honey."

He wins.

As we drive up Benedict Canyon in Beverly Hills, I point out *for sale* signs on every block. "See? You *are* obsessed," Adolfo says.

"Maybe a little."

I am balancing a tray of pumpkin cupcakes as we enter Lorna and Mitch's fabulous four thousand-square-foot home that looks like it belongs on the pages of *Architectural Digest*. Mitch hands us crystal goblets of champagne and pomegranate seeds.

A buffet is set up in the formal dining room, and they even have those little cards in front of each dish to explain what it is, including vegan dishes and even vegan gravy. How thoughtful of them. The occasion is elegant and low-key at the same time. I think I could fit a place like this into my lifestyle.

+'+

I'm in the bedroom at home and hear Adolfo in the kitchen swearing in Spanish.

"What happened?" I shout, running to see what happened.

"*Puta madre!* These damn ants!" He is frantically wiping down the counter with a sponge.

I had saved one cupcake for Adolfo on a small plate covered with Saran wrap. Ants have managed to get inside, completely covering the cupcake. There are also ants swarming all over the counter. Damn ants!

+'+

I have Friday off, and Adolfo and I decide to go out one more time with Linda to look at houses. Adolfo is starting to feel pressured and a bit stressed. Linda has been so amazing and patient, taking us around town all day long. He feels guilty that she drives all the way from Orange County, and spends her time and gas, and we haven't picked a house yet.

"Mi amor," I say, "we can't spend four hundred thousand dollars just because our real estate agent took us around three times. When you work in sales, sometimes you make a sale and sometimes you don't. We'll buy a house through her, but we can't feel pressured. It has to be right."

Linda only has a few houses for us to see today. We decide to go back to the house on Clifton for the third time just to make sure. We have measured our bedroom and Adolfo's studio and also our dining room table to compare with the Clifton house and discover that all of our furniture would fit. The lack of closet space still bothers us, but we love the backyard and the pool and can totally picture enjoying life here.

We take a walk down the street, and the big towers with power lines are still hideous-looking. All of the brown lawns still depress me.

We take off to see the other three houses she has on the agenda, but they don't appeal to us, and we're completely confused about what to do.

Affirmations

I am thankful for the abundance in my life.

My book is selling like lattes across the country.

The right home will come into our lives at the right time.

The "H" Word

The decorator knocked himself out with the Christmas tree in the foyer, carrying out the theme of pink poinsettias, dusted with sparkles of bronze and gold. Dating in early December packs an extra kick of glamour with all the holiday attire and festivities. It's another Monday morning and my first email is a couple of photos of Nate and Kimberly, the couple facilitated by a psychic. They look gorgeous at a holiday party. What a stunning couple. They've been dating since July and are still going strong. I am so blown away. If they get engaged or married, I'm calling that psychic for a reading.

I open the next one. It's from Greg, Mr. Personality Profile who was crushed by Cheryl. He's actually still seeing Kendra, the Asian girl who works as a corporate translator. There isn't one word about her Myers-Briggs score. I click on the attached photo. Wow. She's radiant. That porcelain skin of hers against her straight black hair. He looks like he doesn't quite know what hit him, but, judging by the way he's squeezing her shoulder, he's not going to let go. This seems to be working. Good for them.

Here's one from Ralph, the older guy who wants an heir and a spare.

Dear Marla,

I've had a nice relationship with Denise, but I realized going into the holidays that this isn't the woman I want to be with next Christmas and the next, raising kids. She's a lovely young woman,

but we just have too little in common. I find myself excited to
meet someone new.

Ralph

Isn't it strange how long it takes a man to figure out that a
thirty-year age difference creates a commonality gap? Helllloooo
in there!

I browse the files, searching for capital Bs in the lower left
corners for *Baby*. Lucy, Rita, and Carrie are eager for children,
and over thirty. I get to work on these connections.

Burt is a new client, and he's sent me his first feedback.

Dear Marla,

Here is my reaction to The Monica Show. She's intelligent as well
as beautiful, and I learned a lot about the world of modeling. Most
of the conversation was about her, including the trials of sharing
joint custody of her pet turtles with her ex. She talked a lot about
their personalities and how she even sleeps with one of them. I just
don't think we're a match.

Burt

Wow, that's a first. Sleeping with turtles. I love it. I need to
match him with someone I'm sure is a bit more together.

My cell phone rings, and it's Adolfo. He is over in North Hollywood driving around Clifton Street and the whole neighborhood. Bless his heart.

"Honey," he says, "you're right, those power lines are really
ugly, and the street is just not that nice. The next street over is
better, but in general, it just isn't that great of an area. I just don't
picture us living in that neighborhood."

"I totally agree. We've always lived in really nice neighborhoods, and I don't feel like downgrading. We can wait to start
looking again after the holidays."

"Okay honey, see you tonight."

"Bye, Ricky!"

He admitted I was right. Amazing! I can't resist pulling up
real estate listings online just to see if the house I adore on
Craner is still on the market. Nope. It sold for ten thousand less

than we would have paid. Ooooh, if only Adolfo could see when I'm right a little sooner. Clenching my jaws, I try to do hasty loving affirmations, but I'm brushing tears from my eyes and can't make myself think the good thoughts yet.

+‡+

I take the peacock-blue ashtray down from my desk—*again*—and place it on the coffee table. If we had a house, there might be a little more room for me to have things I love around me.

"Marlita, where in the hell are my socks? Why are there six socks without a mate?"

I've not been able to solve the mystery of the missing socks. We often have this conversation after a load of laundry is done.

When he's in his studio, I grab the pile of orphaned socks and peek out the bedroom door to make sure I won't be seen. Quickly, I tiptoe toward the front door and then run down the hall to the garbage shoot to get rid of the evidence. I feel terrible about it, but I don't know what else to do other than buy him new socks for Christmas. I'll tell my mom to get him some as well.

It's the first Saturday in December, and I'm doing a lot of organizing. Since we are still planning on buying a house, we have both been trying to purge, although I notice that all of the bric-a-brac on the coffee table hasn't been packed up for Amvets.

Adolfo takes a box of trash out. There on the top, I spot some of my magazines.

"I haven't finished reading those. Don't throw them away, please!"

"Why do you want to keep old magazines?" He looks disgusted. "We're trying to clean the apartment!" He continues toward the door.

Suddenly, tears fill my eyes. I grab frantically for my beloved magazines, screaming, "How dare you touch my things? Mind your own business! Give me those magazines right now!" The tears stream down my cheeks.

He looks at me calmly. "Are you getting your period?"

My voice goes into an even more frenzied pitch. "No, I am *not* getting my damn period. You are driving me insane! GIVE ME MY MAGAZINES RIGHT NOW OR I WILL KILL YOU!"

He continues looking at me like I've just arrived from Mars.

"FINE!" I shout. "You want me to throw them away? No problem." I grab the magazines and walk out the door towards the garbage shoot. *What nerve!* My mind is racing. *I'll show him. I will throw out every magazine in the place. I will throw away all of my possessions as a matter of fact. What do I really need anyway?* I throw the magazines down the dumpster shoot, slam the door, turn around, run back to the apartment, and blast my way into the bedroom. Tears spill down my face like the wall fountain in my office. I'm hyperventilating. I grab all of the magazines in the room as well as some decorative things of mine. I stop and grab the peacock-blue ashtray and head back toward the front door. Adolfo comes out of his studio.

"What is going on? What are you doing?"

I glare at him and announce, "What do I really need while living on this earth? Nothing! All I actually need are my clothes, so I am throwing out all of my possessions! That way you can't complain about one damn thing. Get out of my way!" I grab a beautiful multicolored throw pillow.

"Calm down. Stop! Put these things down," Adolfo says. "You don't need to get rid of everything. Don't be silly. If those magazines are very important to you, then keep them. I'm sorry. Calm down. I didn't realize. What's wrong, mi amor? Is it your hormones?"

Did he just dismiss my meltdown with the "H" word? I drop everything and wipe the tears from my eyes. My throat hurts from screaming.

And then I wonder why I do, in fact, care about small things? Why are possessions so important? Material objects are suffocating me. We live in a small space surrounded by all sorts of useless objects that we have attached some emotional importance to. I decide that if there is no room for those few possessions I cherish in this apartment, so be it. Adolfo will have to find something else to complain about.

I wipe my tears and head out the door for a walk, leaving

Adolfo looking utterly baffled. *I've made a logical decision. Why don't I feel good about it? Adolfo loves me,* I tell myself. Some little part of my brain adds: *Yeah, as long as you don't take up any space.*

Affirmations

I love and am loved.

I love and am loved.

I love and am loved.

twenty-three

The Glam Fix

"Hey, Marla!" Alana says, all perky on a Monday morning. "Guess who I saw over the—" She is staring at me. "What's wrong?"

"I'm transparent? How can you tell something's wrong?"

"It's obvious. So, what's up?"

I head into my office, and she follows. I turn on the wall fountain and boot up the computer.

"Adolfo and I got into a huge fight."

"You and Ricky?"

"Yeah. I was screaming at him, and he was looking like I'd smashed his studio up or something."

"Why were you screaming?"

"Oh, looking at it from this side of the moon, I guess you could say . . . you know when you have a big dog and you try to have one teeny patch in your backyard to grow flowers, and the dog just goes and digs them up?"

"Adolfo trampled your flowers?"

"Magazines. And when I screech about it, he thinks I'm hormonal."

"Well, you are . . . a little . . ."

I glare at her and start deleting spam. "I know. I'm embarrassed. We kinda made up Sunday, but I'm still weird and shaky." I'm glancing at an email while we talk. "'Butterface?' Does that mean *fat*?"

Alana shakes her head. "Has to be a guy. What does he say?"

I read her the email aloud.

Hello Marla,

    I want to let you know that my new age limit is thirty-years-old and under. Beyond that, I'll need a photograph to be sure the gal's not a butterface and doesn't look too weathered.

    Hope you had a nice weekend.

Brent

"These men!" Alana says. "Yeah. I thought it meant *fat* when I first heard it, but it means a woman who might have a nice body, *but her face . . .*"

"Butterface. Charming. Who'd you see over the weekend?"

She prattles about being at Whole Foods with Arthur and seeing Alicia Silverstone without makeup.

Somehow, I don't care so much this morning. I get busy and put Brent, who now goes into the C.D. category, with a couple of *femme fatales* who I know won't give him a second date.

Hi Marla,

    I called Monica on Friday, and in the scope of 10 minutes, she told me about her dysfunctional family, her dislike of people in Palm Beach (where I have a condo) because 'the people are strange and fight in restaurants,' her dire financial situation, and her love of her pet turtles. TMI!

    I'll just move on to the next name on my list.

Kenneth

I debate whether to have a chat with Monica. She's in her late thirties, no kids. She desperately wants to get married, but she clearly has no boundaries. I see this happening again and again. I give advice in my dating books, and I will counsel if asked, but I've had too many angry and aggressive women blow up at me for trying to give them some unsolicited advice, so I decide to mind my own business.

Hi Marla

    Without going into another essay here, I really haven't found any

of the girls that cute. Unfortunately, I'm still a shallow, visual guy and I need a "look" that attracts me. Sometimes I wish I could look past it, but I can't. I've had the good fortune to have dated some very beautiful women in my life, I've just never found the one that I considered a good enough match to spend the rest of my life with. ☹ I'll keep going with this, but I really hate just dating to date.
Richard L.

I email Richard and tell him that he just hasn't had the right chemistry yet with someone. He's only met three girls through us so far and needs to be patient.

I can't concentrate. All I can think about is my meltdown with Adolfo. I email Bobbie and tell her a little about it, but when I think of all these men with their insistence on perfection in a woman, my gratitude for Adolfo's love wells up in me. I add in my note to her:

> Bobbie, I know that if anything happened to Adolfo, that would be it for me in the dating arena. I could not sit across from a man on a date at my age in Los Angeles, knowing that he is analyzing my weight, age, anatomy, and wrinkles.

Marla,
> I know you two will work this through.
> Love to you, Bobbie
> P.S. You must always keep a good bottle of wine in your office.

I have an incoming email from Matthew, the guy who was so excited about his first date with Angie that they both forgot to eat the dinner they ordered. If he's telling me he's decided one boob is higher than the other and can't be with her anymore—right before Christmas—I will have to puke. I can't take the chance. I'll face it later.

On my lunch break, I head out for a bit of window-shopping to lift my spirits. Beverly Hills looks gorgeous all decked out for the holidays. Rodeo Drive sparkles all year round, but never more than when twenty Baccarat crystal chandeliers line this dream drive. They shimmer by day and glisten by night.

Across the street at Two Rodeo, I meander along the charming cobblestone pathway, all decked out in red and gold, the trees and garlands weighted with lights and ornaments. I look in the windows at the jewelry and artwork that is way beyond my means and imagine Rod Stewart selecting a diamond necklace or sapphire earrings for his wife to open on Christmas morning. Then I walk over to Wilshire Boulevard and walk one block to the Beverly Wilshire. The hotel where *Pretty Woman* was filmed draws tourists from all over the globe. Now, UNICEF's twelve thousand-prism crystal snowflake floats above this eighty-year-old iconic hotel.

With its $35 million renovation a couple of years ago, this queen mum of Beverly Hills began to draw younger and hipper crowds. I notice the tables at the hotel's outdoor café, The Boulevard. Yes, darling, for my power lunch today, I'll be munching a lobster on brioche sandwich and an endive salad sprinkled with walnuts and pomegranate seeds.

Not. I'll get just get a soy protein smoothie at Jamba Juice. Slurping on it as I walk back to the office, I realize I don't have to actually own stuff to have it in my life. It isn't like I need diamonds so I can just gaze at them all day. I'm lucky to be able to get a little glam fix without having to buy it, lock it in a safe, insure it, and then hire a bodyguard on each of the two occasions a year when I wear it. I actually smile at how happy this thought makes me.

"Hello," a handsome business-type with silver hair says to me, smiling back.

At the office, I open the email from Matthew. Oh, thank God. He and Angie have gone exclusive and included a picture of them walking arm-in-arm on the beach. Jeez, I'm tearing up over this. In fact, I put my head down and have a good boo-hoo. Guess I am hormonal.

✦✦

By Wednesday, the holiday spirit finally fills me. I come home from work in a festive mood and open a bottle of bubbly, crack open a pomegranate, and enjoy a glass or two with the red seeds catching the light like rubies. This will probably be our last

Christmas in this apartment. I play some music on the Internet and venture into the man cave to dig through Adolfo's studio closet, carefully moving file boxes and noting exactly where they were. There's the two-foot fiber-optic tree I bought at Rite Aid three years ago. I replace the boxes perfectly, set up the tree, and set a live poinsettia alongside assorted colored Christmas balls in a crystal bowl on the coffee table—beside the peacock ashtray. I dance to the music as I hang some strands of gold stars on the mirror behind the dining room table, and, *voilá*, Christmas glam of my very own.

+¦+

Saturday, Adolfo and I go to American Burger on Sunset Boulevard for lunch. I'm enjoying a delicious veggie burger, but Adolfo and I are arguing about real estate. Again. We'd driven past a house on Gardner Street on sale for a million dollars. He swears we've both been to it.

"No," I say, "that was the house on Stanley. We went to the open house. I still have fantasies about that house."

He shakes his head. "Are you losing it? We went inside. A blonde lady gave me her card."

"Yeah, at the Stanley house," I insist. *Losing it?* Ooh! "I will bet you $500 I've never been inside that house on Gardner, Ricky Ricardo." We shake hands.

"Okay, get ready to pay, because I am right."

American Burger has great food, though the place is basically a dump with pinball machines in the corner and a TV hanging on the wall above the garbage can, blaring away in Spanish.

A dude walks in, parading in a miniskirt, platform sandals, blue toenail polish, and a purse slung over his chest. I can't help but stare a bit because he isn't like a man who wants to look like a woman; he's clearly a man. Well, this is Hollywood.

On the way home, we drive by the house on Gardner again.

"I have *not* been inside that house!" I insist. I'm right, of course. "I win," I tell him.

"Yeah, but not fair and square," he says. "You have to win fair and square to collect."

"Not fair and square?" Can you believe this guy? One way or another, I'm collecting on this.

✢

Sunday morning is glorious! The sun is shining and the birds are singing. Apparently no one told them it's December. My friends in Chicago are probably shoveling snow. I'm at the bank, depositing a residual check of thirty dollars for a part in a movie I did some twenty years ago. Then I head up to Runyon Canyon, which goes all the way up for miles into the hills of Hollywood and has spectacular views of the city. You often spot celebs here in sweats, baseball caps, and expensive sunglasses. I manage to hike up quite a way this morning. A young Asian man asks directions, and I tell him to follow me since I'm going back that way. Tall and thin, nice face, he's wearing trendy sweats and a baseball cap. A quality camera hangs around his neck.

"Are you in L.A. on vacation?" I ask.

He smiles. "Yes, vacation, from Korea." His name is Hwang.

We eventually discuss my book and its Korean translation.

He wants to pose for a photo with me, and a hiker snaps us, Hwang's arm around my shoulder, smiling and looking very proud. I look a mess, no makeup, hair in a headband.

Hwang is twenty-six and studying electrical engineering. "You write because you love it," he says. "In Korea, people write a book just wanting to get the money. Then if they do not make money, they commit suicide."

"You wouldn't do that, would you? It's awfully final."

"No!" He shakes his head emphatically and then laughs.

At some point, I ask, "How do you say hot cakes in Korean?"

"There are many kinds," he says. "But maybe *pa jun.*"

"Thank you, Hwang." *Very, very much.* He's made me feel like an internationally famous author. I love that.

Affirmations

My books are selling like *pa jun.*

I write because I love it.

I collect five hundred dollars from a sore loser.

Law of Attraction

irectly after work Monday night, I meet my friend Estee at Mastro's for a little holiday fun. The place is already packed, but I grab two stools at the piano and wait for her. Adolfo is playing one of my favorite original instrumental pieces as I order a glass of Chardonnay and a yummy scallop appetizer. I'm starving and can't wait. It's early but already Adolfo's tip jar is filling, a generosity that comes from good people who appreciate the extra zing of Adolfo's music. How could he think his job might be in danger? The Beverly Hills economy isn't in trouble. Adolfo says I'm too optimistic, too trusting. It's going to bite me, someday, he says.

A middle-aged woman with big, dark, curly hair—oh, it's a brunette Dolly Parton wig—and wearing a low-cut silver blouse walks over to the piano and sits down on the stool to my right. I smile. Expensive cosmetic surgery has created some odd hybrids. This lady spent her bucks on implants. The rest of her is a bit wrinkly and droopy, but her boobs are perky as a teenager's.

"Hi, honey," she says.

I nod a hello. *Honey?* Strange. The waitress brings my wine.

"Do you work in the area?" the wig lady asks.

Oh, no. Not *this* conversation. "Yes, for a recruiting firm." Pretty good answer, huh?

The waitress sets down my food.

"Oh, I think I will order that, too!"

Catching the sparkle on my right hand, the woman grabs it before I reach for my fork. "Is this your wedding ring?"

I'm wearing a ring I found one day when Adolfo, my mom, and I were in a gift shop at the Grove, admiring their gorgeous jewelry. Adolfo told me to pick one out. The style was a copy of a six-carat Tiffany ring. It cost $150, but the real thing would cost $80,000. I didn't care about that. I just liked the bauble.

I jerk my hand from the wig lady's grip and wave my left hand with my actual wedding ring.

"Well, what is that one, then?" She points, eyes bulging, at the Tiffany knock-off.

"A gift from my husband." I take another bite of scallop and dip the bread into the sinfully rich and delicious garlic sauce. Adolfo blows me a kiss, and I return it. "My husband," I say.

She appraises him. "Where else does he work?"

You a lady dick or what? "Just here, and in his studio," I say. How can I get away from her? Why do some people have no sense of boundaries? Did I attract this gal? Where is Estee?

One of the managers walks by. I smile and wave, but he gives me a distracted nod.

"Ooh, that was a bit cold," the wig lady says. "Where are you guys from?"

Oh my God. If I hand her a résumé, will she go away? "Seattle. Adolfo is from Mexico."

"Really? You can't tell. He doesn't look Mexican."

Aarrgghhh. I'm officially fed up. Why can't I just tell her to leave me alone? Oh. Maybe this is why I attracted her. She can tell I'm not the type to just say, "Piss off."

Hallelujah. Estee is walking up the stairs. She waves to Adolfo and hugs me.

"Excuse me." I say to Ms. Wig, as I turn my back on her to chat with Estee.

After an hour or so, Adolfo motions to me. "Honey, I almost forgot. Call your mom. I talked to her today."

My mom will be coming next week for Christmas, and I'm so looking forward to it. I call, and we talk a minute, and then she requests her favorite song, "The Lady Is a Tramp." She loves the song so much that she wants it played at her funeral. Sometimes when I'm at Mastro's, I call her and set the phone on the piano so that she can hear Adolfo sing for her.

"This song goes out to Donna Reed, my sweet mother-in-law in Seattle, Washington!" announces Adolfo. *"She gets too hungry for dinner at eight, loves the theatre but never comes late . . ."* he croons into the phone.

No Sinatra fans tonight? There is usually someone in the crowd who bursts out with *bravos* after this song. Again the manager looms, and the bartenders and waitresses seem watchful. What's with the negative vibes?

+ᵗ+

Beverly Hills restaurants are still doing big business, but the economy and the holidays have drastically curbed new male clients at the Double D, and Gary is on edge, looming, double checking on us, making us all nervous. On top of that, the members that do have money are off to exotic destinations for the holidays: Paris, London, Bora Bora. The Tahiti trip destination is one of those dreamy huts that jut out into the clear blue sea with floors made of glass, allowing a direct view into the ocean of colorful fish swimming by.

Though I don't have many new guys today, I still have to face a lot of feedback. The first one is from Damian, a client in New York. My last note to him teased that in order to provide him with the slimmest women, I'd be trolling the morgue for choice corpses, and I was optimistic about finding the perfect match.

Hi Marla,

Well, I'm not that bad! I have seen some walking corpses in L.A.! I go to Maha Yoga in Brentwood all the time and have seen quite a few examples of the body type I am really attracted to. Plus a knockout face is kinda nice too!

I know you are only poking fun at me! I have received all of your emails about the girls; frankly hard to know based upon your descriptions. By the way, I am on Millionairematch.com as well; "hotelierdamian" is my username. I think you have a good feel for me, but feel free to look at my profile again.

Thanks

Damian

Breathe, Marla breathe. I stand by my lighted candles and breathe. He's met at least thirty-five women so far, and only one has been thin enough for his taste. Reading his profile again won't make any damn difference. I will keep trying to find him an attractive skeleton before the dot com does—which is what he has in mind.

I actually feel a certain compassion for these men who just long, desire, yearn, and fantasize about a perfect woman much younger than themselves. I see them spend year after year, alone and frustrated because they haven't been able to hook up with their notion of beauty. Do they think they'd rather have a momentary shot at biological perfection than a lifetime with a loving mate? Are they victims of biology or what? Their obsession seems as insane as those male bugs that live just to have one shot at fertilizing an egg, and then they die.

Attraction may be something we have little choice over. On one end of the spectrum, you have men happy to have sex with sheep. At the other end, you have guys like Richard L., who noted in his email that he feels guilty for being shallow because he can't make himself be attracted to any woman he'd rate at less than a 9.

I believe you attract a mate that matches the vibes you put out, and I like to think I know what I'm talking about. This doesn't mean that a sex-obsessed guy will attract a nympho. He might attract a woman obsessed with some other form of gratification—like diamonds. You put out superficial energy, guess what you get back?

So, what am I putting out? Ambivalence. Some focus on the good side of things but also a *lot* of frustration. So, what is that vibe bringing me, career-wise? I need to think about this.

Romantically, I'm so lucky that Adolfo and I had that instant mutual attraction; that he thinks I'm a goddess, a perfect 10.

"Those men are sicko!" he tells me that night when I tell him about the guy who wants a skeleton. "A real man wants some flesh on a woman, curves, not bones!"

I love my Ricky!

++

My positive vibes definitely attract friends too, like Megan. I'm meeting her for a holiday lunch. Megan lives in Australia, and the last time I saw her was almost a year ago when we met at Mastro's. We were hanging out then with my friend Aura Imbarus, Adolfo's friend Burke, who is a TV producer from New York, and Mom. I was chatting about—of all things—the French fleur-de-lis symbol. An Olivia Newton-John look-alike, wearing a top with a fleur-de-lis on it, walked up to me and said, "Hi, my name is Megan. I'm from Australia. My friend stood me up for dinner. Can I hang out with you guys?"

I thought it was unusually brave to do that, and I totally liked her approach, her vibe. I can't help but compare her M.O. that night to my recent experience with the woman in the wig who began with an inquisition. The wig woman may have been looking for a little company, as Megan was, but her invasion-of-boundaries routine offered all the wrong energy.

So now Megan is back in L.A. with only a few days until Christmas. I reach Prego, a wonderful Italian restaurant a few blocks from the office. She's not here yet. Greg, the bartender, is a good-looking fellow around forty-five. He waves me over, and we strike up a conversation.

There is a beautiful three-foot Christmas tree at the end of the bar, and he brings me his "oakiest" Chardonnay, the Rodney Strong.

Greg was an actor on *The Bold and the Beautiful,* among other things, and we share some Hollywood memories.

I see Megan coming in the door. She runs over and we embrace. She looks great, of course!

"Hey, is this Olivia Newton-John?" Greg asks. "Ladies, sit here at the bar. I'll spoil you!"

Megan blushes. "I'm fine with that." Her accent is so damn cute as she orders a glass of wine and offers a toast. "To spoilage!"

The Bold and the Beautiful is so popular in Australia, Megan calls a girlfriend on the other side of the planet to say she's with a guy who played on it.

We both have salads, and Greg keeps refilling our wine glasses. After the meal, we're working our way back to my office, and she sees a sale going on at Gucci.

"Oohh, let's go inside and see what they have. I'm in vacation mode," Megan sings.

The day has been slow at work, and it's Christmas after all. *Why not?*

The store buzzes with women virtually frothy-mouthed in their determination to buy "bargain" designer goods. Megan appraises a knee-high black boot with a spike heel and rejects it. I try on a belt with a heart buckle. *How darling!* Perfect for a matchmaker. I don't even own a belt. It fits perfectly. It wants to belong to me. I love it.

"Wow, that looks great on you," Megan gushes in her adorable accent.

I take it off and look at the price. $250. Ugghh.

I definitely do not need to be spending that kind of money, especially for a belt, but my intoxicated mind prods me: You won that five-hundred-dollar bet fair and square. And it's Christmas, buy yourself a present. I find myself floating toward the cash register and handing over my credit card. If Adolfo finds out, he'll blow his top. Here we are trying to save for a house, and I'm spending recklessly on a belt! Well, he never has to know.

Advice during an iffy economy: Never drink and shop.

Affirmations

Gifts attract more gifts to me in abundance.

Money flows to me from expected and unexpected sources.

Adolfo thinks I look great in my new belt; he's happy for me.

Adolfo's Christmas Present

Mom is here and we celebrated a quiet Christmas. Adolfo looked at Mom and me funny when he got socks from both of us. His real present is coming today. While we're waiting for him to finish some recording in his studio, I'm chopping fruit for the brunch I'm fixing.

"What's this nice Christmasy-looking bottle?" Mom asks, picking up a bottle from the counter that is full of a beautiful lime green liquid with a label in Spanish.

"Absinthe," I answer. "We should have had some on Christmas Eve. It's an anise-flavored liquor made from an herb called *Artemisia absinthium.* One of my clients brought it back to me from Spain."

"Oh, I've actually heard of this," she says. "Isn't it illegal here in the U.S.?"

"It's legal in the States now as long as it is thujone-free. That's what was responsible for the psychedelic effect."

"Well, you'd better be careful with this then. All you need is to be wandering around Hollywood hallucinating." She laughs.

I go over to my computer and pull up some info on Wikipedia. "Well, this sexy drink inspired prominent artists, writers, and poets—like Vincent Van Gogh, Toulouse-Lautrec, and Pablo Picasso. It says, Oscar Wilde once wrote, 'A glass of absinthe is as poetical as anything in the world. What difference is there between a glass of absinthe and a sunset?' And, Ernest Hemmingway wrote *For Whom the Bell Tolls* under the influence of absinthe. So as an aspiring bestselling writer, I'll feel pretty high-brow when I sip a little of this magical green stuff as I start working on my next *oeuvre*."

"This is the stuff they called the Green Fairy!" Mom says.

I read the article further. "That's right! In Paris, the cocktail hour even became known as *L'Heure Verte*—the green hour. It's making a comeback. Here, Mom, I want you to taste it." I take two shot glasses from the cupboard. "Let's live a little!"

My mom takes a sip and a grimace comes over her face. "Tastes like licorice," she says.

"Yeah, it's pretty good. I like it."

We are about to spend the day shopping for Adolfo's Christmas present. Last week he said, "I've never had a new car in my life! My brothers all had brand new cars that my dad bought them, but I didn't get one. And I was the one who sent money month after month, supporting them! So I deserve to have a new car."

I hugged him. "Of course you do, sweetie. You don't need to justify it. Let's go get you a beautiful new wagon." He needs to tote around his equipment, so he needs a car with ample space. His '96 Ford hatchback could fall apart at anytime—like mine did two years ago on my way home from Mastro's at midnight. (The axle actually fell off! Talk about scary!)

So, as soon as we eat, we'll go look at a couple of car dealerships. Of course, we'd be doing this whether it was Christmas or not.

Adolfo comes into the kitchen. "What are you doing? What's that?" He's talking about the green beverage in our glasses.

"Just tasting the absinthe," I say innocently.

"Are you out of your mind?" He confiscates the bottle. "This stuff makes people go insane; you two will be messed up all day." He's looking around the kitchen for a place to hide it, as if Mom and I were naughty children. "I just hope you two aren't too loopy when we go look for a car."

"No. We're fine. Good to go," Mom says.

We eat our absinthe-enhanced brunch and then go straight to the Volkswagen dealership. Mom and I seem to see a lot of humor in everything.

Juan, the salesman, greets Adolfo with a smile and a contagious laugh and shows us a silver Volkswagen Jetta. We all pile in and take a test drive. Mom is in the front with Adolfo, and I get in the back with Juan.

"Very smooth ride," says Adolfo.

Mom and I find the sunny, post-Christmas weather amusing.

Juan babbles on about Jettas, turbocharged diesel engines, rail direct injected horsepower, pounds of torque, mileage, maneuverability, bucket seats, manual lumbar support, fully adjustable heating, and optional panoramic sunroof.

I lean forward, giggling and whisper to Mom, "I feel like I'm inside a TV commercial."

"Yes, he's really got his spiel down." She cracks herself up. Our wit amazes us.

"I love the car," Adolfo says looking at me with a boyish grin on his face. "Have any errands you want to get done this morning, mi amor, as long as we're checking this baby out?"

"No, I'm good," I say. "Amaaaaazingly good. How about you, Mom?"

Knowing I'm jerking Adolfo's chain a bit for treating us like children, she plays along. "Oh, yeah. When you got a great bottle, you can never start early enough, that's what I say."

Adolfo looks a little faint.

Back at the dealership, he takes some measurements to see if his keyboard and equipment will fit in the back, and they will. "What do you think?"

"If we can afford it, I say go for it!"

Those were the words the salesman wanted to hear. They crunch numbers in the little office while Mom and I wait patiently. At first.

"When I bought my Toyota, I was in and out within an hour," I say. "It was a breeze."

"Well, men just loooove to make a deal," Mom says. "They don't want to think that someone is putting one over on them. It's an ego thing."

I'm laughing, thinking we should go on stage.

Adolfo futzes around with the measurements some more, and

then, "Wow!" He spots a gorgeous Audi wagon and wants to test drive it.

"Sure," Juan says.

The four of us pile into the car and head out for a test drive.

"Rides like a dream," Adolfo says.

Juan-the-salesman begins his pitch: one owner, lacquered wood dashboard, sunroof, power windows, leather seats, immaculate . . .

"I'm confused," Adolfo says. "Should I save $7,000 and buy the used car, or go with my dream to buy a brand new car?"

"Sure glad I had a drink this morning," my mom mutters just loud enough for all to hear.

I giggle.

Adolfo dithers another forty-five minutes with the measuring tape. "Okay," he says, "It'll be a tight fit to get the keyboard into the Jetta, but it'll just slide right in the Audi."

Mom and I watch as the guys walk—for nearly thirty minutes—between the two cars, back and forth, forth and back, pointing and talking. Then they go inside and crunch more numbers. The guys stay in the damn office for an entire hour more.

Then—picture old-time movies in fast motion—we all climb in one car, test drive, get out, get another, test drive it, and get out.

Adolfo has a huge smile on his face. "I'm buying the Jetta."

Once again the guys disappear into Juan's office. By now several hours have gone by, and mom and I start dancing around the dealership to a song by Pink. Her popular song, "So What" is coming over the speaker system. It's a roaring beat and Mom and I get into it.

"So what, I'm still a rock star, I've got my rock moves . . ."

We're singing at the top of our lungs and a couple of the salesmen peek out of their offices to see what the hell is going on. We pay them no attention, and continue dancing as we keep belting it out along with Pink.

In the middle of the song, someone turns the PA down, obviously because of us. We practically die laughing.

Meanwhile, Adolfo is applying for financing online to see if he can get a better rate than what the dealership is offering. Bored out of our ever-lovin' minds, Mom and I start doing exercises to the insipid elevator music that has replaced the rock station. We work our legs, then start butt exercises.

And still they blather over window tint.

Mom and I are twitching and jerking as we have a simultaneous nervous breakdown.

Adolfo calls to me, "What about floor mats, honey?"

"Oh my God, can we just go already?" I ask.

"Are these good mats?" I hear Adolfo ask. He's grimacing, obviously racking his brain, trying to think of anything else he can ask to make sure he is getting a good deal.

Mom and I sit on the couch against the wall, staring like zombies.

Another guy is trying to talk Adolfo into buying a Lo-Jack for $1,000.

"Buy it later, honey. Please take us home before I slit my wrists," I plead. "Mom and I can't take any more of this."

The sales guy goes into overdrive: what if the car is stolen five minutes after you buy? Taken over the border, into Mexico and, blah, blah, blah. . . .

"I need a drink," I yell out.

"You really should consider the paint protector," says Juan. "It protects your car from being damaged by bird droppings. And there's a special going on today for $495."

Mom and I can stand it no longer. We start laughing and making bird calls and rude pooping noises. We are crying from laughing so hard, rolling on the couch, kicking our legs in the air. Only five-hundred smackers to protect the car against bird shit!

José glares, and Adolfo asks us what the heck is so darn funny.

"We are delirious from being here all day long. We just went over the edge."

"Let me take these two women for some food," Adolfo says. "I think they were in the sauce or something this morning."

We leave. Thank you, God!

Affirmations

I am an adoring and patient wife.

We buy a new house more quickly than it took to buy Adolfo's car.

The FDA, in its wisdom, keeps absinthe legal.

Judicious encounters with the green fairy attract my muse.

Imagine My Surprise

The office Christmas tree is sagging like it has an absinthe hangover. "I know just how you feel," I tell it. Mom is out and about amusing herself today, but we'll get together this evening. What little between-holidays business I have today is with clients who don't celebrate Christmas.

I'm chatting with Mahmoud, an Iranian client, in my limited Persian. My dad worked in Iran for American Bell International for six months when I was in high school. I just loved the country, the people, the music, seeing their films, and eating the food. I find it so interesting that Persian is spoken throughout Beverly Hills, aka *Tehrangeles*. My biggest concern when matching Iranians is remembering whether they're Jewish, Moslem, or Baha'i. Good thing I know the nuances of the culture. I promise Mahmoud I'll find him someone special.

Next, I do a telephone interview with a new out-of-state client, a brilliant, young Chinese brain surgeon who is just too busy to find the love of his life, especially one who looks like Gisele Bundchen

The next email I open is from Dina, who I matched up with a thirty-eight-year-old guy from India who lives in L.A. The man manages a plush company in the textile industry.

Hi Marla,

    I went out with Fareed last night. He's not someone that I'd be interested in, however I do believe him to be a good-hearted man, so I'm giving you a heads-up about something. During dinner, he mentioned that his brother was getting married on March 7. He then told me that his mother had given him a deadline of that same date to find a wife. I just kind of smiled and laughed, figuring that he was telling me what his mother wanted.

At the end of dinner, he said to me: "So, I have a deadline of March 7. What do you think?"

He wasn't joking. I understand there are cultural differences and that there are many arranged marriages in India, but this is Los Angeles!

Dina.

This is a surprising first. Most women complain that it takes so long for a guy to commit, and here is one who proposed on the first date. His mother probably just wants to save on her florist bill.

Tuesday is an even slower day. Gary's vacationing on Catalina, so I take time to do some tallying. Over the year, I've matched almost two hundred men, averaging fifteen contacts each. Some sixty-five or so have resulted in long-term relationships, including twenty-one marriages. Not bad. Of course, the stats lose their glow a bit when I consider the cluster of unremitting C.D.s and gold-digging airheads that tend to account for three quarters of my problems. Is *this* my life's work?

On Wednesday, I'm planning on working only in the afternoon for a few hours. It's December 31, New Year's Eve day. Adolfo, Mom, and I climb into the new Jetta and head to Adolfo's favorite place for breakfast, Norm's Coffee Shop in West Hollywood. The giant sign on top of the restaurant says, NORM'S! WHERE LIFE HAPPENS. The place is always packed with interesting characters, ordering two thousand-calorie artery-clogging breakfasts. The staff is friendly, and the coffee is good.

Inside, we're seated right away, and Mom and I immediately order coffee. I watch the waitstaff scurrying around, serving coffee, calling out orders to the cooks, delivering steaming platters of great-smelling chow. I could do this blindfolded. I almost feel envious of their work. The food arrives, and I dig into my oatmeal with raisins and nuts.

"What if I were to take a job in a coffee shop and hang with the 'real' folks a while?" I say, mostly to Adolfo. "We're only a couple of miles from Beverly Hills, yet not one person here is trying to show off with their designer clothes or shoes. No more dealing with unrealistic clients and exhausting myself. And best of all, I could work a few shifts and spend the rest of my time writing."

Adolfo holds a forkful of hash browns in midair. "Are you out of your mind? You have a great job in Beverly Hills! Why do you think you made a vow not to be a waitress all your life?"

Mom concentrates on her eggs Benedict.

I heave a big sigh. "For a second there, I was remembering only the good side of waitressing. I had my fill of it eons ago. But," I look him in the eye, "I can't keep on like this."

"My God, Marla. If you lost this job, we might have to move to Seattle."

Mom and I both stare at him.

"What are you talking about? There aren't any jobs up there. How would that help?"

"It's bad out here." His gesture includes Greater L.A. "I'm telling you Marla, hang on to your job. You're lucky to be working in Beverly Hills. Things are only getting worse."

"No need to be negative." I mention my Law of Attraction stuff. "Pessimism isn't helping anything."

"You live in fantasy land," he tells me. "I live in reality. It's *bad* out there!"

We glare at each other and finish eating in silence.

A woman screams at the top of her lungs. The whole place goes quiet. There is a couple standing at the front, along with about a dozen other people, waiting for a table. The woman looks more like someone you would see at Mastro's than at Norm's. She is probably in her fifties, has bleached-blonde hair worn in a braid that falls down to one side over her shoulder. She has obviously had a serious facelift, and she's wearing big dark glasses. Her designer baby-blue sweatpants are tucked into a pair of pink suede Ugg boots. She continues screaming at who we assume to be her unfortunate husband—a homely old guy wear-

ing a very bad toupee and a black leather jacket. Did I say there
were no pretentious types in this place?

"I will not sell all of my good clothes! How dare you ask me to
do such a thing," she screeches! "I'll take a taxi home if you don't
say you're sorry and promise to never bring the subject up again."
She continues screaming as though she is having a heart attack—
and of course, everyone, including her husband, is hoping she is.

"I am sick of this shit!" the poor guy says and walks out.

And so the woman starts screaming yet again.

"Just an old bat having a tantrum, nothing to be alarmed
about," Ms. Donna Reed offers to those within range.

Everyone resumes eating. It's another day at Norm's. I guess I
was romanticizing "real people" as well as waitressing. Life happens wherever you are.

After breakfast, Mom and I drop Adolfo at home, and head to
an appointment to get our hair done at Fantastic Sam's with
Mimi—who has probably already been coached by Adolfo.

Mimi is Korean and in her cute accent, she tells me, "Oh, yes,
Adolfo say yesterday, 'Mimi, do no cut Marla hair too short.' And
I say, 'Okay, Mr. Adolfo. I do no cut Mrs. hair too short!'" Then
she laughs, knowing she'll cut it my way.

Mom, Marvin, and I go to Mastro's for New Year's Eve since
Adolfo is working that night. We have a great time. I have Thursday and Friday off and then the weekend, so the time with her
and Adolfo has been wonderful.

Sunday, we take her to the airport. She gives me one of those
looks, like when Bobbie said, "Excuse me, your soul is limping."
She's worried about me. I tear up a bit and hug her goodbye.

+‡+

Now the Christmas tree is gone from the office entry, and an
elegant spray of dainty white dendrobium orchids has replaced
it. I only have a single sprig in a pink glass vase in my office. Gary
must be cutting back on the flower budget. I refill the water in
my wall fountain, turn it on, and light my candles in honor of
the New Year. I consider the day's beginning auspicious. I open
my first email and can hardly believe what I'm reading.

Dear Marla,

As you know, I've dated all the women you referred me to. I appreciate that you tried hard to please me. By New Year's Eve afternoon, I broke my date with Jen for the evening. The holidays had a lackluster feel to them as we went to parties and took a trip to Santa Barbara. I just felt like the midnight kiss would seal a deal I didn't want. Truth is, I missed wild and crazy Natasha. I called her to see if she was doing anything that night. She was, but she said she'd break the date, and we went out. Well, we wound up in Las Vegas and tied the knot on Friday! Thanks for knowing me better than I know myself on this one.
Phil

I print it out and hand it to Alana. "No *way!* OMG!" She turns to me. "You totally rock!"

We laugh and carry on. I send congratulations from Alana, Gary, and me, and demand that Phil and Natasha send a wild and crazy photo for my chocolate wall.

And then in another email, Lewis and Cass, the couple that went biking up in the Redwoods have gone exclusive. What a great start to the year.

The third email breaks the roll. Brandy, the friend and client who did my hair and makeup for my first signing, is dating again after her heartthrob romance fell through. She's disappointed now in Patrick, annoyed, and trying to laugh it off.

You mentioned he works out five to six times per week. No, I work out that much. He works out five hours a month. And a kick-boxer? Well maybe 20 yrs ago. He is also 45 going on 30 and stared at my breasts while he was drinking. Cheesy as a Levitra commercial. Saving the best part for last: he tells me "I think I'm too young for you."

Yeah, right. I'm sending him a TTYN on this one. Marla, will these men I meet get any worse? LOL. Can't wait to meet the others!
Brandy

TTYN? Oh, yeah. *Talk to you never.* The last time I saw Patrick, he really was in great shape and awfully sexy. But it's been about a year and a half since our meeting in the office, and life has clearly happened. Funny how my clients never email me a BTW, saying, "Hey, Marla, I'm packing an extra twenty-five these days because I've been hitting the cognac since business is down. The old pony's a little off his polo game, and I've lowered my expectations." Right.

Alana pops her head into my office to alert me that my appointment is here and filling out paperwork in the lobby.

I check another email before she comes in.

Hi Marla,

Thanks so much for the introduction to Tami. We had dinner at the Peninsula Hotel. She is indeed gorgeous. Actually she is the most beautiful woman that I have ever met. She is bright, has a college degree. She's down to earth, well traveled, and has a fabulous "natural" figure. She really knocked me out, so thanks again!

Barrett

Hallelujah! I love it. I note Barrett's feedback in his file and email Tami asking for her feedback. I go into the kitchen and pour myself a cup of coffee and then Alana brings in my appointment—a pretty woman named Cynthia in her early thirties, slim, wearing black slacks, a baby-blue cashmere turtleneck sweater, and black patent leather pumps. She has dark blonde hair worn in a bob and red lipstick. I tell her how we work and then look over her questionnaire.

"Cynthia, what is the highest age that you would consider dating?" I ask.

She crosses her legs and puts her chin in her hand. "Well, let's see; I am used to dating older men. I actually prefer it. I guess if he could satisfy me in the bedroom, I would be open to date a man in his early eighties."

Wow, I wasn't expecting that.

Then she says, "Now, he wouldn't necessarily have to satisfy me with his genitals, but you know, if he was able to with toys and stuff, that would be fine I guess."

After choking on my coffee, I reply, "Okay, no problem," and make a note in her file. "We really don't have any men in their eighties right now, but it's good that you're so open."

We chat about her lifestyle and what type of a man she is looking for, and I actually find her a match, which surprises me because she is looking for a man with no children among other specific things. Most of my older male clients have kids already. I match her with a sixty-year-old Jewish attorney who has never been married who is looking for a much younger woman. Even though Cynthia's requests seem a bit bizarre, she is quite charming, artistic, and cultured. I really hope that I can help her.

My cell phone rings. I check the caller ID and see that it's Shelly, my girlfriend from Washington. I pick up.

"Hey, happy New Year!" I say.

We chat a bit, and I ask, "How's the new business?"

To supplement her income, Shelly has recently bought a laser and is slowly building a clientele of people who need hair removal. She's been working at the front desk at an accountant's office, and the pay just doesn't cut it.

"I have a housekeeper now," she gloats.

"What? How can you afford that?"

"Well, one of my clients is a tranny. His name is Marcus, but he goes by Michelle. He basically lives as a woman, but has a huge problem with back and chest hair. The problem is she can't afford my services, so we are doing a trade. She cleans my house twice per week, and I do her laser treatments. I leave the key under the mat. It works out quite nicely. Just imagine my surprise when I came home from the grocery store the other day to the sight of Michelle, a six-foot-one transvestite in a French maid's outfit and platform shoes vacuuming my living room!"

I just about split my seams laughing.

From my intercom, Alana announces, "Marla, Frank Stein on line three."

"Oh, sorry, Shelly, I've got to take this call. I'll talk to you later. Love you."

I emailed Frank a match earlier in the week, and he probably wants to discuss it. Frank is a fifty-nine-year-old attorney who lives in Orange County. He is no prize in the looks department but seems to be a nice enough guy. The problem is I'm tapped out of younger ladies who will date his age and height, which is *not tall* at best, so I have now matched him to a lovely forty-eight-year-old dermatologist who lives near him. I pick up the line.

"Hi Marla, this is Frank Stein. So, you sent me a fifty-year-old woman?"

"Well, no actually, she is forty-eight." I can already see where this conversation is going.

"I don't date forty-eight-year-old women. They don't look good," he barks.

"Well Frank, all of our ladies are very attractive for whatever age they are, and I assure you that Dori is lovely. She is a former Ford model."

"I don't know what that is."

"Well, Ford is one of the largest modeling agencies in the world, and they represented Dori. She is still stunning, as well as accomplished, sophisticated, and awfully funny!"

"Listen, I have fifty-year-old women chasing me all the time. I am not interested! I signed up with you guys because in the sales meeting I was promised that you had plenty of younger women for me to meet."

He is really getting on my nerves now. His voice is raised and he seems pretty mad.

I respond calmly. "Frank, I'm looking at your questionnaire that I filled out during our face-to-face meeting a few months ago. You said that the age range you are open to is thirty to fifty. I think that you should be more realistic. After all, you want to find someone to spend your life with, correct?"

"What? You obviously heard me wrong!" he yells. "I don't want fifty-year-olds! Are you telling me because I am old, I should date old women?"

Actually, yes, I am. "Well—"

"I'm going to sue you! I'm a litigator and let me tell you, I win my cases. I can sue you!"

I am just plain pissed now. I've given this guy excellent service. "Frank, we have lots of attorneys here as clients. I've heard that threat before." I tell him.

He continues to rant. "I have plenty of hot younger women after me, it's not a problem!"

"Well then, why are you here?" I snap.

He rants and raves some more, and I finally cut in with an upbeat and calm tone of voice. I am trying everything I can think of.

"Hey, Frank, listen; I'm looking at your file now, and let's review the ladies I've introduced you to, shall we? Margo, thirty-three years old. Janet, forty-four years old. Camille is thirty-eight years old—and you absolutely flipped over her."

He interrupts, "Yes, she was an 11 on a scale of 1 to 10, amazing!"

"Yes, exactly, and then the fourth lady you met was Patricia who is forty-one. I'm reading your feedback, and you liked all of the ladies you met. So Frank, I've never matched you with a fifty-year-old woman. I don't know what you're yelling about. I'm really on your side. If you want to call Dori, go ahead, and if not, no problem; we'll move on," I tell him in a soothing voice.

"Yeah, okay." He is calm now.

"Okay, we had a bit of drama just now, but we're okay, right?" I ask.

"Yeah, I guess I'll give the Ford model a try."

"Okay, I think you'll be pleased."

"I mean it doesn't mean she's a model Ford now, right?" He's actually laughing.

"Right. She's more of a Lexus." Chuckle, chuckle. "Bye, now."

Oh. My. God. I feel tears welling up behind my eyes, but I manage not to cry. Over the years, I've been yelled at and threatened because the male clients have been oversold in the sales meeting, and then it's up to me to deliver the young supermodels to them. Each time, I hold my ground, but it always shakes me up. I look through the books of available women, and I find one more, much younger woman for Frank to meet, but only if she agrees. I really only have to match him once per month. After this next one, though, I honestly don't know what I am going to do. I just don't have anyone else in the database to match him to.

I really need to win the lotto or rack up book sales in the millions so I can just stay home and write in a wonderful new house.

Affirmations

I am an expert marksman at shooting arrows into appropriate hearts.

I'm such a good diplomat, I could negotiate world peace.

I get a tranny maid of my very own.

twenty-seven

Shift Happens

ori, the former Ford model who dated Frank Stein, has driven up from Laguna Beach for a Wednesday appointment with Dr. Walden. She used to live up here and refuses to go to anyone else. "No one does Botox like he does," she insists. "I would drive to the ends of the earth to see that man. His skills are nothing short of magic."

So on my lunch break, I grab my purse and head for the restaurant where I'm meeting her.

"Marla! Hi, honey!" Dori is wearing four-inch heels. Her shoulder-length auburn hair is meticulously blow dried, and her periwinkle sweater set plays up her coloring. She air kisses me, and the hostess shows us to our table.

"Now don't even look at my forehead," she says. "He really shot me up. It will look amazing in a few days though."

I tell her I have a great Botox guy as well. "So, what happened with Frank?"

Between bites of her poached salmon and jasmine rice, Dori recounts the details of their date. "He's a jockey! I'm five six, and I was towering over him. Can't you find me someone that I can wear my heels with?"

"Really? When I met him, he told me that he was five nine."

"Marla, I'm telling you, he barely came up to my nose."

"Dori, I'm so sorry. I know that you like a guy at least a bit taller than you, but what about his personality? Was he a nice guy? Did you have a good time?"

"He was all right. But he chewed with his mouth open. My ten-year-old has better table manners." She takes a sip of her green tea and looks at me intently. "All these guys are so old. Don't you at least have someone in my decade?"

Poor Dori. I have explained to her before that the only men in our service who will date her are the guys in their upper fifties and beyond. "Oh say, what about Martin Simpson from Laguna Beach? Did you go out with him yet?"

Pushing aside her plate with a perfectly manicured hand, she gazes at me again. "He told me that he is bisexual."

"Whaaaat? I can't believe it. Are you absolutely certain?"

"Yes, we spent three hours together over lunch. We talked about a lot of things. I'm not interested in someone like that."

"I am completely blown away. I have gotten feedback from at least five other women and no one said anything like that."

"Honey, men tend to spill their guts when they're with me. Guess I just have that *je ne sais quoi.*"

And she definitely does. The men her age capable of appreciating it will probably never meet her though because of their infernal prejudices.

I'm back at my desk, opening emails. I don't believe this:

> From: Ashley Madison**sexually explicit**Dating Community
> Subject: We guarantee you will SLEEP with a married person
> Are you married or in a relationship and want to have an affair?
> Are you single but want to have an affair with someone who is married or in a relationship?
> Join our Married People's Dating Community right now for NO COST at all, and we GUARANTEE that you will have a sexual affair with a married woman or man! WE GUARANTEE this!

No wonder the divorce rate is over 50 percent. I heard the owner of this site in an interview on the radio recently. He sure was full of himself, thinking that he is filling a desperate need in our society by helping married people cheat on their spouses anonymously.

My next email is from Nate, the guy who consulted the psychic and is dating Kimberly.

Hi Marla,

I just got back from a couple of business trips and finally got to see Kimberly after spending too much time apart. We had "the talk" and we are officially planning a future together! Thanks again for everything.

Nate

Woo-hooo! I get up and do a little dance around my office. Go Marla, go Marla! This is great! Maybe I should call that psychic. Wow! Here's another exciting email!

Dear Marla,

You introduced me to Alana about four years ago. I want to let you know that we got married last month. We are very happy. Thanks for all that you do.

I'm glad you're still with the agency. We've recommended the service to many people. I remember being somewhat stern with you after the first couple of matches, even over this one with Alana because I didn't want to date anyone under thirty-five. Alana convinced me on the first phone call that she was okay with our age difference (16 years) and she has never wavered. So, thank you for putting up with me and introducing us.

Richard

Someone who wanted to date age-appropriately! What a reversal. And how wonderful to be appreciated for having had the right instincts. Let's hope that proves to be the case with some of my current crusty clients—like Frank Stein. I've introduced him to a lovely lady named Priscilla.

The next email typifies what people write me or call me to discuss at least once a month:

Dear Ms. Martenson,

I'm wondering if you need any help in the office because I'd like to be a matchmaker myself, and I'd like to learn how you became one. I'm always matching my friends up, and everyone says how good I am at it. It seems like so much fun, I'm sure I would just love such a fun (and easy) job. You are so lucky. Thank you in advance for your help.

Shirley Adams

Dear Ms. Adams, do you have access to many clients who look like and have the income of Brad Pitt and Angelina Jolie *and* who for some reason are having trouble getting dates? If that is your situation, you will find matchmaking easy. Go for it, girl.

Unfortunately, my fabulous-but-can't-seem-to-get-a-date list is quite short and demands are long. Yes, I'm proud of the many deliriously happy couples I've introduced. Yes, I do meet amazing people and even develop personal friendships with many of them. My "Impossible to Match" client files are getting thicker, however, so if you know a lot of Megan Foxes who'd like to date short, pudgy, bald men, do come and help me out.

Sigh. Sigh again. Relight candles. I'm lucky to have this job. Lucky to have this job. Lucky.

Actually, I have a very polite standard email that I send out to reply to people like Shirley.

✦✦

Saturday morning, I take the peacock ashtray from my desk and return it to the coffee table. Annoyed, I'm sitting at my desk in the living room, and I shift, just a simple turn to the right. I somehow pinch a nerve in the right side of my back. It hurts like a cut with a red-hot razor. My back remains stuck for the rest of the day. By Sunday, it's no better, and since the chiropractor's office is closed, I opt for a deep tissue massage. It doesn't help.

Monday morning, I'm still in pain, but I figure it should work itself out in a few days. I've heard shift happens, but this is ridiculous. I struggle to get through each day, and by Thursday, I'm out of my mind in pain. I finally go in for an adjustment at the chiropractor's. It doesn't help one bit. I consequently go two more times, get two more massages, and take drugs that my doctor recommends with no results.

So, here I am, days later, still in excruciating pain as I drive to Balboa Island to meet a new client, Dan Jackson, for the purpose of seeing his home and lifestyle. I'm putting hundreds of miles on my car, beginning with driving from Los Angeles to Balboa Island, and then down to La Jolla, and then back to Los Angeles, much of it in bumper-to-bumper traffic.

I've given myself plenty of time to get down to Newport, and I have my new TomTom—this one's male voice guiding me in a British accent that Bobbie thinks sounds like Matt the Bachelor. So we name my TomTom's voice Matt-Matt. I figure there's no way I can get lost.

I want to get to my first destination with enough time to find a place to eat and use the bathroom. I see a Mexican fast food place. Perfect. I park and go in and order food.

This leaves twenty minutes to get to my client's house. I get back in my car, my neck and back in searing pain. It hurts too much to really turn my head to look behind me. I do my best and proceed to back up slowly. Slowly. . . . Crash!

Fresh pain jolts me, but it subsides enough for me to step gingerly out of the car, and make my way around to the back. I have managed to slam into a pole. At least there's no damage. Oh, wait. Big dent on the left-hand side near the bumper.

Just what I need. That will be hundreds of dollars to repair, I'm sure. I yell at the car and then sob. At this point I'm completely disoriented, upset, enduring the shooting pain up my neck, all while trying to program the address to Dan's house into my TomTom. Once I get the thing programmed, I dial Adolfo's cell.

"Mi amor?"

"What's up, baby?" he asks.

"I just crashed my car."

"Ay, Marlita, what now?"

"It hurts to turn my head, and I smashed the car into a pole."

"I can't believe this."

"We'll have to call the insurance company. I'm upset, and now I have to find this place, and I am running late."

"This is the second time this year you crashed your car," he says helpfully.

"No, the first time I was rear-ended. Not my fault at all," I remind him.

"You have to be more careful. Your car is practically new and you're trashing it!"

"I know, I know, anyways, I have to go. My client is waiting."

I get in the car and follow Matt-Matt's voice. It takes me to a trailer park. Something tells me this is *not* Dan's neighborhood. Damn it, damn it, triple damn it. I am lost.

I call Dan. He is so nice and gets a map to guide me to his home.

However, I am utterly befuddled. I turn the wrong way down a one-way street right into oncoming traffic. I can see the other driver's expression of sheer surprise and shock and start screaming right into my hands-free headset and into Dan's ear. He's still on the phone with me.

The tear reservoir bursts.

"Can you make a U-turn?" Dan asks, his voice sounding even warmer and more mellow than Matt-Matt's.

There is a lull in traffic. "Yes." I make the hasty maneuver before the next onslaught of traffic.

Dan calms me down with his soothing voice and guides me to his home. When I arrive, he gives me a hug and a warm smile. I am completely embarrassed and feel totally unprofessional.

"Hi, Dan, I'm so sorry! Nothing like this has ever happened before," I assure him. "Honestly, I am usually not this discombobulated."

"Well, I was wondering . . ." he says with a smile.

I'm trying to put the harrowing experience behind me and ignore the pain in my neck so that I can give him a good impression. Dan proves to be someone very matchable. I'll find him someone soon. Somehow by the grace of pain pills, motivational CDs, an improved relationship with Matt-Matt, and prayer, I hold it together for two more clients down in La Jolla.

Thankfully, I make my way home after a long day of hob-knobbing with the rich and lonely.

The next morning, Friday, it's pouring down rain. I drive my car to the body shop and Adolfo follows. Jimmy, the owner of the body shop, is a friend of Adolfo's and says that the car will be ready in a week, and insurance will cover all but three hundred dollars. So far, between the chiropractic adjustments, massages, painkillers, and the car accident, this pain in the neck is costing me over six hundred dollars.

The pain has not let up, so we go downtown to St. Vincent's hospital for a neck and upper back X-ray. Adolfo finally drops me off at work, and I arrive harried and wet. I proceed directly to the kitchen to get myself a cup of coffee. Alana always has it ready since I'm not allowed to make it myself. The last time I made an attempt, the pot leaked all over the counter, and the coffee tasted like mud. So now, whenever she sees me going toward the kitchen with a mug in hand, she jumps up from her desk.

"I'll make the coffee! Stay away from the pot!" she yells, dead serious. Since my disastrous week, she's even more leery of allowing me near the machine.

Luckily, the X-rays showed no serious damage; all I had was a pinched nerve that eventually worked itself out over a few more days.

⁺⁺

The following week offers just the repair job my soul needs. Adolfo and I have tickets to go see Wayne Dyer at the Egyptian Theatre on Hollywood Boulevard for the screening of his new film, *Ambition to Meaning*. This is Hollywood, so there is a red carpet and photographers, and don't forget those beautiful and skinny models, all posing.

A cocktail reception before the film is held in front of the theatre in a lovely courtyard—bar set up on the left, a long table of food on the right. Adolfo gets a glass of red wine, and I opt for champagne. We take a place in the growing line for food.

"See anyone who looks familiar, honey?" I ask.

"Just you, honey."

We load up at the food table and then find a seat near the red carpet for a prime view of arrivals. The paparazzi are buzzing around, poised with their cameras, waiting for Ellen and Portia to arrive.

Ellen DeGeneres often has Wayne Dyer as a guest on her show, and Portia de Rossi is starring in tonight's film. Cameras begin flashing like fireworks as Dyer arrives. Next comes Portia de Rossi, sans Ellen, and she looks incredible in chic black, her long blonde hair pulled neatly back in a ponytail. Now Dyer is right in front of us. I hand Adolfo the camera and instruct him to make a video. The crowd swarms, but I manage to get his attention for some individual shots.

Adolfo and I enjoy the film, set in beautiful Monterrey and showcasing a few character-driven stories that dramatize Dyer's messages. In the car on the way home, Adolfo and I discuss what an inspirational film it was. Its message, that if you trust in yourself, you trust the very wisdom that created you, moves me powerfully. I should quit obsessing on my limitations. In trusting my own strengths, I attract the same in my life. Adolfo and I both thought it was just a lovely evening.

He's quiet for a moment and says, "I worry that you're too trusting when you give out so many business cards."

I laugh. "Well, that's why I have them, for networking and promotion."

"There are a lot of weirdoes out there. I'm just protecting you, mi amor."

"Gracias, yo te quiero con toda mi alma," I say. Thank you. I love you with all of my soul.

Affirmations

I am pain free.

As Matt-Matt guides me through traffic, I trust my inner guidance through life.

I trust in the splendor of my very being. (Repeat sincerely and often.)

twenty-eight

Volumptuous

During a break at work, I go online and start looking at houses again. I can't believe the new year is almost a month old. I see myself as a housewife extraordinaire, cooling my freshly baked cupcakes on a granite counter, living in the Valley in our new home with hardwood floors and plenty of closet space. I find several places that look like real possibilities. Adolfo keeps saying that in a couple more weeks we'll go out looking. I'm thinking maybe around Valentine's Day.

My phone rings. One of my favorite VIP clients, Josh Bennett, is giving me feedback about his date with Carmella. She's the gal that I had to give advice to after she asked Jack to buy her an expensive handbag in Vegas. She's so incredibly gorgeous. I decided to risk introducing her to Josh, hoping she'd gotten the message about not pressuring dates for expensive gifts.

"She is hot, that's for sure," Josh says. "Definitely a 10. I just love her long, silky dark hair and her full lips."

"I knew that you would like her Josh. How many times have you seen each other now?"

"We've gone out four times, but honestly, I've decided that I won't be calling her again."

"Why not? What happened?"

"She keeps trying to get me to buy her expensive purses. The last time we were out to lunch she whispered all seductive in my ear, 'Let's go over to Gucci. There's a sale, and I just need a tiny handbag.'"

"Well, did you buy her one?"

"No, she was trying to get me to take her to Gucci on the first date. I told her maybe next time, but I was turned off, so I made an excuse that I didn't have time. She doesn't give up. I think she'd probably sleep with me just to get that handbag."

"Wow! Why did you see her four times then?"

"Marla, she is so volumptuous that I put up with the behavior. She is the most volumptuous woman I have ever met."

I chuckle. "Josh, I think the word you are looking for is *voluptuous*. There is no *m* in that word."

"Well, however you say it, she's got it."

"Okay, well thanks for the information. I guess I can't match her anymore. I'll find another exciting date for you. No problem."

Volumptuous. A natural blend of sumptuous and voluptuous. Somehow it captures my male clients' dream of fantasy sex with a trophy woman. But somebody like Carmella?

Dear Carmella,

I am writing you because I have to say that I don't think that we're the right service for you. I was so excited to have you in our database, not only because you are gorgeous, but very charming and sweet as well. However, our male clients come to us to find a wife. A woman they perceive as being willing to exchange a bedroom visit for a handbag doesn't come off as marriage material. I wish you all the best.

Marla

And then, while in this frame of mind, I get an annoying email from Jasmine, a twenty-eight-year-old brunette who works as a sales girl in a Beverly Hills boutique.

Marla,

Daniel picked me up in a 1997 GM truck, and I'm pretty sure that he doesn't make more than 60K per year. Like I said when I met you, I want doctors and lawyers and don't need you to fix me up with a guy in a truck. If it is not the right match, then I don't want to waste my time. If I'm being too difficult, maybe this agency is not for me.

Jasmine

Dear Jasmine,

I understand perfectly what you are looking for, and you are correct. This agency is not for you. I wish you all the best.
Marla

And then we have another entry in the "Will Wonders Never Cease?" file:

Dear Marla,

Thanks for the introduction to Pricilla. She is absolutely gorgeous and perfect in every way. And I think she likes me too. Can you believe it? We have seen each other at least six times so far. And her age is perfect for me. 42 is just right. You can hold off on setting me up with anyone else for now. I am really hoping that things will develop with her. Thanks again and have a great day.
Frank

Yippee! I feel like doing a Broadway dance with high kicks and a top hat around my office. I cannot believe that sophisticated, gorgeous, much younger Pricilla, has gone out with Frank six times. My fingers are crossed that this lasts. Any scenario would be fine by me as long as I don't have to match up Mr. Lawsuit slap-happy Frank Stein again anytime soon.

✝✝

At home that evening, an important-looking envelope has arrived from my publisher. Adolfo is with me, watching me open it. My pulse speeds up a bit. "It's too late for them to ask for the advance back," I say, "although they could delay the publication date."

"Where is your optimism?" Adolfo teases. "It might be money."

I open it to find a letter and two checks. I read the letter first.

Excuse Me . . . second printing doing well . . . attached royalty check after having earned back the advance . . . !

I scream.

"How much is the check?" Adolfo yells over my frenzy.

I carefully tear open the first check. It's for $6,000. "This is great! Not quite super sales, but great! And they're going into another printing, so there will be more!" I'm jumping up and down.

"What's the second check for?"

I'm thinking expense reimbursement, but no. "Oh, a royalty check from sales in Korea!" I hand Adolfo the second check for $500. "Sixty-five hundred bucks into savings for the house!" I squeal.

"No, honey," Adolfo says. Six thousand for the house. That five hundred—it's for you." He kisses me and looks sheepish. "I sorta owe it to you from our bet. This money is yours, fair and square, and I want you to have it."

This day, this money, this feeling of success—it's simply volumptuous.

Affirmations

My books go into many printings.

Mi amor and I easily and quickly find a perfect home.

Miracles flow, and wonders never cease.

 *twenty-nine*

Slings and Arrows

alentine's Day is great when you are in a relationship, but otherwise I think it is just another reason to feel bad about being alone. I remember when I was single and living in Chicago, I never seemed to have a boyfriend on Valentine's Day, and I always felt so depressed about it. As a waitress, I had to witness dozens of couples nuzzling and canoodling, women accepting proposals, and then going home to snuggle with their sweethearts. In the meantime, I, having taken myself out to lunch with a lonely glass of champagne, would be going home alone with nothing to do but watch an old movie with my dog.

Or at least that was how I once felt. Now, I see Valentine's Day as just a commercialized holiday invented to sell cards, chocolates, and overpriced dinners in restaurants. It has an odd power, though. It often prompts some of our clients to go exclusive and others to realize that if they don't want to spend a Valentine date together, it's a good indicator that the relationship is going nowhere. Often, clients who'd gone inactive come back into the fold. Quite a few previously steady daters are asking for new referrals today. This comes in from Francesco:

Hello, Marla,

I'm still in contact with Tate, though we aren't dating. She told me that she revealed our sad story to you. I know now that I handled things badly. I have great respect for Tate. She's a better person than I am, obviously. I can't quite give up on her, but I'm also

a practical man. I want a woman in my life, and so, would you please resume our agreement? Tate has made me realize that I do want a woman who has more going for her than just her looks.
Francesco

I decide that I'll try him out with Cheryl. Just doing my job. Later that day, even good old Karly decides she needs to get back in the swing.

Hi, Marla,
    What a frigging nightmare this has all been, huh? I'm thinking about suing that asshole Francesco. He ruined the holidays for me. You know he conned me into an abortion? Kinda makes me appreciate the old farts that I can wrap around my pinky. So, send 'em to me. G2G.
Karly

G2G. Got to go. Well, I have a few C.D.s that should be just about right for you, honey. As Bruno used to say, *plus ça change* SOSO (same ol' same ol').

✝

I want to tell Adolfo about some new house listings on our Valentine date tonight. We haven't called the Realtor for a while, and house-hunting seems to be the last thing on his mind as we circle the parking structure at the Grove, where we are going to have dinner and see a movie. There is not one parking space available.

"This is ridiculous," says Adolfo with steam coming out of his ears. "Valentine's has become like Christmas. They were talking about it on the news yesterday. People should leave it to couples. Why are single people, old ladies, and little kids celebrating Valentine's Day?"

I start laughing at Mr. Grump. "Let's just valet."

Adolfo agrees and we are soon having dinner at our favorite French restaurant, Monsieur Marcel, situated in the Farmers Market. The staff knows us, since we eat there at least a couple of times per month. It's busy, but they find us a cozy table in the corner. Their musician plays the accordion to serenade all of us lovebirds. I have the mussels and Adolfo has the duck confit. This is our eighth Valentine's Day together. We always do something special, nothing big, but always special. The point is just to celebrate how lucky we are to have each other.

We hustle over to the movie theater so that we are there thirty minutes in advance to make sure we get to sit next to each other. The place is a madhouse. We are seeing *He's Just Not That into You,* starring many of my favorite actors. The film is adapted from the dating advice book by Greg Behrendt, which gives me hope that my books can make it to the big screen, too.

After the film, I walk through the crowd, hand in hand with my Valentine, on our way to Barnes & Noble to "visit" my book. I feel like the luckiest girl in the world.

+¦+

Two nights later, Adolfo comes home about midnight.

"Hi, honey," I say, my sleeping mask still covering my eyes.

"Hi, baby."

I ask my usual question. "How was work?"

"Well . . . I'm outta there in two weeks!"

"What?" I pop up from the pillow, ripping my mask from my face. "What are you talking about?"

"They're making changes over there. I think they might be trying to cut down on expenses. Maybe they're going to pay someone else less than what they pay me. They really wouldn't give me a straight answer."

"Wow, this is unbelievable. You have been there over six years and have a huge following. All of your regulars. . . . Celebrities come in to see you! They're making a big mistake. You're the best piano man in town."

"I know. I'm shocked. Thank God we didn't buy a house. Can you imagine what trouble we would be in? Remember when I told you that I had a feeling that I could lose my job?"

"I know. But I thought you were just being negative. I didn't think—really think—that was possible. Why would they do this?"

Mastro's has been a part of our lives for so long. I flash back to all the birthdays when friends have met me there to celebrate with Adolfo's wonderful music. My mom and I have been hanging out there for years whenever she's in town, watching the celebrities and posers, laughing and singing, eating our two thousand-calorie scallops with a glass of Chardonnay.

I was dreaming of staying home in the near future, in my role of Hollywood writer, working out of my office, which I would decorate the way *I* wanted. My life is rearranging itself superfast. My dreams are pushed aside. No house. Trapped in my job at Double D.

"Well, maybe it is for the best. Change is good, right?" Adolfo takes off his jacket and sits on the bed. "This will force me to pursue more studio work." He gives me a quick look and then stares at the floor.

I want to be furious and kick things and swear. Lightning has just struck my world, but if I show any of what I'm feeling, Adolfo will feel a thousand times worse than he already does. I fake it. "Yes, absolutely!"

✛

At work the next day, I call Bobbie and try to explain things, but, I don't know, the tears . . . they just happen, despite all my trust in Adolfo and in our future.

"He's the best piano man in Los Angeles," I say to Bobbie, sniffling, trying not to sob. "Thank God I didn't cry in front of Adolfo. My disappointment is not with him, never."

"What an opportunity," Bobbie says, showing not one lick of sympathy.

"What? Adolfo is feeling sick about this. Six years. Six years! And they let him go." I have to stop and blow my nose. "Oh, I wanted a house so bad!"

"When he hired on at Mastro's, did he think it would be for life?" she asks.

"Well, no."

"So it's on to another chapter for Adolfo. A terrific opportunity. You know, the 'one door closes, another opens' thing."

"Right. Of course. And I know this. And he does, too."

"His fans will follow him elsewhere. They have before," she points out.

"Things happen for a reason, and I am certain that better things are ahead. We'll be positive and attract new opportunities."

I affirm all this to Adolfo that evening.

Affirmations

New and wonderful opportunities are opening up.

The universe has bigger and better things in store for everyone.

Creativity flows easily and effortlessly.

Divine health, prosperity, love, and peace are ours.

thirty

Rollercoaster Boogie

I kiss Adolfo goodbye, ready to leave for the office. He's enjoying working on music for commercials and TV soundtracks in his studio. He has some private gigs going. The restaurant bar scene is still slow, so another steady job may not come right away.

My new books have arrived, and I'm all tingly again. This time my promotion in Portland will be before the Barnes & Noble signing at The Grove. Life cranks into a high-speed boogie again as I get ready for the trip.

I'm speeding on my way to work, and Life's Grand Scheme hits me. I've had serious relationships in three different countries, lived in at least twenty different apartments in three major cities, worked in at least twenty-five different jobs, traveled eleven times to Europe, speak three languages, and now have two careers. I scurry about so that couples can climb into the mini-railcars, lower the lapbar, and soar and plummet on their thrill rides of the heart. Our high hopes carry us into the clouds, and reality drops us so fast our stomachs are in freefall, and yet somehow it's thrilling, and on a Monday morning like today, we're back for more.

As soon as I walk in the door, Alana says, "Something's come up with Gary. And Frank Stein is on the line."

"Good morning to you, too," I say.

She looks nervous. "I'll come in after you talk to Frank."

I pick up the phone in my office. Please God, let it not be that Frank is back on the market. "Hi, Frank, Marla here."

"Oh, hi, Marla. Listen, I have some bad news about Pricilla and me."

Kee-rap. "Really, Frank? What happened?"

"Well, I feel just awful. I totally screwed up. Everything is my fault. Pricilla and I were getting along great. I'm absolutely crazy about her. But one day I was fiddling around on the Internet, and since I never closed out my account on match.com, they still send me profiles on possible matches. Well, they sent one woman's profile and a photo that was dynamite. She was local, young, and a looker like you can't believe, and loved to surf and golf. She looked like a perfect match, so I just thought that I would email her and make contact. Well, wouldn't you know, she's a friend of Pricilla's."

"Frank, no!" *You monumental idiot!* "I can't believe this. What are the chances?"

"I know. So, of course, she told Pricilla that I contacted her, and well, as you can imagine, Pricilla is furious and says that she's been humiliated in front of her friends and can't trust me. I totally understand her feelings. But, Marla, I am crazy about her. I don't know why I did what I did. I really messed up."

"Yes you did, Frank. But have you tried to win her back? Have you sent flowers? Written her letters?"

"Yes, I've sent three bouquets of flowers and emails apologizing. I have done everything that I can think of. She just keeps saying that she doesn't know, and she is confused and hurt. But until she tells me to absolutely leave her alone, I feel like I have to keep trying to win her back, although it doesn't look like she's going to take me back."

"Frank, I'm so sorry about this. It *is* a big lesson, isn't it?"

"Oh, you'd better believe it. Well, I just wanted to let you know about this because I might be back soon wanting to be matched up again." Might? There is such a lag time between hope and the reality adjustment.

"Frank, I hope that she takes you back. I'm rooting for you." *More than you will ever know!* However, I'm getting out my big black book.

Alana is at my door the second I hang up. "Gary wants to take us to lunch today." She looks stricken, as if she's just been fired. "What do you think it means?"

He's never done anything like this before. We speculate for a few minutes on the possibility of downsizing or flat out going out of business. "He *has* been complaining about rising costs and fewer clients in this economy. And he cut back on flowers," I say.

"Or maybe he wants to move us all to the Orange County office?" Alana says. "Or fire one or both of us?"

My cell phone rings. It's Bobbie. Alana and I shrug, and she goes back to the front desk. I take Bobbie's call. Last week, I'd done my absolute best to send her a great guy to compensate for the bird shit man.

"Well, did you go out with Sloan last night?" I ask.

"Yes, I did, and thank you very much, Miss Matchmaker. He is adorable. So sexy."

"Mm-hmmmm. Details please."

"Okay, well he picked me up at seven and took me to a fabulous restaurant in Del Mar at the L'Auberge. I'd never been there. Get this, he'd called in advance and had a chilled a bottle of Veuve Clicquot champagne waiting at our table."

"That's your favorite. How did he know?"

"Yes, that's what I'm thinking, Miss Smarty Pants."

"Okay, I *might* have casually mentioned what your favorite champagne was." I'm grinning.

"He was such a gentleman, and we have so much in common. I don't think we stopped talking the whole night. We closed the place down. The waitstaff was stacking chairs around us when we finally noticed and got the hint that we should probably leave."

"Ooh la la," I say. "It sounds like there is real potential here."

I get back to work, scrambling to get ahead because tomorrow morning I'm leaving for Portland to do the press for my new book.

By midday, I've done two radio interviews over the phone for my book, recorded a dozen email feedbacks, and had a meeting with a frustrated client.

Gary walks into my office at twelve thirty. "Ready?" He's chipper, always dashing in his expensive suits, worn with crisp white shirts and no tie.

Alana and I are cordial, but a bit grim as we head for a final meal before the ax. We step inside Lola's, a wonderful little Mexican restaurant nearby, and Gary starts off with an order of margaritas. So, is he really loosening us up so we won't cry? Or screech at him in public?

He orders guacamole and then big meals, more than I'd eat in a week, and starts talking about who he thinks is in love with whom and who I might try with whom, reminiscing over some fabulous bloopers. Gradually, Alana and I get into the spirit, and I reveal how Dee Dee was engaged to her old sugar daddy while Scott and Jerry were so smitten with her. We're all three laughing about this. The lunch is remarkably enjoyable. At the end, Gary cheerfully picks up the tab, and says casually, "You gals are doing a swell job, and I want you to know how pleased I am."

Alana and I look at one another, in complete and total shock at Gary's sudden appreciation of us.

"Thanks for the compliment, Gary," I say. "It really means so much."

Alana agrees and then excuses herself to use the restroom.

Gary says, "I'd also like to take you and Adolfo out to dinner one evening next week. How about Prego?"

"Fabulous!" I tell him. "Love the seafood pasta there."

Alana and I both feel relieved, and it shows in our moods. In the afternoon, I interview five new girls, set up ten matches, counsel a client named Mike about whether he should break up with Cindy (whom he's been dating exclusively for five months), and have a training session with three new recruiters. It looks like I will be getting out of here half an hour late. I still have to do laundry and pack tonight. I answer a few more emails and take a couple of calls, tidy up my desk, and manage to slip out the door.

✝

I am finally packed, the laundry done and put away, the dinner dishes washed, and I am lying in bed, watching Larry King ask Dolly Parton if the press should be commenting on Jessica Simpson's recent weight gain. Dolly wants everyone to leave her alone.

"Marlita!" Adolfo yells from the bathroom. "Every time I have to bend down to lift the lid on the toilet seat, it hurts my back."

"Wow, Ricky, you are really out of shape if you can't bend down to lift the lid."

The toilet seat has been a matter of much discussion during our seven-year marriage. Adolfo likes the lid to be left up, to air out the toilet, he says. I, on the other hand, prefer that the lid be left down at all times. It looks like we'll be disagreeing on that subject for the rest of our lives.

"Lucy, honey, just leave the lid up at night so that when I have to get up to go to the bathroom I don't have to lift it. And you can close it during the day."

"No problem, mi amor. Good compromise."

And it is. Just like our marriage.

Affirmations

My book promotion launches mega book sales.

Life is a dance, and boy can I boogie.

I can accept compromise with grace.

Love keeps the heart's rollercoaster ride on track.

Showtime

I have a million bees in my hive this morning. It's Monday, and I am back at my desk with a steaming cup of coffee Alana has freshly brewed. I sold eighty books up in Portland at a signing, and Mom has flown back down to L.A. with me for the signing on Thursday at the Grove. Afterward, we'll be having a cocktail party at a nearby restaurant. I've invited battalions of people, including my cousins Jodi and Wendy who are driving up from Orange County. Bobbie will be driving up with another friend from Del Mar. I'm hoping Gary will reschedule an appointment in La Jolla that afternoon so that I won't be racing up the freeway in rush hour traffic to get to my own bash.

Now, I must focus. Here's an email that requires no effort at all.

Dear Marla,
    Two months ago Yogesh and I got married. Here are some pictures of the wedding. Thanks so much for finding me the absolute love my life. You are an angel.
Love, Linda

How awesome. Yogesh, originally from India, is an amazing man: intelligent, spiritual, and gentle. He lost his fiancée in an accident a few years ago, and when I met him, he told me that more than anything, he longed to share his life with a soul mate, but he was afraid that he'd had his chance and would never find true love again.

As if fate stepped in, I was introduced to Linda, a beautiful and charming educator, whose dream it was to one day work or study in India. I told her that I'd like her to meet someone. And that is how Linda and Yogesh came to love one another.

The photos of their marriage are simply breathtaking, especially the one on the beach where they are reciting their vows, and others showing them toasting with champagne in front of a three-tiered cake with red roses, and of Linda wearing an Indian veil on her head and a ruby bindi on her forehead. Love seems to have made the already vibrant colors dazzle the eye. I marvel that it is through my hands that their happiness has grown.

In spite of all the ridiculous requests and expectations I often put up with, Linda and Yogesh are proof that the agency is also serving a beautiful purpose. And so I too am serving a beautiful purpose. Is there anything in the world that can be more worthy than helping soul mates find their way to one another? To find love? To have someone to experience the world, life, family, and even with whom to grow old? How could I ever accomplish anything more important than that?

I email Gary the wondrous photos. I tap on the door of his plush office. He calls me in, and I tell him to check out the photos of Yogesh and Linda.

"Another success story!" I announce.

"It's why we do it," he says, smiling and giving me a high five. "Congratulations, Marla."

+¦+

Wednesday brings another high point. I am sitting across from Ariana at Prego. "Two glasses of champagne, please," she tells the dishy Italian waiter with the closely shaved goatee.

"*Subito, Signorina.*" He bows and disappears, returning *molto subito* indeed with two flutes of bubbly.

"Soooo?" I think I know what this is about.

"First of all, I want to propose a toast to you: to the best matchmaker in town!" She clinks her glass to mine. "I thought for sure that I was a hopeless case, but you never gave up on me, even after years of dating disasters, spilling my guts after too many cocktails, not having good listening skills, and becoming too intimate too fast. You gently set me straight and now: ta-daaahh!" She shoves her left hand under my nose.

I gasp for air at the size of the rock. "Holy cannelloni! Is that what I think it is?"

"Billy proposed. Last weekend. He took me to the Montage resort in Laguna and proposed on the balcony of our room under the moonlight. I am so happy. You have to come to the wedding."

"When is it?"

"Not until next year. We want to have a super-big wedding, and it will take time to plan, but you will be the guest of honor. Thanks a million, Marla."

My eye plumbing must be shot. It keeps leaking. I am beaming like I've just won the lotto.

"Order anything you want," she says. "Lunch is on me."

The work day is over and I pack up my things and head to my car. Filled with gratitude, I am thankful to be going home to a loving husband. Mom is out with Marvin and some friends tonight at Enoteca Drago in Beverly Hills. I stop by the store to pick up a bottle of wine and some fresh salmon to make Adolfo a nice dinner. Tonight we will celebrate. I turn on the radio and just before arriving at home, I hear a song I like so much that a few weeks back, I tracked down Thriving Ivory and asked the lead singer, Clayton Stroope, if I could use the lyrics of "Flowers for a Ghost" somewhere in one of my books. It feels like cosmic validation that choosing love is important to both the male and female of our species. On this day, the lyrics really come to life for me.

Who will bring me flowers when it's over?
And who will give me comfort when it's cold?
Who will I belong to when the day just won't give in?
And who will tell me how it ends and how it all begins?
Don't ever say goodbye,
I'm only human . . . only human.

At work Thursday morning, I'm trying to stay as calm as I can. I have been looking forward to this day for over a month. Tonight at seven thirty is my big book signing at the Barnes & Noble at the Grove in Hollywood. I beg and argue with Gary to let me reschedule the trip to San Diego to see a new client's home—obviously so that I can be impressed and tell all the women that he has a fabulous house—but he is adamant. What a complete and total jerk! But alas! I am a worker first and a glorious author second.

So after three hours of driving, I pull into the driveway of Eric's fifteen thousand-square-foot mansion—which I guess Bobbie would call a big-ass palace—overlooking the water. Gary is meeting me here as well—which I find interesting. I'm not sure if he wants to see the client's fabulous house or is just checking up on me. So I've made the 110-mile drive, me in my car and Gary in his.

I get out of the car and stretch my legs, already dressed for the event tonight with my hair in a sleek ponytail and a black headband, just the way Gary hates it. I dare him to make a comment about it.

The house caretaker, a lovely British woman, leads us up some stairs into a spacious room with a full bar. She offers cool drinks and salmon hors d'œuvres. Yum.

Eric saunters into the room barefoot, wearing jeans and a black T-shirt. He is a handsome guy around fifty with intelligent dark eyes and tousled chestnut hair. He will be easy to match, a real dreamboat. Eric proceeds to give us a room-by-room tour: a full-blown gym, gourmet kitchen, library, formal dining room, and more. His bedroom is bigger than my entire apartment and has French doors leading out onto a balcony facing the Pacific. From there, I look down on the backyard where a Jacuzzi spills into one of those gorgeous infinity pools. It is majestically peaceful and serene here. I look at my watch: 3:11. I need to hit the road no later than four to make it to the bookstore on time, assuming nothing goes wrong.

"You have your book-signing tonight, right Marla?" Eric is leading us downstairs toward the front door. "I *cannot* believe you drove all the way down here today."

"Right, it's at seven thirty."

He turns to Gary and says with a grin, "Boy, you might lose Marla as an employee soon if she keeps publishing like this."

Oh. My. God. Did he just say that to my boss? I remain silent.

Gary turns and says, "Gosh, I hope not."

"Well, thanks for coming all the way down here. If I'd known about the signing, I'd have rescheduled, since all days are the same for me. In fact, tomorrow or early next week would have been even better for me. But once you said you were both coming, I didn't want to ruin your schedules."

We stroll for another half an hour around his fabulous house and yards, then shake hands and say our goodbyes. I wave to Gary, open the trunk of my car, pull off my black knee-high boots in favor of comfortable flats for the long drive, and jump in my car. All this way for a forty-five minute tour.

I'm praying that there are no accidents or construction work to slow down traffic. I take a deep breath. *Calm down, Marla; you have plenty of time to get there.* Three and a half hours until the event starts. *Relax!*

I open the glove compartment and select a positive and uplifting audio book. The San Diego freeway traffic is as slow as a bale of tortoises. Orange County traffic makes me think I'm in the parking lot at LAX. Finally! I'm finally approaching downtown L.A., but it's seven o'clock. It looks like I'm going to miss my own book-signing! I'm hyperventilating.

At a dead stop, I speed dial Bobbie's number.

"Marla, where are you, girlfriend? There must be a hundred people here already. And more still arriving—though we're short an author!"

"I'm stuck." I can hardly speak. I blow out my breath slowly.

"I can talk about the publisher and the book and keep everyone interested until you get here."

"You're a doll. Thanks. See you soon."

I finally get to Melrose Avenue and take that exit, hitting every stoplight. I pull into The Grove parking structure and circle on up to the top floor like I'm in the Indy 500 and find a spot. It's 7:29 when I run to the back of the car, open the trunk, and change back into my knee-high boots.

Adolfo is waiting for me at ground level, and we walk into Barnes & Noble.

A good-looking young man greets me at the front door. "Marla, how are you? Right this way," he says. "My name is William."

Wow, how did he know who I was? I wonder.

We take the escalator up to the third floor.

"I'm going to take you to the green room," says William, "where we always let our star authors hide out, so they don't get mobbed before taking the stage."

Wow! He considers me a star author.

Sitting in the green room, I feel like quite the celebrity. I open a bottle of water and take a swig. My mom and Julie, my editor, come in, and we're all a bit gaga looking at each other.

"Would you like a glass of champagne?" William asks.

Two full minutes of sipping and relaxing, and it's time to greet my crowd. We make our way out to where the signing is to take place, and I spot Bobbie. "Oh, thank goodness you didn't have to stall for me. William said these things never start on time. If I'd known that, I wouldn't have been such a nervous wreck."

"You look great," she says.

I say hello to a few people and then look up to see William at the podium, telling everyone about me, and . . . it's show time!

The signing is great, a standing-room-only crowd. I speak for about twenty minutes and read a chapter. The question-and-answer period goes on and on until William has to cut us off. Last time, the same thing happened. Dating is such a hot topic that people just keep on asking questions that could go on all night. I love it. I really need to develop an interactive seminar about dating because people just can't get enough of this topic.

After signing my last book, I head toward Marmalade, a nearby restaurant with a cozy back room that secludes guests inside velvet curtains in a space lit by crystal chandeliers. I've ordered fancy hors d'œuvres to be served buffet-style with white and red wine. I have to admit, this is my favorite part, so far, about being an author—the book signing, my one night to feel like a rock star.

I walk in and everyone applauds. I have all of my favorite people around me, celebrating with me that my dream has come true. The atmosphere is fabulous, with little tea candles glowing all around, and I flit around trying to talk to everyone. Four television producers are there, and three film agents.

A waiter wheels in a huge cake full of candles and everyone applauds again. I start to cry when I see the decoration. My girlfriend, Aura Imbarus, who ordered that special cake at my last signing, commissioned the new artwork confection, depicting the covers of *both* of my books along with the words, "And many more to come!"

It's so incredibly thoughtful. What a great way to end an amazing evening.

Lying in bed that night, I think, Okay, maybe I'm not a full-time writer yet, and maybe I'm not my own boss, calling the shots and making my own schedule, but slowly and surely, my dreams are coming to fruition. I am truly thankful.

Affirmations

I am a human enabling other humans to find soul mates.

I am a truly successful author.

My husband, family, and friends are a vital part of my success.

I am a star.

thirty-two

"How It Ends and How It All Begins . . ."

Today Adolfo and I are attending a wedding—one that is taking place because of me. A year and a half ago, I introduced a couple who fell in love on their first date. Timothy is a forty-five-year-old hotelier, and Dawn is a feisty, outgoing thirty-two-year-old real estate agent. Neither has been married before, although Dawn has been engaged twice. The match was a no-brainer. Timothy was looking for a sweet, intelligent, sexy, classy, worldly, ultra thin, wrinkle-free woman, and yes, he specified a cup-size preference: at least a C. Dawn is all of that and was interested in meeting the top 1 percent of our financially successful men under fifty and over six feet tall. That was Tim.

The night they got engaged, they both called me from the famous Man Ray restaurant in Paris. Timothy spends money like drunken royalty when vacationing, dining, or shopping, and Dawn is the kind of gal to help the Timothys of the world do just that.

It's four o'clock on a Sunday, and as we sit in the pew, the bridal march begins. Outstretched branches of fifty white birch trees arch over the aisle as the bride makes her entrance. Three hundred attendees are witnessing the exchange of vows in a wonderland filled with twenty thousand melon-colored roses, fragrant tuberoses, gardenias, and lilies-of-the-valley. Dawn's beauty and joy radiate in a lustrous, shell-white, silk Vera Wang gown with a halter bodice topping gathered tulle, the skirt just brushing her diamond encrusted Stuart Weitzman four-inch heel shoes. Her hair is in a French twist with a shoulder-length tiered veil, the scalloped edges beaded in tiny pearls. She is carrying a bouquet of melon roses and orchids. Her ten-carat, emerald-cut, three-stone, Tiffany diamond ring sparkles like a mini-klieg light, and the five-carat diamond earrings match perfectly.

Timothy takes her arm when she reaches the altar. He's smiling and looks pretty good in his black Armani suit with his newly darkened hair slicked back. He is clearly in awe of the vision that he is about to marry.

As the wedding march ends, a trio starts to sing "Ave Maria" a cappella.

Eight bridesmaids—all in satin Vera Wang A-line gowns in a soft green—attend to the bride. Their sweetheart necklines, side-draped bodices, and asymmetrical fabric corsages at the waist are reminiscent of old Hollywood glamour.

As I take Adolfo's hand, I think about our modest but elegant wedding in Mexico. This couple with their over-the-top displays, however, isn't any happier than we were on our wedding day. I still wear my zirconium with pride, but I'm also wearing my Tiffany knock-off ring that looks like a five-carat diamond. They make me as happy as Dawn's ten-carat pebble.

After the ceremony, the couple dashes out to a waiting white Rolls Royce. A violinist has followed them to the curb, serenading them. Two dozen white doves are released into the air, and the couple is on their way to the reception at one of Timothy's hotels in Beverly Hills.

As we enter the reception hall, a harpist picks up where the violinist left off, and we stroll into the dining area. Tiny glass vases, each with a single white rose, mark individual place settings, and white rose petals are scattered around a ball centerpiece of white roses. Pearls in the vase glow with candlelight. There are four crystal glasses per person. Silver hearts hold the place cards, and silver letter-openers engraved with the word *love* are offered as wedding favors.

At my place setting, a beautifully wrapped gift and a card sit on top of the dinner plate. I carefully unwrap the fancy gold and silver paper to find a chrome bottle stopper with a crystal heart. The message inside the card tells what a blessing I have been in their lives. The final line: "It is because of you, Marla, that we have found true love."

I wipe away a tear.

"What's wrong, honey? Are you okay?" Adolfo's brow frets with a look of concern.

"I'm fine, mi amor. I'm just happy for them. It feels so good that it's through my job that this is possible for Timothy and Dawn."

"I hope they'll be as happy as we are. You are the best thing that ever happened to me." He kisses my forehead.

A string quartet plays in the background as we feast on fresh asparagus and a Bibb lettuce salad with a champagne vinaigrette, followed by lobster bisque, then a choice of halibut, roast duck, or filet mignon. Each course is served with a different French wine. After dinner, Tattinger champagne is served, along with fresh raspberries dipped in chocolate. The wedding cake is a five-tier wonder, coated with white chocolate, roses, and a gold-leaf trim.

The bride and groom get up for their first dance to the song "At Last" by Etta James. It's a great opener, but it can't match the first dance at our wedding to the song that Adolfo wrote for me, "Tu Eres Mi Estrella." And later that evening, Adolfo grabs my hand and presses his cheek to mine, singing softly just for me a verse of his song in Spanish:

> You're the taste of enlightenment,
> And after all these nightmares
> You have rescued my life,
> And in this constellation, you're my guide, you're my path
> I follow the light in you.

He tells me I look so good in my sage-green strapless cocktail dress that I bought on sale at a boutique in Hollywood that he's been waiting to get his arms around me since we hurried out the door. It has been a magical evening, and I'm looking forward to

going home with my Latin lover, climbing into bed, cud-
dling . . . and eventually watching our favorite shows that we
Tivoed.

Dawn and Timothy make their way over to us, and Dawn gives
me a big hug.

"Oh, Marla, thank you for everything. You have changed my
life. I am so lucky to have such a wonderful man to spend my life
with."

"My pleasure. I wish you many years of health and happiness.
What an exquisite wedding. Thanks for inviting us. Where are
you going on your honeymoon?"

Timothy talks about Rome, the Amalfi Coast, Greece, and
ultimately Paris, "so that Dawn can get some shopping in." He's
laughing.

"Sounds like a dream," I say.

Standing in front of the hotel, we watch as the Rolls whisks
the couple away, and the valet brings around Adolfo's silver Volkswagen Jetta. I chuckle to myself, knowing that none of the ladies
here would accept a date with a man who drove a Jetta. The least
they'd allow their fabulous fannies to sit on would be a BMW 4
series coupe with leather seats. Adolfo grins, kisses me, and I
touch up my lip gloss. The fruity scent retrieves a memory of
something he did when we'd only been seeing each other for a
month.

I've loved lip gloss since I was twelve when my best friend Jill
and I carried around our giant Bonne Bell Lip Smackers in our
handbags. I've been slathering the stuff on my lips day and night
for three decades. Cherry, strawberry, root beer, mango—it's all
good. I can't sleep unless there is a tube next to my bed to keep
my lips from drying out. Before I met Adolfo, I was dating a guy
who hated the fact that I used it, and he constantly made rude
comments to get me to quit. I mean, what did he care?

I went over to Adolfo's apartment and into the bedroom.
There, sitting on the nightstand on my side of the bed, was a
brand-new cherry lip gloss. That little pot of gloss meant more
to me than a diamond necklace. For a guy to pick out a lip gloss
and put it by the bed was so damn cute and thoughtful. I made

my choice that evening, and the universe lined up with it: love matters more than wealth. Sometimes you get both, as I hope Dawn and Timothy have.

On the short ride home, I say to Adolfo, "I can't wait to see what happens on *The Tudors* tonight."

Before watching the show, Adolfo says, "I'll make you a cup of hot tea, honey."

"Sounds perfect, sweetie." I set the peacock ashtray back on the coffee table.

Perfect, indeed.

Affirmations

I accept that I am human. Only human.

I love. I am loved. I am love.

Ricky and Lucy live happily ever after.

About the Author

Marla Martenson is the bestselling author of *Excuse Me, Your Soul Mate Is Waiting* and *Good Date, Bad Date.* Marla is a dating coach, matchmaker, and speaker and has appeared on numerous TV shows including *Today*, WGN Chicago *Morning News*, *San Diego Living*, and *Better TV.* When not busy writing or coaching, she can be found sipping vanilla soy lattes, getting Botox injections, and nagging her husband to put the toilet seat down.

She can be reached at www.MarlaMartenson.com

BETTIE YOUNGS BOOKS
PUBLISHING COMPANY, INC.

. . . books that inspire and celebrate remarkable journeys

VISIT OUR WEBSITE AT
www.BettieYoungsBooks.com